WHO ARE WE?

VOLUME – 1

KALIM ULLAH KABIR

INDIA • SINGAPORE • MALAYSIA

Copyright © Kalim Ullah Kabir 2025
All Rights Reserved.

ISBN

Paperback 979-8-89133-964-4

Hardcase 979-8-89498-611-1

Dedication

DEDICATED to my beloved Mother, Father and all my ancestors.

It is for the whole world and my motherland "BHARAT" to understand "WHO ARE WE?"

READ, UNDERSTAND & ACT.

"Who are we?" book has been written brave heartily by Mr. Kalim ullah Kabir. I heartily congratulate him for writing this splendid book. The author is multi-talented and has written thoughtfully with his versatile knowledge and experiences about Human, Humanity, Religion, Sects, Hindustan and Hindustanis. Today whole world needs Humanity, Hindustan and Hindustanis. Till how long will human hate each other in the name of Religion, Cast, Creed and Progress? All Religion teaches only humanity. All the humans in this world are creation of Allah. All Humans are the generations of Adam, the generations of Noah. All People of different religions need to live amicably and needs to share happiness and sorrows with and in each other's festivals, occasions and in difficult times. All this is possible through the right education and guidance. Religion is not for hatred or for show-off, it is for proper understanding all aspects of humanity and it needs to be implemented.

This splendid book gives the message of Co-Existence, Nationalism, Patriotism, Faith, Acceptance and love. The author has emphasized on the harmony of all religions and sects, using the example of the great Prophet Mohammad peace be upon him. This book should be read by every person, so that everyone can analyse and evaluate themself and improve. The author has rightly written, "Truth can be supressed, but it cannot be erased." I pray to almighty Allah for peace and tranquillity to prevail in Hindustan and in the whole world? I pray to Allah for all the success to Mr. Kalim Ullah Kabir and his book "WHO ARE WE? Volume 1. Ameen

Dr. Imam Umer Ahmed Ilyasi,
Chief Imam, All India Imam Organization, New Delhi. India.

"WHO ARE WE?" written by Shri Kalim Ullah Kabir is with me and is a must read for all. This is not a story, it is more a 'document'. After reading "HAM KOUN? In Hindi and "WHO ARE WE?" in English, I understand that the writer and humans are in pain for some reason. Whoever has created the sunlight, has created it for every living being, from insects to humans, not for any particular Religion, Caste, Creed or Gender. But some elements have erected bushes, shrubs and walls at such places, as a result light is not able to reach everyone's courtyard completely. It seems that Kabir is suffering from this problem, and wants that the bushes, fences and those walls should be demolished, so that the divine light can reach everyone's courtyard, over which everyone has the right. The day when this becomes possible, human will become a true man and woman!

The book "WHO ARE WE?" volume 1 in English and "HAM KOUN?" BHAG 1 in Hindi will establish religious tolerance. This is a commendable step taken by the author to understand the root cause of disputes among different religions and sects. Man is not made for religion but religion is made for man, this message awake the tendency of humanity in every human being. The mention about the truth of Islam and the existence of Sanatan Dharam for ages is a symbol of the superior knowledge of the author and existence of humans only for humanity. This book has positive energy that gives the light of love and peace to the world by highlighting the truth to attain MOKSH. I appreciate it and pray to God for all the success of this book and the author.

दिनांक :- 23·10·2023

Dr. Indresh Kumar,
Guide (Margdrashak), New Delhi, India.

The Kabir! Kalimullah too!

These days, the principles of tolerance and co-existence are being disregarded in the world. So their relevance is increasing day by day. In such a situation, there is a need to properly understand not only one's religion in the context of science and human values, but also proper understanding of other religions is necessary.

Through this book, the author Shri Kalimullah Kabir has tried with all his might to understand and explain Islam in the light of Sanatan Dharma, which means protection and adherence to eternal values. His effort is noteworthy and is commendable. The author aim is to present the basic information's about Islam to the general readers through this book. Along with Quran-Hadith, the author has also tried to quote facts from various books. Some topics may look new to the general readers but is worth reading. Muslims cannot ignore the provisions of other religions with the reverence to all the 124000 Prophets.

Mr. Kalimullah Kabir was introduced to me as a consultant engineer. In his professional life designing buildings & structures that are pleasing to others, providing specialised construction solutions and decorations is his hobby. With this view of assessing people requirements and sentiments, the method of subtle observation and study, probably became a factor of inspiration for Shri Kalimullah Kabir for intensive study in the context of diverse religions and sects.

The continuous movement of this universe through the ages is the direct evidence of eternity. Being multi-talented there is strength in the thoughts and expressions of writer. In the light of geographical and natural diversity on earth, diversity of ideas is a natural phenomenon. Like animals, humans too are in search of facilities. Nomadic tendency to dominate and expand influence is a natural nature. In the light of nature's diverse favourable and unfavourable conditions, the human mind's concept of some invisible governing power is also the reason for the expansion of cultures in various forms. All humans are made of bones, blood and flesh. Then what is the difference and why? "Who are we?" This question in the author's mind holds special importance in today's scientific era in the context of our responsibilities.

Today, various wars and conflicts are taking a monstrous form. In such a situation, this book presentation of the thoughts of Shri Kalimullah Kabir is the age-appropriate emergence of Indian thinking and personality in the light of the current situation, is the grace of God. Through his book, the author has made a logical and legal effort to reconcile the inconsistency of beliefs and sects.

The meaning of life lies in making it useful. In the race to become more powerful people are becoming consumer, man is engaged in giving the earth the form of Karbala in the competition of limitless materialism. It is my opinion that this book will prove to be useful as Coramine (lifesaving medicine) and the author will receive global encouragement for his magnificent effort. This is our prayer to God.

Regards,
Siddhinath Singh,
Patratu, Jharkhand, India.

My heartiest congratulations on the publication of the book "Who are we?" Volume 1. This book is a good attempt to understand the major religions of the world in the context of India from historical and sociological perspectives. The author has touched upon the conservative approaches of some ignorant Muslims living in India which have nothing to do with Islam, its teachings and values. Islam, as embedded in the word itself, is a religion of peace, tolerance, and reconciliation. The author has emphasized that having a true interpretation of the Islamic teachings in the light of the Quran and authenticated Hadeeth contributes to a nation- building process which is based on mutual collaboration and respect between the components of society to ensure social harmony and constructive interaction among different faiths, cultures, and races.

At a time when humanity and human dignity is being violated in countless ways in countries and societies throughout the world, often in the name of religion. It is imperative that we re-emphasize this important value and more importantly apply it in our daily lives. It is indeed inevitable for a country to evolve itself into a nation by promoting mutual understanding and increasing acceptance and tolerance for all religious belief. This task can be achieved through inter- faith dialogue for ensuring co-existence, peace building and societal harmony. Last but not the least, I hope this book will serve its very purpose of removing religious ignorance and to help all communities specially in India to go back to their authentic religious sources of humanity to feel the real taste of our societal harmony. My best wishes to the book and the author for all success!

Diwan Rashid Khan,
Media & Communication Officer,
Qatar General Electricity & Water Corporation, Qatar.

 This book "WHO ARE WE?" written by my great Indian friend Mr Kalim Ullah Kabir, is a precious stone. I heartily congratulate my friend for his redolent effort in writing this significant book. I knew my friend is a multi-talented person, with his versatile knowledge and experience the author presented valid points in a logical manner for the betterment of mankind. Today, when there are differences of opinions among people in the name of country, religion, sects, colour and creed, which hampers the peace and humanity comes under stake. In such a typical time the author has dared to bring the facts and unify the society and world with humanity through this book. I know the great country India, my friend being an Indian has given a ray of hope for the whole world, which needs the spirit of harmony. India gives energy to live and let live other peacefully. The name of this book "Who are we?" itself creates curiosity within oneself. People starts relating their self with the word "WHO ARE WE?" The author has rightly said that "religion is only by, of and for humanity". Holy Quran and Prophet Mohammad speaks about humanity and peaceful co-existence.

I pray for the immense success of the Author and this book. I firmly hope that every person will read this book and get positive vibes, which will bring acceptance, love, peace and harmony in the world.

Quadratullah Taghabi,
Baghlan, Afghanistan.

Contents

Preface

Since ancient times, when human started thinking beyond the fulfilment of his natural primitive needs, many questions came in front of them. Chief among them was **"WHO ARE WE?"** From where and how did we and this world began? An attempt has been made to find the answers to these questions from the point view of a "BHARATIYE Muslim".

Since time immemorial, "BHARAT" has been a country of various religions and cultures. Human history is of millions of years. People call "God" by different names. In the history of mankind approximately 124000 divine messengers or avatars has come in different parts of the world and taught the same lesson of humanity. Prophet Mohammad Sahab pbuh has given examples of love and respect even to his enemy. The Prophet Pbuh said "Hubbul watan minal imam" which means "Loving one's country is an integral part of faith". During international events we are known by the name of our country. Prophet Muhammad pbuh said contemporary education makes a person capable and efficient. **Today the most powerful weapon to change the world is education**. In the name of religion or sects, blindfolding, putting cotton in the ears, sealing the mouth, sitting with folded hands is the sign of foolishness. Few People have changed the religious teachings for little benefits and the result is that the true spirit of religion is lost for ever.

This book takes through an intellectual journey of history and religion to understand "Who are we?" What we are doing?" "Where we are dragging our generations?"

I am thankful to my parents, teachers and mentors who made me worthy human being. It is because of the proper upbringing that "I am not spoiled in good times and I am not broken in bad times". I am thankful to almighty GOD who has made me experienced different situations so that I can bring facts in front of the society. Peace and tranquillity can be established in the world by making sincere efforts. The darkness of ignorance can be overcome only by the light of knowledge.

I am thankful to all those people who has guided me in my journey of writing this book and increased the usefulness of me and this book. They all deserve my special affection. I am grateful to all those authors whose book I have read and understood. In the present "volume 1", I have tried to put few facts in brief. If there is any mistake of terminology in this book I apologize to all for that. May be my knowledge is limited, so I cannot even dare to say that my views are irrefutable. My main objective is to bring attention of common people towards this important topic "Who are we"?

Who are we?
Few words

"Hind" which we know as "BHARAT" has been a great nation and a centre of attraction since time immemorial because of its unique features. From time immemorial people from every corners of the world have been attracted towards "BHARAT". The civilization of the world started from the BHARATIYE subcontinent. We find people of all ethnic groups, religions and sects of the world in "BHARAT". BHARAT has been a source of inspiration. One who came here became of here. This is the truth, "truth can be suppressed for time being but cannot be erased". Biased history given by the Westerns has tried to suppress and maligned the true image of BHARAT.

BHARAT got independence in the year 1947. But BHARAT was not made on this day, BHARAT was liberated on this day. Vasco da Gama did not discover BHARAT in 1498, he discovered the sea route to reach BHARAT. No one can tell when BHARAT started or born? We the people of BHARAT consider the BHARATIYE civilization as eternal and our land as sacred, according to Vishnu-Purana even the **deities' wishes to take birth here**. That's why even the Prophet Mohammad pbuh praised Hind (BHARAT) in many occasions. Many countries are made or born, the one who is born his death is also certain. BHARAT in the field of religion, thoughts, acceptance and literature has developed independently since ages. BHARATIYE soil is evident.

It is said in the book "Sanskriti ke char adhyay" (page no. 115) written by Ramdhari Singh Dinkar, Alexander invaded BHARAT in the fourth century BC. After the collapse of the Mauryan Empire, a large group of Greeks came. Yuchi, Shak, Huns, Abhirs, Parsis, Turks etc. also came and settled in BHARAT. Today they have no separate existence. All of them have settled and absorbed themselves well according to their works in the society. BHARATIYE culture has been prepared by the combination of cultures of many ethnic groups, religions and sects who came and settled in this country. Aryans did the work of decoction. Aryans took herbs from all groups, religions and sects and mixed all of them in proper quantity. The result is the fragrance of BHARAT.

Thousands of years ago, when Parsis came from Persia (Iran) to escape attacks of Turkish invaders, the then king of a kingdom sent them a glass of milk. The leader of the displaced returned the milk mixed with sugar. Today the Parsis are real minority in BHARAT, the most respectable, prosperous and educated people. Where have the Kirats gone, where have the Unanis, Yuchis, Shakas, Huns and Abhirs gone. They all have become sugar in milk. Many people came from abroad one after the other. Sometimes the society had also experienced slight tremor upon their arrivals, but in the end they all merged in the ocean of BHARATIYE culture. Those cultures have given BHARAT a universal image.

It has come in a research that the oldest stone on the earth which came above the water is in Saranda (Jharkhand) forest (The Indian Express dated 12 November 2021).

In the medival time which is called dark age, there was misery everywhere in the world, the condition of women was pitiable, girls baby were buried alive. Evils were everywhere, there was darkness in the world and in that darkness Prophet Mohammad pbuh came with a ray of light. The light of humanity, i.e. "ISLAM". But today Muslims have diluted the true spirit of ISLAM. Prophet Mohammad Sahab said God has sent different Prophets to eradicate the evils and corruption from the society. All the messengers taught the same lesson of humanity in different forms. The path may be different but the destination is the one. Even in the prestigious Gita, Lord Krishna says that when evils increases in the world, he incarnates to destroy the evil and establish the good.

Prophet Mohammad pbuh had set an example of love and peace even with his enemy. The Prophet Pbuh served the old Jew lady humbly with medicine and water, whereas she used to throw garbage upon the Prophet. This is real Islam i.e. love and respect for all. Another example, during the lifetime of the Prophet some businessmen were passing through a road, many stones and dirt were scattered on that road, one among them said "it seems that Muslims do not uses this road that's why here stones and dirt is scattered". This was the true spirit of Islam which is all the activities of humanity but it is missing today among Muslims. BHARATIYE Muslims are very fortunate that Allah has given dual responsibilities to Muslims in BHARAT that is to be a BHARATIYE MUSLIM. Prophet Mohammad pbuh used to say that he gets cool breeze from HIND i.e. BHARAT.

The Prophet said "Hubbul Watan Min-al Imam" which means "loving one's country is a part of faith". During International events people are known by the name of their country, not by the name of their religion. Prophet Muhammad pbuh has said that if require then one shall go too far off places to gain knowledge and become wise. Just as water is known by different names in different languages, so is God known by different names in different languages. The Quran itself mentions 99 names of Allah. **"Truth is one, the wise call it by different names".**

Updating and reformation is a continuous process required in everything and in community. It starts from oneself, one's home, then the society and the country comes automatically. For real Islam i.e. peace, love & humanity all have to improve. Small sacrifices have to be given. All have to keep patience. Sacrifice means to stand for truth like Prophet Mohammad pbuh and Shri Ram Ji did. Sacrifice means giving up one's comfort and facilities for others like Gautama Buddha did. Like Prophet Abraham who was ready to sacrifice his beloved son on God's call. Forgiving people like Prophet Yusuf. Sacrifice means loving people, live and die for humanity, like Jesus Christ. Jesus sacrificed himself for humanity, love and peace. Jesus never converted anyone's religion. He simply gave the message that was given by the earlier Prophets.

Off late some people have brought changes in religious teaching due to selfishness, hence the true spirit of religion has been lost. There are 6 different Hadith books which were compiled and written about 200 years after the death of Prophet Muhammad (Pbuh). Muslims are neither understanding nor following the Holy Quran properly but they have become more dependent upon Hadith. Sahih al-Bukhari had collected about 600000 Hadith, out of which he considered only 7275 to be authentic. He had rejected the rest i.e. non-authentic. There has been a lot of controversy about the authenticity of Hadith since the beginning. Enemies of BHARAT mislead our youth through misinterpretations of fabricated Hadith.

It is the fact that Muslims have diluted the true spirit of Islam. For small benefit, many Muslims uses and misuses Sharia law and Indian law as per their convenience. If sharia law is beneficial then many Muslims follow it. If sharia law harms then many Muslims go with Indian law. In BHARAT, Muslims have been made a tool kit. Jealousy and hate speech are the major destructive factors, which have entered through wrong education systems.

From history we come to know that after power passed into the hands of Turks, they invaded BHARAT. Few Turks then distorted the word Jihad and made it their business and few called themselves Al Ghazi. Turks invaded BHARAT many times and plundered. **The scattered remains of the invasion are the cause of intense hatred towards Muslims.** There are many reasons for the backwardness of Muslims. Few among them are that Muslims consider themselves as superior. They limit themselves considering themselves as superior beings, not taking knowledge from others, some believe that there is no religion like them. According to them, there is no one like them in the whole world. This is the reason why some Muslims, instead of living like sugar in milk, have kept themselves dispersed. Because of this isolation, they have become easy prey for vote-bank hunters.

Today few Muslims in BHARAT are being humiliated and looked upon with suspicion. The question arises why? Muslim can easily find the answer within themself. Some Muslims have also distorted the meaning of Jihad. If a Muslim in the name of Jihad dies, he is told that he will get hoors in heaven. A question arises? That if a man dies then he will get hoors, on the other hand if a woman dies then what she will get?

I think that if Muslim takes care of their characters, everyone will respect them, like it was in the time of the Prophet. Few things has to be ignored. Everyone has to embrace humanity. Islam talks about love, peace and respect for all religions, sects and all living beings. The holy book Quran mentions the plant of Tulsi (Rehan). Sanatani people worship Tulsi. What greater proof is needed that what is considered sacred and is worshiped in other religion, is praised in the holy Quran? According to the holy book Quran, the system of ages i.e. Yuga's is justified through Noah's ark deluge event. It is believed that Sanatan Dharma is the oldest religion. Sanatan means eternal never ending.

I say "If circumstances makes you fall due to any reason, then fall like a waterfall, though falling from height it spread beauty in the environment". "Human is not made for religion, religion is made for human". Through religion humanity tendency comes in human, religion keeps man away from devil and devilish activities. Religion is neither a word nor a doctrine, it is an action. It is to be and become, not to listen and believe. The soul is neither male nor female, it lives only as long as the body it wears of which it becomes. As many souls that many can be the path to reach God.

Quran 6:108 surah Al-Anam says: "Do not despise those they invoke other than ALLAH, otherwise they will begin to despise Allah out of ignorance."

Those looking for equality among humans and religion, if they study the true spirit of all religions, they will definitely find similarity in the spirit of all religions and sects. There is more need to emphasize on that equality today. The darkness of ignorance has to be dispelled by the light of knowledge.

There is no solution without coordination of science and religious philosophy. Science has to be freed from materialism and religion from orthodoxy. Today's civilization will have to be universal. There is no conflict between science and spiritual knowledge, both are engaged in the search for TRUTH. Just because of the difference of directions, there seems to be a conflict. Science searches for 'this', spirituality for 'I'. Science searches for 'effect' whereas spirituality for 'cause'. Science searches for 'means of happiness', spirituality for 'joy'.

The most important thing is that the BHARATIYE Muslims will give the ray of light for the whole world. This book is the initiator. This book is going to make everyone to relook inside oneself and ponder "who are we?" Anarchy spreads due to the storm of hatred and peace spread due to the storm of love. People shall not run after the external ostentatious rituals of religion.

Chapter 1
Human!!! Who?

"Human" is one who belongs to the genus Homo. "Man" is derived from the word Manu. Scientists still haven't been able to pinpoint the exact time when and how the first human evolved, but they have identified some of the oldest humans. We have found some human fossils that are of more than 300,000 years old and as technology advances we are able to learn more and more about the humans who lived in earlier eras.

One of the earliest humans we know from history is Homo Habilis, who lived in Africa about 2.4 million to 1.4 million years ago. Others include Homo Rudolfensis, which lived in East Africa about 1.9 million to 1.8 million years ago (its name comes from its discovery in East Rudolph, Kenya); and Homo erectus, which ranged from southern Africa to modern China and Indonesia from about 1.89 million to 110,000 years ago. 1

One very important question comes from the story of Adam and Eve? That if all humans are descendants of Adam and Eve, then the DNA should be the same in all humans. But then why and how Neanderthal DNA contains Homo Sapiens DNA and Homo Sapiens DNA have Neanderthal DNA. Europeans have an average of one to two percent Neanderthal DNA. When that DNA passed from Neanderthals to humans and vice versa? We call them "gene flow events," which is a hilarious euphemism, because what we're talking about is cross breeding! Much later a little finger bone and teeth of a teenage girl were found in a cave at Denisova in Russia. This proved sufficient to obtain the complete genome from this creature, which was not Homo sapiens, not Homo Neanderthalensis and nothing else we knew about that! We call these people Denisovans. They are a different human species, but not us, not Neanderthals and not what was previously known. We've found that our ancestors interbred with Denisovans, and they interbred with our ancestors. The further east you go today, the more Denisovan DNA you find in people alive today and the less Neanderthal.

This story is so close to magic that it is hard to believe. When you analyse the amount of DNA from the three species that we know to interbreed (Denisovans, Neanderthals and Homo sapiens), they do not add up, leading us to believe that we also carry DNA from another human species for which we have no bones and no DNA. The shadow of another human species—its mark—is still within us all. This is very special. 2,3,4,5

Now come to the point that we read Adam and Eve (in sanatan Manu and Shatarupa) came from heaven. But till date no one has been able to tell the date of birth or death of Adam and Eve (Manu and Shatarupa). Adam and Eve had sons and daughters. In the beginning a brother killed another brother to marry his sister. But the question arises that how did Adam allow them to marry their own siblings? Come on, if it was okay for that time, then why are there different races and different DNA? Here it means that there is a missing link in today's written history. We have to find out the missing links of history, and try to bring the truth in front of everyone.

If religious belief is mixed with science then all the answers will be found. Science says that our ancestors were chimpanzees, apes. This seems to be true according to our skeletal system and many other things. Then the sons of Adam may have cross-breaded with other human species or chimpanzees or apes, or with other Homo genes, or with Neanderthals, or Denisovans . Whose skeletal remains have been found? It is believed that Adam was thrown from heaven to earth and he landed on Adam's peak in present day Sri Lanka and Eve was also thrown from heaven and she landed in present day Saudi Arab land. Adam walked towards Arabia through present BHARAT and after few centuries Adam met Eve in present day Mecca place in Saudi Arabia, and there Adam bowed down and worshiped God for the first time on this earth. But then nothing is known as to where they went from there. The story of Adam is often considered an allegory.

Concept of Adam, Lilith and Eve are one segment of humans: The puzzling verse of Genesis 1, which states that God created man and woman together. God created Adam from clay, he also created a woman out of clay and named her Lilith. But the two could not agree, because Adam wanted Lilith to come under him, and Lilith insisted that Adam come under her and so she separated from him. And then Eve was created from Adam's rib. 6, 7.

In the story of Adam and Lilith, Lilith and Adam were created together from the same substance. This represents equality between men and women. Then Lilith and Adam disagreed because both Lilith and Adam wanted to see each other under them. That means both Lilith and Adam wanted to dominate each other. Both did not accept each other's dominance and they both separated. Then God created Eve from Adam's rib. **"The woman was created from Adam's rib. She was not made to rule over, nor to be trodden down by feet, the woman was made by his side as his equal. Just under his arm and nearby the heart to give equal love and equal respect".**

Coming back to ADAM and EVE meeting at present day MECCA. Africa is very close to Arabia so they might have migrated to Africa where Eve gave birth to sons Kabil and Habil and others. It is said that the most ancient humans and civilizations come from the continent of Africa. We also cannot deny about the movement of humans from Africa to Europe because Neanderthal also lived in Europe for more and more than one lakh fifty thousand (150000) years. At the same time and before that, there were another human species the Denisovans. Today according to the research and existing written records, it is also proved by the fossil remains of humans. The oldest known evidence of anatomically contemporary humans (as 2017) are fossils found in Jebel Irhoud, Morocco, which are approximately 300,000 years old. That means humans were on earth for more than 300000 three lakh years. More history is yet to come. As technology is developing, we are learning more and more.

Now coming to the most common story. According to Bhagwat, the king Satyavrat was the hero of Mahapralaya, the same hero of which Christians and Muslims consider as Noah. According to Sanatan Dharma, when Lord Vishnu assumed Meenavatara. This Satyavrat lived in Kamandalu and it was Satyavrat who left him one by one in Kamandalu, then in the lake, then in the river and the sea. Vishnu made him **Vaivaswat Manu.**

According to the time-calculation of Hinduism, there is a chaturyuga of four Yuga's. There is a manvantar of 71 Yuga's. 14 manvantars are considered as 1 kalpa. 1 kalpa means 1 day of Brahmaji's. The total age of the universe is about 4,32,00,00,000 years, it is divided into total 14 Manvantara. There is a Manu in each Manvantara.

The names of the 14 Manus are as follows:-

1. Swayambhu

2. Sawrochish

3. Uttam

4. Tamas

5. Raivat

6. Cackhash

7. **Vaivaswat**

8. Savarni

9. Dakshsavarni

10. Brahasavarni

11. Dharmsavarni

12. Rudrasavarni

13. Devsavarni

14. Indrasavarni

Sanskrit developed in the middle country i.e. ZAMBODWEEP. It was influenced by the language of Rig-Veda. All humans were Destroyed only Manu survived. Veda drowned in the waters of the holocaust, then Vishnu saved it. These are the two main signs existing in the said literary tradition. There is no mention of the holocaust in the Rig-Veda. The question of the destruction of mankind in it No. The flood is mentioned in the Atharva Veda. The source of research in this direction is MacDonnell book on Vedic God tales. The Shatapatha Brahmana (1.8.1,1-10) states that the flood destroyed all other human beings. Only Manu's family were saved in a boat. The story of the deluge is also in the Avesta and may be Indo-European.

McDonnell believes that the Aryans came from outside and settled in BHARAT, therefore, the mention of the deluge in Avesta is considered to be older than Arthveda. Aryans were in Zamboodweep when this incident had happened, so in the opinion of McDonnell, it is the Indo-European era. He did not give any explanation as to why there is no allusion to that event in the Rig-Veda. The poets of the Rig-Veda are extraordinarily conscious of the movement of water.

That event must have happened before his composition and they don't even hint towards him, this situation is very surprising.

If the deluge was of the Indo-European era, then McDonnell did not tell where it happened. But there are two assumptions involved in his interpretation, and they are important: (1) Atharvaveda was composed before the Bible. 2) There is no indication of the deluge in the Rig-Veda. Hence, the event is post Rig-Veda. But did not consider that the BHARATIYE Aryans would have received this story from the Sumerians. But with the present knowledge of the Sumerian records, if we pay attention to the fact that the reference to the holocaust story is not in the Rig-Veda, it is in the Atharvaveda, then this possibility is worth considering. The Sumerians may have received this story from the BHARATIYE Aryans at some point after the composition of the Rig-Veda.

If it is in the Atharvaveda, it is a possibility that the Sumerians may have received this story from the BHARATIYE Aryans at some point after the composition of the Rig-Veda. In the Atharvaveda, the reference to the holocaust story is as follows to tell the place where the boat descended from the peak of the Him (mountain). People must have been well-acquainted with the story of Manu reaching the top of the Hill in a boat in the deluge and that particular place in the Himalayas. The boat landed, where the peak of the Himalayas is, it is considered sufficient to say this much. In Shatapatha Brahmana, that place is called the descent of Manu (Manoravasarpanam). He must have been known by this name.

The story is elaborated in a mythological way in Shatapatha Brahmana. When Manu was washing his hands in the morning, a fish came in his hand. He said to Manu, take care of me, I will protect you. All the people will be swept away but I will protect you from it. Manu asked, how can I raise you? He said, small fish are eaten by big fish, raise me in a pitcher. When I grow up, then take me to the sea. In a certain year there will be a storm, then you make a boat as I say. When the storm comes, then go inside the boat. I will protect you. As the fish said, Manu raised it, then put it in the sea. In the year for which he said, Manu made a boat and sat in it when the storm came. That fish is now big Matsya came to the boat, Manu tied the boat's rope to its horn. In this way he reached the northern mountain, Matsya said tie the boat to the tree and come down when the water subsides. Later Slowly Manu came down from the mountain and saved himself from the storm. All the subjects were swept away in the storm, only one Manu survived. (Shatpath, 1.8.1,1-6)

According to Manusmriti, the land created by the Gods between the rivers Saraswati and Dishwater was called Brahmavarta. It was on the banks of the river. In his descendants there was Prithu, who established villages and cities, developed agriculture and commerce.

The basic historical linguistics is that there is a great deal of similarity between Greek, Latin, Sanskrit etc. languages. Once it is understood that the Rig-Veda was composed before the development of the Harappan civilization, the relationship between ancient BHARAT, Sumer and Egypt is established. There will be no difficulty in recognizing the relationship between Rig-Veda culture and Harappan civilization, the relationship between Harappa and Minoan civilization. Crossing the area through which Apsu reached Sumer, Indra, Marut Mitra etc. Vedic Devgan reached West Asia. 14

In this era, humans have been divided into different groups.

Ethnographic division of races from Meyers' Conversations' exikon of 1885-90 is listing: Meyer's Conversations' Lexicon from 1885–90 lists the ethnographic division into races:-

Caucasian (Aryans, Hamites, Semites)

Mongolian (Northern Mongolian, Chinese and Indo-Chinese, Japanese and Korean, Tibetan, Malayan, Polynesian, Maori, Micronesian, Eskimo, American Indian),

Negroid (African, Hottentots, Melanesian/Papua, "Negrito", Australian Aborigine, Dravidian, Sinhalese)

Another popular division recognizes 4 major race. In a 1950 statement, the United Nations opted to drop the word "race" altogether and speak of "groups". In this case, a 1998 study published in Scientific American according to one study, there are more than 5,000 castes or groups in the world.

As social animals, man started living in groups and gradually developed various ways of living a comfortable life because of his power to think and adaptability according to the environment. Later a major development took place to make people to remain good and that is "religion". People invented the word "God". And different types of religious rituals were started. Actually Supreme God is there, but he is not concentrated in Mosque, Church, Synagogue, Temple, Gurudwara etc. He is inside everyone's heart in the form of soul. It is proved by this, like if someone does wrong or illegal work then there is a feeling of guilt inside soul that it is illegal or it is bad. This the inner voice of the soul is God. After death, the soul goes back and reunites with the divine soul from where it came. In Hindi Atma goes back to Parmatma.

GOD particle is in everyone's heart and is present everywhere and it is for the whole universe and not for any one particular religion or community. Supreme GOD loves all human beings very much irrespective of their religion, caste, creed or gender etc. That's why the Lord does not harm humans immediately while committing crime or illegal act. God has given man the freedom to do anything good or bad. God gives chance to all human beings to improve. But if a person still does not improve, then his deeds only punishes him. This can be found in everyone's life if one start thinking deeply. Punishment is not given by God, punishment is given by person own deed i.e. karma.

The incident associated with Prophet Lut in the Middle East is a great example of punishment for bad karma. Prophet Lut settled in Sodom after receiving the divine order from God. Located on the border of present-day Jordan, Palestine and Israel. Sodom was then a large prosperous city, but also the most corrupt city with the most criminal activity at the time. The Prophet Lut began preaching the humanity in Sodom. Prophet Lut approached the people of the city and reminded them of God. The men and women of Sodom were enraged by Lut's speech and made plans to banish Lut from their city. Prophet Lut became very disappointed. Distressed, Prophet Lut raised his hands to the sky and prayed.

The Lord sent three angels disguised as men including the angel Jibraiel. The angels went to Sodom disguised as handsome youths. The Prophet Lut welcomes them to the city of Sodom, first trying to persuade them to leave the city. But Prophet Lut was too embarrassed to ask the guests to leave, then he quietly and safely brought the guests to his home so that no one would see the three men.

Lut wife who was unbeliever and evil-doer saw the men entering the house. She went to the people of Sodom and told them about the youths. The whole city of Sodom gathered at Lut's gate." Prophet Lut was helpless against corrupt people. Then three men (God's angels) said: "O Lut, verily we are the messengers of God; they will never reach you". The light went out. Everyone became angry and shouted: "What is this magic that has just hit us? Where did it come from? O Lut! You will see what we will do to you tomorrow morning." Then the blind men returned to their homes. God ordered Lut to go out of the city with his family same night and told not to look back. As dawn broke, there was a loud noise in the city. There was a sound of screaming and crying. Their deeds then caused stones of fire to rain from the sky, ending the futile lives of the inhabitants of Sodom. God had commanded not to look back towards the city, but Lut wife looked back and started crying seeing the destruction. Upon this a burning stone hit her and she died on the spot. 10

Prophet Lut left Sodom with his daughters and returned to his uncle Prophet Ibrahim. Ibrahim along with Lut continued to spread the message of the Lord till his death.

Today, the Dead Sea is located at the site of the city of Sodom. There are a total of 17 verses in the Quran that mention Prophet Lut. Surah Anam (6:86) Surah Aaraf (7:80-82). 10, 11

This incident is mentioned in every religious text of all the Abrahamic religions. It was from that incident that the name Dead Sea came. Dead Sea is a land locked water body. Actually it should be a lake or a river. But due to the curse of deed (Karma) the water became extremely salty and even the fish cannot survive in it. At about 1,400 feet below sea level, its shores are the lowest land point on Earth. According to Islamic belief the Dead Sea also stands as a sign of Allah's punishment. According to scientists, this area is covered with large deposits of sulphur. There is no life to be found there and the area stands as a symbol of destruction. Sulphur is an element that appears as a result of volcanic eruptions. The Quran states that this place of punishment has been left as a sign for those who observe it: "Surely there are signs in it for those who understand. And certainly they (the cities) are on the road." Verily in Him is a sign for those who believe. (Quran 15:75-77). 12, 13

Allah loves humans very much and has given many relaxations (leverage / comfort) but when a person goes beyond a certain limit, then person gets punishment according to their deeds. Punishment comes in different forms. Today man is facing destruction in various forms due to human deeds in almost all parts of this world. This is a warning to all of us to reform or else we all will perish. People are themselves responsible for the problems they are facing today.

Now a doubt arises that there are many such natural incidents in this world like earthquake, Tsunami, war etc. due to which thousands of human beings and animals are affected or killed. Do their sins deserve equal punishment? In addition to this, thousands of millions of human beings and innocent animals are killed in religious ceremonies or other types of wars imposed by some people. Why is the punishment for these sins meted out to the general public and not to the leaders who inspired them for those wars? In answer it can be said that what we consider to be inert nature and animate being, both of them are bound in an unbreakable strong relationship.

The creation of the universe is not meaningless, it is said in the Quran (3:151) - Those who surrender to God, sitting and lying down and contemplating the creation of the sky and the earth, O Lord! You have not created all this in vain and aimlessly. Similarly, the creation of life is also not in vain. Quran (23:115) says - Have you imagined that we have created you in vain? And that you will not return back to us? It is inevitable to get the result of the deeds. There are good results of the good deeds and bad results for the bad deeds. It is said in the Quran (17:15) - He who follows the right way shall do so to his own advantage; and he who strays shall incur his own loss. In addition to this (39:10) it is said, there is a good reward for those who do good in this world and the land of God is vast. Indeed the patience will be given their rewards without account.

The Bhagavad Gita says that God does not see the outer form of your actions, but he sees your intention. God knows all your intention. Nothing is hidden from Him. Quran (6: 59) says "And with Him are the keys of the unseen, which no one knows except Him." And he knows what is on the land and in the sea. Not a leaf falls but that he knows it. And no grain is there within the darkness of the earth and no moist or dry (thing) but that is (written) in a clear record.

God is not only the witness of all our deeds but is also witness of the feelings in our hearts. Earthquakes, tsunamis and various other natural disasters are not determined by some divine arbitrariness, but by the inner intention behind our outer actions. Today we have evolved from cave man to modern man but have we all really become (human)? God has given us both heart and brain. But we are engrossed in worldliness. We have to turn towards God.

Reference

1. https://www.history.com/news/humans-evolution-neanderthal-s-denisovans

2. https://humanorigins.si.edu/evidence/human-fossils/species/homo-Neanderthalensis

3. http://ngm.national geographic.com/2013/07/125-missing-human-ancestor/shreeve-text

4. https://www.hindustantimes.com/books/book-excerpt-adam-s-first-wife-wasn-t-eve

5. https://en.wikipedia.org/wiki/Y-chromosomal_Adam

6. February 18, 2011 World-Mysteries Blog http://bl og.world-mysteries.com/science/how-many-major-races-are-there-in-the-world d/

7. https://www.britannica.com/topic/Yahweh

8. https://al -injil.net/2012/06/10/taurat-Quran-to-injil-l esson-4-the-sign-of-l ut/

9. https://myisl am.org/story-of-Prophet-lut/

10. https://www.ligions.com/the-dead-sea-in-isl-amic-tradition-2004359

11. https://knowthestraightpath.wordpress.com/2012/01/13/truth-about-the-dead-sea-mentioned-in-quran-is-confirmed-by-geolists/

12. Babu Ram Vilas Sharma on West Asia and the Rig-Veda, h 150 – 151

Chapter 2

Where and How we Have Come From?

The beginning of the earth is believed to be about 4.3 billion years ago. As per todays record human development is only a small event in its long history. The Prehistoric Period - when there was human life before record documented human activity roughly dates about 2.5 million years ago. 1

Genetic measurements suggest that the ape lineage that dates back to Homo sapiens is closer to that of chimpanzees and bonobos, the closest living ancestors of contemporary humans, about 4.6 to 6.2 million years ago. Earlier lived on earth.

The Palaeolithic period is also called the Old Stone Age, is a period in human prehistory distinguished by the original development of stone tools that covers 99% of the period of human technological prehistory. It spanned from the use of stone tools, 3.3 million years ago to the end of the Pleistocene.

The timing of human control over fire remains a matter of debate, with few attested claims of regular fire use by early humans in Africa around 1.6 million years ago. Fire may have been used in Europe but the year is yet to be confirmed. About 350,000 years ago, fire was an important part of human life. The increase in the number of sites with good evidence of fire in the Late Pleistocene suggests that European Neanderthals had fire management. 2

We have found anatomically contemporary human remains of eight individuals of 300000 years old. They are among the oldest known remains classified as "contemporary" (as of 2018). These oldest known evidence of anatomically contemporary humans (as of 2018) are approximately 300000 years old fossils found in Jebel Irhoud, Morocco.

Many older human fossils have been found in different parts of the world, which carbon dating millions of years back describes the different HOMO species. As

a). Peking Man dating period 680000 - 780000 years old were HOMO ERECTUS discovered fossils discovered in 1921 in Zhoukoudian, China.

b). Java man Homo erectus was discovered in Indonesia in 1891, which dates the fossils to about 1 million years old.

c). Turkana Boy, Homo erectus is notable for being the most complete early human fossil ever discovered in Kenya in 1984. The fossil is estimated to be 1.5 to 1.6 million years old.

d). Damanisi Skulls Five skulls found at Damanisi, Georgia are some of the oldest fossils belonging to the Homo erectus line Age: about 1.8 million years old.

e). Homo Erectus georgicus Location: Damanisi, Georgia, Twiggy (OH24) Age: 1.8 million years

f). Homo Habilis Location: Tanzania Year discovered: 1968. KNM ER 1470 Age: 1.9 million years.

g). Homo Rudolfensis Location: Kenya, Year Discovered: 1972. KNM ER 1813, Age: 1.9 million years.

h). Homo Habilis Location: Kenya Discovered: 1973. UR 501 Jaw age: 2.5 - 2.3 million years. 3, 4

Despite some claims by some researchers of bear worship, belief in an afterlife and various other rituals, the archaeological evidence does not fully support the presence of religious practices by contemporary humans or Neanderthals during that period.

This means that humans, may be a little different but were present in this world from 1 to 2 million years ago. Anatomically contemporary humans may have originated in Africa. Most scientists think that a small group may have spread slowly from Africa to different parts of the rest of the world.

The oldest known human burial has been found in the Middle East dating back to 100000 BC. The oldest known Homo sapiens burial of a child has been found at Panga or Saidi, East Africa, 78000–74000 BC. Neanderthal graves found from 70000–42000 BC have been found in Europe and the Middle East. And traces is slowly getting into more research with the help of technology.

According to today's history, physically contemporary humans evolved and flourished behaviourally about millions of years ago. In this Yug today we have written history from around 3500 BC. There is a huge gap in history. Due to improvements in technology, we are slowly finding evidence of the existence of life and cities before 5000-6000 BC. It means to say that the incident of Noah / Manu's terrible flood also proves to be a true incident which is mentioned in the texts of almost all religions. At the same time due to the development of technology the discovery of many submerged cities in the world is the proof of that civilization which existed before in earlier Yug's. The exact dates of the events of Ramayana and Mahabharata are yet to be confirmed. With the help of technology, we have been able to locate Dwarka, the city of Lord Krishna submerged in the Gulf of Cambay.

The researchers have given the following results after their study:-

Several underwater complexes and cities have been found in different places. There is a Neolithic settlement off the coast of Israel in the Mediterranean Sea, which is believed to be more than 8000 years old discovered in 1984 in 30 feet deep water buildings where even odd skeletons have been found. But the most amazing discovery is the seven megaliths arranged in a circle like an underwater Stonehenge. The settlement is believed to have been submerged as a result of the earthquake and/or subsequent tsunami. 5

Scientists used variations to build a more reliable molecular clock and found that Adam would have lived between 120,000 and 156,000 years ago. A comparable analysis of the mtDNA sequences of some men suggested that Eve may have lived between 99,000 and 148,000 years ago. 6

In 1987 population geneticists first demonstrated the existence of such a 'mitochondrial eve'. After analysing mtDNA from 147 people around the world to chart their genetic relationships, they used a 'molecular clock' based on the number of DNA mutations that arise with each generation to estimate Eve's age. This woman, the researchers concluded, probably lived in Africa about 200000 years ago. The discovery provided evidence for the theory that contemporary humans evolved in Africa before migrating to other continents. Yet comparable studies later found that Adam, the common ancestor of the part of the Y chromosome that is passed from father to son, lived 100000 years earlier. It is possible that Adam and Eve lived apart for ages. 7

Carlos Bustamante, a population geneticist at the Stanford University School of Medicine in California who led one of the latest studies, says chance could explain the discrepancy between the ages of Adam and Eve. He says that polygamy may also help explain the difference. The calculation of whether Adam or Eve lived depends on the number of reproductive adults in the population, and polygamy reduces the number of males who pass on their Y chromosomes thus reducing the estimate.

Bustamante and team sequenced the Y chromosomes of 69 men from around the world and revealed nearly 9000 previously unknown DNA sequence variations. They used these variations to build a more reliable molecular clock and found that Adam lived between 120000 and 156000 years ago. A comparable analysis of mtDNA sequences from the same men suggested that Eve lived between 99000 and 148000 years ago. "This idea of a common ancestor of all men is not true," says Bustamante.

A team led by population geneticist Paolo Franclaci at the University of Sassari in Italy reached a similar conclusion by studying the Y chromosomes of 1200 men from the island of Sardinia. The team identified nearly 7000 previously unknown Y-chromosome variations and used that detail to build their molecular clock. The clock helped to indicate major events in Sardinian history, such as the rise of a Neolithic population there and the arrival of Africans as part of the Roman slave trade. It also suggested that Adam lived 180000–200000 years ago, similar to early estimates of Eve's age. 8

"Adam," our oldest relative so far, finally has an approximate date of birth. According to two Israeli researchers, the first humans walked the earth 209,000 years ago – 9,000 years earlier than scientists thought. The study was carried out by Dr Eran Elhaike of the University of Sheffield and Professor Dan Grauer of the University of Houston and Tel Aviv University. Their findings contradict a previous study that determined that the discovery of the Y chromosome (present only in males, while females have two X chromosomes) predated humans.

"We can say with some certainty that contemporary humans must have emerged millions of years ago. It is also clear that 'humans' were not one, but groups of humans lived side by side, and roam together in our world. This means it is clear that many ADAM and EVE (Eve) were present on the earth. **So we can conclude different species of human lived in this world. And God created Adam as referred to a Homo sapiens.** In the events of changes upon the earth, all the other species become extinct and only Homo-sapiens survived on this earth. **Homo Sapiens were made by GOD with special mind power different from other homo species.**

History of contemporary behaviour of few other human species has been found. From hunter to great explorer. As per the current records available with us till 2022. It is that the fittest living apes from Africa may have gradually started to evolve or co-existed with other contemporary human species. God made special Homo-sapiens means intelligent individuals, which had been created by God as Adam and Eve, would have gone and lived a very harsh and difficult life. Were forced to live at the mercy of nature. The other human species tribes followed migration routes and spread out. Somehow they survived the difficult situation. They must have spread gradually from the peninsula to all parts of the world. Humans in Europe came into contact with indigenous people known as Neanderthals who had been living in Europe for more than a million years. They were bigger and stronger than us. They mingled with each other. Much latter the Neanderthal population declined and slowly the Neanderthals became extinct. Only survival of the fittest homo sapaines survived and lived.

Earliest known discovered 40000 BC the remains of one of the anatomically contemporary humans were found as a cremated remains, buried near Lake Mungo in South Whale, Australia. It means that people were living in this world even before 40000 BC. 9, 10

Other hominids such as Homo erectus had been using simple wood and stone tools for millennia, but as time progressed, tools became far more sophisticated and complex. Ice age started in Europe and life came in danger. Various revolutions took place for the inventions of survival, and often small inventions kept happening. It has been found in southern France whose carbon dating is more than 17000 years old. Human beings became inventive and started looking for only things that could survive. A record of our ancestors 26,500 years ago exists in the Garga caves, fingerprints have been discovered in caves in southern France. Cave painting, Lascaux, France 15000 BC "Venus of Willensdorf", Austria 26500 BC. The ancestors were giving the universal message of their existence. The same type of fingerprints are found in South America, Australia. 11

Animals were domesticated long before the Ice Age. This can be said because human's fossils of more than 300000 years old has been found. Also we have found the ruins of the city of Dwarka, and carbon dating of debris tells us that the city existed even before 9500 BC. Various agencies gives various dates of even older than 12000 BC. The carbon dating system proves that the present history that we have now is incomplete history. The findings from the city of Dwarka confirm the different eras that we see in Sanatana Dharma. Islam also confirms about the era through the Noah arc (ship) incident.

Many remains of the settlements of the oldest cities have been found in Turkey. There are still many settlements yet to be discovered. The settlement has been found at the site of the mysterious mountains of the Anatolia chain. Turkish city of Catalhoyok has been found to be of around 11000 BC. A very old temple has also been found there, which is 11000 years old. The archaeological site located in Turkey south-eastern province of Sanliurfa was added to the UNESCO world heritage list in June 2018. A beautiful small town tells a lot about a person's life. The settled village, settlement must have given free time to some people. Catalhoyuk Settlements developed as a potential spiritual centre of Anatolia. Presumably practicing worship in temples, its inhabitants left many clay figurines and impressions of phallic, feminine and hunting scenes for history. The Minister of Culture and Tourism there has called Anatolia the cradle of civilization. 12, 17

According to the observations and history the word God must have been in existence. The fear factor must have led to the emergence of the word GOD. But we also know that when Adam met Eve, they prayed and thanked God long ago. So the word God existed since the time of evolution of mankind. There must be some other great civilization in different parts of the world. Specially like the city of Dwarka whose remains have been found submerged in the Gulf of Cambay. There are many more yet to be discovered.

Later on the community developed. The numbers grew and expanded and the barter system began and various systems developed. Priests and kings were made, society developed and divided, gradually caste system developed, discrimination started, love and hatred entered. God sent messengers to different parts of the world to eradicate evils and corruptions and to show the right path to the human beings.

During the different ages great development took place in different parts of the world. Engineering system emerged. With suffering and sacrifice a new engineering's was invented and the taming of nature started.

In the present age the Minoans, a great civilization in Europe flourished from 3000 BC to 1400 BC. They were trailblazers from the west and traders from the Mediterranean to the east. Ruins of Minoan cities have been found in Europe. Archaeologists describe them as ideally living noble lives but the Minoans were not able to control disasters. Rituals performed to please the Lord, human sacrifices were offered. A temple was excavated at Keonosis in which evidence of human sacrifice has been found. **Many ancient civilizations used to sacrifice humans**. The temple was buried in an earthquake and the city was destroyed. Where the remnants of that civilization went is a moot point. Some migrated from Europe to the East and other parts of the world. The Egyptian civilization began to flourish in the other part of the world around 3500 BC. Early civilizations emerged first in Lower Mesopotamia (3500 BCE), followed by the Egyptian Civilization along the Nile (3500 BCE), the Harappan Civilization in the Indus River Valley (in present-day BHARAT and Pakistan; 2500 BCE), and Chinese Civilization as well as the Yellow and Yangtze Rivers (2500 BC). These societies developed a number of unifying characteristics, including a central government, a complex economy and social structure, sophisticated language and writing systems and distinct cultures and religions. Entities such as the sun, moon, earth, sky and sea were often deified. Temples developed, which developed into temple establishments, complete with a complex hierarchy of priests and other functionaries. The specialty of the Neolithic period was the tendency to worship anthropomorphic deities. The earliest surviving written religious texts are the Egyptian Pyramid Texts, the oldest of which date to between 2500 and 2300 BCE. 14

And in this Yug it is from this period of civilizations that we have written records. Now it is concluded that when the present history was written during 18th and 19th century, we had limited resources due to which we could not discover many ancient things. Gradually, as technology developed, we are getting many new discoveries about old civilizations. It is only through technology that we came to know that the city of Dwarka is submerged in sea. Similarly we are getting many new things which prove that many other civilizations existed even before 5000 BC. The submerged city of Dwarka is the city of Lord Krishna's. The underneath measurements of the city confirms the truth of the Dwarka city area as is mentioned in the Sanatani religious text books.

Biggest recent discovery of a 'Dragon Man': Human skull found in China forced scientists to re-think about the evolution of humans. The skull was first found in late 1933 by workers building a bridge over the Songhua River in Harbin. At the time, the region was ruled by Japan and to prevent it from falling into Japanese hands; Chinese labourers wrapped it up and hid it in a well, where it remained for more than 90 years. The skull was found when a labourer narrated the story to his grandson in 2018. After being found by the family, the fossil was donated to the Geology Museum of Hebei Geo University. The team of researchers then carried out **a geochemical analysis of the skull and dated it to be at least 146000 years old**. Due to a long, difficult and confusing history since the discovery, information about the fossil's exact geographic origins has been lost, the researchers said.

Researchers believe that Dragon Man probably lived in a wooded flood plain and humans in an attempt to establish the newly found specimen's position in the tree. They entered it into a database along with 95 other skull fossils. They found that this formed a new branch closer to contemporary humans than to Neanderthals.

It has recently become clear that multiple human lineages co-existed with Homo sapiens. The researchers said the fossilized skull is one of the best-preserved human fossils and advances understanding of previous such finds from the region. 15, 16

The overall conclusion is that there is a vast gap and limitation in the present history. The current history that we read was written when technology had not developed and written with a biased mind frame. As new technology is developing, we are getting many new things from history. The new findings confirm and give us ideas about the era or yug's mentioned in Sanatana Dharma. The holy book Quran also justifies the era or yug's system through Noah's ark flood incident.

Reference

1. https://www.history.com/news/prehistoric-age-timeline

2. https://www.pnas.org/content/108/13/5209

3. https://www.nationalgeographic.com/culture/article/131017

4. https://australian.museum/learn/science/human-evolution/homo-ergaster/

5. https://www.smithsonianmag.com/history/oldest-known-seawall-discovered-along-submerged-mediterranean-villages-180973819/

6. https://avalanchespaces.com/qa/quick-answer-how-long-have-humans-been-on-the-earth

7. https://www.nature.com/articles/nature.2013.13478?fbclid=IwAR2xJhNc7aNRgAUTlzdEHeB8PBIEcaMoU-PGST6zoPYvcD4iQQullXFKPhM

8. http://linguaggio-macchina.blogspot.com/2013/08/y-chromosome-analysis-moves-adam-closer.html

9. https://en.wikipedia.org/wiki/Early_human_migrations

10. https://humanjourney.us/discovering-our-distant-ancestors-section/out-of-africa/

11. https://en.wikipedia.org/wiki/Human_evolution

12. https://www.nationalgeographic.com/history/history-magazine/article/early-agriculture-settlement-catalhoyuk-turkey

13. https://www.britannica.com/topic/Minoan-civilization

14. https://www.oldest.org/culture/civilizations/

15. https://www.livemint.com/science/news/dragon-man-massive-head-in-china-forces-scientists-to-rethink-human-evolution-11624667613147.html

16. https://www.nationalgeographic.com/science/article/dragon-man-fossi l-skull-may-represent-new-human-species-in-china

17. https://favdaily.com/oldest-temple-i%DO%BF-the-world-over-11000-years-old-gobekli-tepe

Chapter 3

How Have we Evolved?

The biased History which was written in the seventeenth century. The author Arch Bishop Usher (1581 – 1653), according to his own calculations he told that the earth was created on 4004 BC at 9 am before the birth of Christ. That day man emerged on the earth. Till the middle part of the 19th century, most scientists believed that the existence of man on the earth is not more than 6 thousand years. But in the second half of the last century and the current century, geological exploration and by the testing radio-active minerals, scientists have proved that the earth is more than 4 billion years old.

Now with the help of technology we have got proofs from some proven researches and techniques, which are as below:

Big Bang started nearly 14 billion years ago. Earliest life on earth started around 4 billion years ago single-celled prokaryotic Archaea. JURASSIC periods occurred 1.7 billion years ago.

Earliest **hominids Apes** came into existence in around 25 million years ago in Africa, earliest hominids (great apes) amongst the **hominoid gibbons** in Asia.

Hominids ***Pierolapithecus catalaunicus*** in Spain and ***Nyanzapithecus alesi*** in Kenya, possible ancestors of hominines and contemporary apes, the former with upright posture around 13 million year ago.

Earliest hominine *Sahelanthropus*, then *Ororin* and *Ardipithecus*, amongst the hominids in Africa: reduced canines, arboreal habit and bipedal capability around 7 million. Replacement of the earliest hominines by *Australopithecus* spp. in Africa: fully upright, bipedal and free-striding gait around 4.2 million years ago,

Earliest human, *Homo* sp., amongst the hominine (Ledi-Geraru, Ethiopia): rounded chin as *Australopithecus afarensis*, but smaller and slimmer molars as the later *Homo Habilis around 2.8 million year ago.*

Earliest stone tools produced by humans (Gona, Ethiopia): Oldowan tools, chopping through flesh, bone, bark around 2.6 million year ago.

Earliest evidence of human ancestors outside of Africa: tool-using hominine' in Shangchen, southern China around 2.1 million year ago.

Early *Homo erectus* direct ancestor of contemporary humans coexisting with *Australopithecus* – soon extinct and *Paranthropus* (South Africa): enlarged brain and smaller teeth around 2 million year ago. Migrations of *Homo erectus* from Africa to Eurasia (Georgia; to Lantian in northern China by 1.63 million years ago; to Java by 1.5 million years ago), replacement of *Homo Habilis* by *Homo erectus* in Africa around 1.4 million year ago. Earliest control of fire by *Homo erectus* (South Africa) → uniquely human capability, extending the day with firelight, raising the nutritive value of food with cooking around 1 million year ago.

Homo antecessor in Western Europe (Atapuerca, Spain), closely related to the last common ancestor of Neanderthals, Denisovans and contemporary humans around 9 lakh year ago.

Rise of *Homo heidelbergensis* in Africa and Europe, possible ancestor of *Homo sapiens* and *Homo Neanderthalensis*; cooking meat and starchy plants 6 lakh years ago.

Rise of Neanderthals *Homo Neanderthalensis* across Europe around 4.5 Lakh years ago, Denisovans diverge from Neanderthals (southern Siberia) → Tibetan Plateau before 160,000 years ago; subsequent interbreeding, possibly also with *Homo erectus* around 4.3 Lakhs years ago. Earliest representatives of our species, *Homo sapiens* (Jebel Irhoud, Morocco): facial and dental structure similar to contemporary humans, yet still archaic elongation of the braincase around 3.1 lakh years ago.

Homo sapiens enters Eurasia (Greece), first of multiple dispersals out of Africa by humans with early contemporary traits, including globular braincase and descended larynx facilitating spoken language around 2 Lakh years ago.

Burial of dead by anatomically contemporary humans in Qafzeh cave, Israel and by Neanderthals in Tabun cave, Israel: mortuary practices around 1.2 lakhs years ago.

Interbreeding of *Homo sapiens* with *Homo Neanderthalensis* (Siberia) → accumulation of contemporary traits through gene flow around 1 Lakhs year ago.

Earliest human etchings on rock: cross-hash decorations or symbols (Blombos Cave, South Africa) and drawings around 1 to 0.7 Lakhs year ago.

Eurasian *Homo sapiens* co-existing with *Homo floresiensis* (soon extinct) and *Homo luzonensis*, interbreeding with Neanderthals and Denisovans 60,000/ till 50,000 years ago, earliest anatomically contemporary humans.

Capacity of Language development remains a mystery

Homo sapiens, established in Europe (Bacho Kiro, Bulgaria), mating with Neanderthals, spreading eastwards around 46000 years ago, earliest musical instruments: bone and ivory flutes (Swabian Jura,

Germany) → concepts of harmony, melody, rhythm, timbre; no human society without music 42000 years ago.

Anatomically contemporary humans replace Neanderthals, our last remaining sibling species 50000 - 40000 years ago.

Earliest migration of humans into the Americas (Chiquihuite Cave, Mexico), along the coast from Siberia around 28000 years ago, introgression of last remaining Denisovans into the contemporary human genome.

Associated skull cult 11500, earliest continuous settlements (southern Levant), including Jericho: stone and mud architecture developing into a walled city of up to 3,000 people → contemporary cities of 30 million people 11000 years ago- 9000 BCE, continental ice-sheets withdraw from Europe and North America 10000 years ago.

9000 BC the settlements of Catalhöyük developed as a possible spiritual centre of Anatolia? Presumably practicing worship in temples, its inhabitants left behind numerous clay figurines and impressions of phallic, feminine and hunting scenes. The first evidence of a worship at present-day Catalhoyuk dates 9000 BC.

Earliest mining of metal, to heat, hammer and grind into tools: copper for projectile points (Great Lakes, North America) about 8500 years ago, beginning of a wave of migration from the Middle East northwest through Anatolia, Europe. Man scattered and settled in all parts of the world. 2

The great flood of the epic of Gilgamesh, the flood of Noah's ship around 5000 BC. This is such a turning point in world history that no one can deny and the whole world was submerged and the old civilization was destroyed. Noah and his family survived.

At that time all old civilization got destroyed and later new world civilization developed from Noah. Before Noah there were different great civilizations in many parts of the world whose history is yet to be fully explored. Slowly the lost history is coming to the fore. Historians did not pay attention to the civilizations that existed before the flood on the earth. Also the boat was made of wooden planks and iron nails. It clearly means that during that time and before that time the iron was in use. Even in Sanatan Dharma, there is a deluge and in it Manu is the super hero.

So the whole history needs to be relooked and needs to be rewritten according to the new discoveries and evidences as we move forward with new technologies. As technology is developing, many things are being discovered. Which is certified by the scientists of America and Europe. Today we have some written history which is somewhat certified but a lot is missing about the earlier history (before 3500 BC). The history which is taught to us today it is incomplete and is distorted. Who are we? We have not been able to trace out properly. There are some other things in history, about which information is coming slowly. Some have come, but authenticity is yet to be included in history.

Research is ongoing and slowly information is being received. Some research give us information about the past ages. According to the Quran also the incident of Noah's Ark justify the concept of different ages i.e. Yug's. We have found that the north and south poles of the earth at different times flipped. The pole has changed its position with the ages i.e. Yug's. After going deeper we come to know in different ages different group of human beings, different species, lived in different places.

Bal Gangadhar Tilak in his famous book **Orion** and **Artic home of Vedas** tried to prove on the basis of several suktas (mantras) of the Vedas that the Aryans lived around the North Pole (that was in BHARAT) during the Vedic period. The Vedic period was before this yug. People who called themselves Aryans gradually spread in all directions. Modern research suggests that in the early period of the composition of Vedic Suktas, the region of Dhruv (North Pole) was inside the BHARATIYE subcontinent. 3

Some have told the Rig-Veda to be of before 6000 BC and some have told Rig-Veda to be of before 75000 BC. A research has come that at one time the North Pole was located in the place of present Bengal, Odisha Jharkhand broader. As the change happened, the direction of the pole changed. The Aryans lived in Aryavarta, which was on the banks of the Saraswati River. Due to the weather and the changing pole, they started wandering and moved away from the banks of the Saraswati River. They changed and moved according to time and then in different era came back to Aryavarta. We all know that change is the law of nature and survival of the fittest. North Pole kept changing from its place many times, similarly human groups also kept changing their place for survival. We find in history that which does not change according to time they perish. 4

A scientist Ivory (Electromagnetism) has done research in electromagnetism and has told that the Earth's magnetic field has been slowly reversing for the last several hundred years and this process is going on and on. This reversal is not something that happens overnight, but over thousands of years. Earth's magnetic field also reversed about 780000 years ago also. According to paramagnetic records, Earth's magnetic poles have reversed at least 100 times in the past 160 million years. The weakening of the magnetic field resulted in more cosmic rays reaching the Earth's surface, causing untold harm to our eco system. 5

Another research done by Mindy Weisberger (Mindy Weisberger February 19, 2021), shows that the Earth's magnetic field also reversed about 42000 years ago, causing a climate 'catastrophe'. Links a magnetic field reversal about 42000 years ago to the climate upheaval that led to the extinction and reshaped human behaviour. 6

A recent study has found that about 42000 years ago, there was a shift in the magnetic poles of planet Earth, which was followed by global environmental changes and mass extinction among other serious effects. Researchers conducting the study used radiocarbon dating preserved in ancient tree rings to narrow down the time period when Earth's magnetic field was reversed and the solar wind recorded the changes. 42000 years ago there was a turbulent period on Earth, characterized by widespread lightning storms, auroras and cosmic radiation seeping into the atmosphere.

After figuring out the time window of the Adams event, the team compared them to observed changes in climate around the world during the same time period. They found that mega fauna in mainland Australia and Tasmania went through a simultaneous extinction 42,000 years ago. Also researchers believe this event may explain the extinction of Neanderthals and the sudden appearance of art in caves around the world. 7

Another research has reported that Australian researchers have found radiocarbon in ancient trees. Australian researchers have analysed radiocarbon records from ancient trees in New Zealand that survived when the magnetic poles were reversed. The trees revealed spikes in atmospheric radiocarbon levels, caused by the collapse of Earth's magnetic field and changing solar winds. But before the flip was a weakening of the magnetic field, causing lightning storms, crimson skies, widespread aurorae and deadly cosmic radiation, which spooked our early ancestors and Earth's wildlife. 8

A reversal of Earth's magnetic poles, coupled with a decline in solar activity 42000 years ago, may have played a role in key events from the extinction of mega fauna to the end of Neanderthals, say researchers.

From the study, we come to know that at present there are many errors in the history which is taught to us. Today, through contemporary technology, the correct and accurate history is slowly coming in front of us. So from the research, we can say that in this earth Humans lived for millions of years. People lived in the present day BHARAT also for millions of years. Those who lived in Aryavarta were called Arya's. Arya means superior. Arya's were not a separate race, they are ancestors of all of us.

The word Arya is not foreign. It is the Vedic language of Gods, which means religious, superior, respectable, generous character, calm, virtuous. Arya's came to be called BHARATIYE – Bharatiya Yantr Santiti (Vishnu Purana 2.3.1) Darshatvya. (The country that lies north the ocean and south of the snowy mountains is called Bharata.) It is not mentioned that Aryans came from outside.

From page number 18 of Ram Vilas Sharma's book "West Asia and Rig-Veda", we find that Aryans entered BHARAT from North West. In the Indo-European forms of BHARATIYE words with voiced aspirated sounds, the consonant and the aspirate do not coincide. This one fact is enough to demolish the theory of the Aryan invasion of BHARAT. 10

A book Ancient India by Megasthnese in page no. 34 Megasthnese has written that BHARAT is a unique country. Not a single person here is of foreign origin. It is neither a colony of any foreigner nor has BHARAT established a colony in any country. 11

Elphinstone has supported Megasthenes. In history of India (elphinstone) and see Aryans (Gordon Childe) page no 35. According the word Arya is not foreign.

There is no such mention in any ancient text that Aryans came from outside and settled in BHARAT. **There is no doubt that a person cannot do justice to himself and his time without being educated.**

According to our present written history which is incomplete. We have the following details:-

The development of systems of governance with the rise of Uruk, a city of 30,000 inhabitants (Sumer civilization, Mesopotamia) in the Indus Valley (BHARAT and Pakistan) around 3100 BCE.

The Great Pyramid of Giza (Egypt) dates to around 3000 - 2550 BC.

Decline of the Indus Valley Civilization, triggered by a 200-year drought around 2000 BC.

The Beginnings of Complex Societies: Babylonian Civilization in Mesopotamia, 1800 BCE; Olmec Civilization in Mesoamerica 1800 BCE; Shang Dynasty in China 1600 BCE; New Egypt 1600 BC

Bronze replacing iron for tools and weapons around 1050 BC, First Jewish Temple (Jerusalem), King Solomon and the rise of Judaism around 950 BC.

Starting centre of higher education (Taxashila University, BHARAT) → Plato's Academy in Greece by 387 BC; Taixue University in China by CE 3; By the University of al-Karouin in Morocco CE 859.

First Olympic Games (Olympia, Peloponnesus, 776 BC). The peak of Greek civilization (Greece), the foundation of ethics, poetry, drama, philosophy; First democracy 508 BCE, First Persian Empire (Cyrus the Great, Persia), connects Mediterranean Sea with Indus Valley → Code of justice that respects others' beliefs around 550 BCE.

Sushruta Samhita (BHARAT, 6th century BCE) described surgery and anatomy in 550 BCE.

A collection of the Torah and other Hebrew scriptures in the Hebrew Bible from about 450 BCE.

Siddhartha Gautama (563 – 483 BCE, ancient BHARAT) better known as the Buddha was a follower and reformer of Sanatana Dharma. His followers named his teachings as Buddhism.

Christianity began after the death of Jesus of Nazareth. - 30 - 50AD.

There was a lot of violence and change in society in the Middle East and Europe. Rome emerged as the central power of the world. The writing of the New Testament Bible began around 250 AD. The New Testament replaced the Old Testament.

The Dark Ages "between" 200 AD to 600 AD. Different kingdoms ruled different places of the world with limited powers. There was chaos and darkness everywhere. Specially in Middle East Asia.

The rise of Islam in Arabia with the Prophet Muhammad (Mecca, Saudi Arabia, 570 to 632) and the Islamic Golden Age of the 7th to 11th centuries.

Birth of renaissance rise of individuality, imagination, innovation, capitalism in late 1400 AD.

European sailors reach BHARAT (Vasco da Gama from Portugal, 1498) → colonial empires in Africa and Asia; Indian Ocean trade; Global multiculturalism 1498 AD.

Scientific Revolution began in 1543 AD, invention of the first cost-effective steam engine (James Watt, UK, 1769) → powered machinery, steamships, Industrial Revolution.

BHARAT was under British colonial rule from about 1750 to 1947.

World War I (1914–18), 32 nations participate, 20 million killed.

World War II (1939–45), 184 nations participated, 60 million killed.

BHARAT became independent in 1947 AD and we are in the present.

Reference

1. History of book science author Samarendra Nath Sen, translator Bhupendra Nath Sanyal

2. https://www.yourgenome.org/stories/evolution-of-modern-humans

3. Bal Gangadhar Tilak's book Orion and Artic home of Vedas

4. Shri Mohan Lal Mahto Viyogi has written, page no 9 book Arya Jeevan Darshan

5. https://www.drbakstmagnetics.com/the-earths-magnetic-field-is-reversing

6. (Mindy Weisberger last updated February 19, 2021)

7. https://www.firstpost.com/tech/science/earths-magnetic-field-flipped-42000-years-ago

8. Muri's sanskrit text book vol 2 p 323

9. Ram Vilas Sharma's book West Asia and Rig-Veda page number 18

10. Ancient BHARAT by megasthenes in page no. 34

11. https://www.space.com/25126-big-bang-theory.html

12. https://www.history.com/news/how-mesopotamia-became-the-cradle-of-civilization

13. https://www.wikiwand.com/en/Cradle_of_civilization

14. https://australian.museum/learn/science/human-evolution/homo-heidelbergensis/

15. https://www.newscientist.com/article/dn9989-timeline-human-evolution/

16. https://en.wikipedia.org/wiki/Timeline_of_prehistory

17. https://humanhistorytimeline.com/

18. https://www.smithsonianmag.com/history/oldest-known-seawall-discovered

Chapter 4

The Missing Link in History

Few extinct animals are yet to be discovered within the evolutionary line as the missing link between modern humans and their ancestors. In the 19th century, a common interpretation of Charles Darwin's work was that humans are the direct descendants of extinct species of apes. To accept this theory and reconcile it with the Hierarchical Great Chain of Being, some fossil ape-human or human-ape seemed necessary to complete the chain. But today it is believed that modern humans are related to apes groups now closely related to anthropomorphism, through a common ancestor rather than by direct descent. Some of it has been identified so far and much more remains to be discovered. 1

When incidentally a 9-year-old boy who tripped over a cliff in South Africa prompted researchers to search for the "missing link" in human evolution, according to a new study. The fossils of Australopithecus sediba were found in 2008 when Matthew Berger chased his dog down a cliff near the Malapa fossil site in South Africa. Fossils discovered in South Africa are one of the 'missing links' of human evolution.

The discovery of an adult female and adolescent male of 2 million years ago has been described as the "Cradle of Humankind" in a discovery that has been controversially debated in the scientific community. New research confirms that this species is closely related to the genus Homo and points toward the discovery of an important missing link in the history of mankind between early humans and most of our ape predecessors.

Writing in the journal Paleo Anthropology found that the species is the bridge between the 3-million-year-old "Lucy" or Australopithecus afarensis and the "handy man" Homo Habilis which used tools between 1.5 and 2.1 million years ago. 1, 2

Most of the currently available histories were written during the 17th centuries, when technology had not developed. History at that time was written by people who were influenced and inspired by a particular place, community, religion and sects. Now as the new technologies is developing rapidly, more and more new discoveries are coming in front of us. We have to look and find out the true and lost history that of before the NUHA Arc incident.

A relic of the old civilization is the submerged city, which we know as the submerged Dwarka. Until the discovery of the submerged city of Dwarka, archaeologists believed that civilization in BHARAT dates back only to 3000 to 4000 years ago. But the findings obtained from the study of archaeological remains found in the sunken city of the Gulf of Cambay, take the civilization of BHARAT to be of before 9000 years ago and beyond that.

According to the epic Mahabharata, Krishna established his mighty kingdom on the banks of Gujarat to avoid endless battles between himself and Jarasandha (in Mathura). Connected by an elaborate network of boulevards, bazaars and temples, Dwarka was evolved in its design and architecture. Around 70 feet below sea level sandstone walls, cobblestone streets, huge pieces of rock were found that were once part of the structures and Copper coins have been found of about 9500 years ago.

The condition in which the buildings were discovered suggests that the city may have been submerged by a tsunami or earthquake. The sea level would have risen. A similar event happened in Bahrain at the same time. This supports the fact that there must have been a busy network of trade between the coastal city of Lothal (near Dwarka) and Bahrain. The sea level rise in BHARAT and Bahrain at the same time confirms that the story of Noah's (Manu's) ark is true and that due to incessant rains the whole earth was submerged.

The city of Dwarka, or "Gateway to Heaven", was found submerged in the Gulf of Cambay in 1988, about 80 - 100 feet below. Ancient structures, pillars, city grids and ancient artefacts have been found. Some consider them to be at least 10000 years old. Either way, it's an underwater city, long lost, full of mystery, legend and spectacular. 3, 4, 5, 6

According to the beliefs and Puranas of Sanatan Dharma, the story of Manu and his boat is as follows.

Our original identity which we get from God gets distorted by our actions. This account is in the Shatapatha Brahmana, which tells how the progenitor (forefather) of mankind known as Manu survived the flood. The Quran the Bible and the Vedas all tell us that all human beings alive today are descended from him. According to the Vedas, Manu was the person who was upon the truth. Manu is referred to in the Agni Purana as Satyavrata ("one who is sworn to truth"). According to the Shatapatha Brahmana, the fish of Vishnu avatar had told Manu about the coming of flood. The Avatar initially appeared in the form of a Shafri (a small fish). The small fish asked Manu to save it, Manu out of pity kept it into the pitcher of water. It grew bigger and bigger, Manu put it in a big pot, and then put it in a well. When the well proved insufficient for the ever-growing fish, Manu placed it in a reservoir. As the fish grew, Manu had to pour it into a river, and when the river also proved insufficient, he put it into the sea.

After which it expanded vastly in the great ocean. This happened when the Avatar informed Manu of a devastating flood that was about to come very soon. As per the instruction, Manu built a huge boat, in which all the species were placed to repopulate the earth. The fish saved the boat during the flood. His boat stopped after being flooded on top of a mountain. Today all the humans on the earth are the descendants of the same Manu. 10

The word 'Manus' (human) comes from the Proto-Indo-European "Manu" (Sanskrit Manu, Avestan Manu). And the English word 'MAN' is derived from Manu. The word 'Manus' comes from the Proto-Indo-European "Manu" (Sanskrit Manu, Avestan Manu).

The religious holy book also tells us that Noah or Manu: offered a sacrifice to God with some of the clean animals and clean birds. It is believed that right after sacrifice God blessed Manu/Noah and his sons and made a promise with Manu that never again would he judge all people with such flood.

Even the Chinese people have the same belief about Noah/Manu and the flood. Each story is the same only the names of the protagonists differ, according to their language and place. Some people called him Noah, Sumerian Utnapishtim, Sanatan Manu, similarly people of every other religion call him in their own language. Other versions of the flood myth have been told by the Mayans, Greeks, Native Americans, Africans, Celts, Australian Aborigines and Chinese peoples. **There is a mention of Noah's Ark in the Holy Quran which means that the Quran authenticates the era (yug) system.**

Like the submerged city of Dwarka, many other submerged cities also exist in different parts of the earth. To the rescue is the legend of Atlantis. Invented by Plato about 2300 years ago. He claimed that this civilization, which allegedly existed 9000 years before his time, was punished by the Gods for being selfish, greedy and immoral and drowned it in the sea.

Manu/Noah and his sons survived the great flood, they may have memorized and spoken the Vedas orally for many generations to generation and later scripted down for the first time around 1500 BCE. But perhaps with the passage of time as well as the large gap between oral and written transmission many real things may have changed.

Sundar Kand of Valmiki Ramayana 9 shlok 4-5, states "After that, the glorious Hanuman saw the best abode of the demons and the house of Ravana, which had four tusked elephants and three tusked elephants. They were guarded by soldiers bearing weapons" Here, sage Valmiki describes elephants with four tusks as well as elephants with three tusks and two tusks.

According to the reckoning of the Vedic period, we are currently in the Kali Yuga and the Ramayana is believed to be an event of the earlier Yuga, Satya Yug.

The Valmiki Ramayana Sundara Kanda [4/27-28] states that Hanuman upon entering Lanka sees four-tusked elephants guarding Ravana's palaces. These elephants were very tall, majestic and were trained to protect Lanka from invaders.

Contemporary anthropologists say that four-tusked elephants existed between 12 and 1.6 million years ago. Gomphotheridae was a diverse taxonomic family of extinct elephant-like animals (proboscis). Referred to as gomphotheres, they were widespread during the Miocene and Pliocene epochs, 12–1.6 million years ago. Some also lived in parts of Eurasia, Beringia, and the Great American Interchange, South America. 12

So the conclusion comes, that the present history is just a small chapter of a thick book. We need to complete the book of history by adding many missing chapters.

As we are developing with new technologies, we are getting all the missing links of our history with relevant facts. We cannot deny this because Quran also says that due to the bad deeds and corruptions of humans, Allah had given the great flood, only Noah and his family were saved from that flood. One more thing is that in the religion of Islam It is said that Allah has sent about 124000 Prophets in this world, among them Noah was also one of the Prophet. It is believed that Adam is the first Prophet of this world but the year has not been yet confirmed. So it is confirmed that from Adam till Noah there is a huge and long history hidden. This history can be of millions of years. After Noah, a new era system has started in which we all are today i.e. kalyug.

A recent study has found that about 42000 years ago there was a shift in the magnetic poles of the planet Earth, which was followed by global environmental changes and other severe effects. There were several types of mass extinctions many times.

After figuring out the time window of the Adams event, the team compared them to observed changes in climate around the world during the same and different time periods. They found that mega fauna in mainland Australia and Tasmania went through a simultaneous extinction 42000 years ago. Also researchers believe that this event could also be the reason for the extinction of Neanderthals. 15

The Bible also describes past pole shifts.

Isaiah 24:1 "Behold, the Lord lays maketh the earth empty, and maketh it waste, and turneth it upside down, and scattered abroad the inhabitants thereof." (Behold the LORD will empty the earth and make it desolate, and he will twist its surface and scatter its inhabitants.

Job 9:5-6 "God moves mountains, they do not know, when he overturns them in his anger; he shakes the earth from its place, and its pillars tremble."

Hebrews 12:26-27 "I will not only shake the earth once again, but also the heavens.

Isaiah 22:23 "I will move the peg in its firm place." This is probably a reference to God establishing a new North Pole after the pole shift.

Scientists believe that the change in magnetic poles had happened many times.

Bal Gangadhar Tilak in his famous book "Orion" and "Artic home of Vedas" has tried to prove on the basis of many suktas (mantras) of Vedas, that Aryans lived around North Pole in Vedic period. Lived nearby. The Vedic period people who called themselves Aryans gradually spread in all directions. It is estimated from modern researches that in the early period of the composition of the Vedic Suktas, the region of Drava was within the BHARATIYE subcontinent. Bal Gangadhar Tilak has also proved that Vedas are knowledge of before 6000 BC. Some other scholars have told Rig-Veda to be 10000 BC old and some have told Rig-Veda to be knowledge of 75000 BC and even older than that.

We are all beginning to know some of the unknown facts of history now and there are many more unknown facts of history yet to be discovered. Recent discoveries from archaeology, astronomy, ancient mathematics and satellite photography as well as bold new interpretations of ancient inscriptions are now in a position to better understand the ancient history of BHARAT and the world. The findings and research show that the Vedic civilization has its roots in BHARAT and the world going back to before 7000 BCE and much much beyond.

When we see the history written with a prejudiced mind-set from some evidences of the Indus Valley Civilizations then the theory of Aryan invasion seems to be correct from that mind-set, but the facts are beyond this. The invasion theory is only two hundred years old when no proper archaeology existed. They actually went with religious and political beliefs. The most important influential figure in all this was the German Ideologist Friedrich Max Müller, a renowned Sanskrit scholar but exceptionally ignorant of science. He also believed in the words that the world was created on 23 October 4004 BC at 9 am. 16

In 1784, Sir William Jones then serving as a judge in Bengal, observed that there were great similarities between Sanskrit and European languages. He is considered as the founder of the field of Indology as well as the Florentine merchant Filippo Sasetti, who after a five-year stay in Goa (1583 - 88) stated that there had definitely been a connection between Sanskrit and the European languages. Jones did a systematic comparative study and found that the Sanskrit "deva" for God becomes "deus" in Latin, "dio" in Italian, "dieu" in French and "Theo" in Greek. In the same way Manu becomes Man. "Agni" in Sanskrit becomes "ignis" in Latin, which gives us ignition. Therefore, for such linguistic similarity, linguists conclude that the ancestors of all the people speaking these respective languages lived in the same region in earlier times in different parts of Asia and Europe. It was called ZAMBODWEEP.

In recent years investigations by scholars from a wide range of disciplines such as archaeology, ancient mathematics, computer science and astronomy have resulted in serious questions being raised about the facts of the Aryan invasion and the various interpretations.

In this age we consider the Ganges as a holy river but in the Vedic period the holiest of rivers was the Saraswati, which flowed in the Punjab west of the Ganges and the Yamuna. As seen, the Rig-Veda praises Saraswati as the holy mother. The word "Mother" is the one who gives life. "Mother" never leaves her children to die of hunger. Similarly, our ancestors used to drink water from the river for their survivals. Plus all the facilities to survive on the banks of the river respectfully, so all consider the holy river as mother, which keeps us alive. Mother is also called Goddess. **In Sanatan Dharma, the word**

deity is considered to have a meaning which gives to us and does not take anything in return. Like earth, sun, moon, water etc.

Saraswati the best mother, the best river, the best Goddess... Rig-Veda 2.41.16

Regarding Saraswati, in page number 12 of the book "**Vedic BHARAT**" by Nav Prakash; there are many references scattered throughout the Rig-Veda. Extensive research done by archaeologists in recent years has shown that the centre of the Indus civilization was not on the banks of the Indus but on the banks of the dry Saraswati. An extensive investigation by Late Dr V S Wakankar with the help of a team of experts from many disciplines showed that the Saraswati had changed its course several times, and finally dried up completely around 1900 BC. The river Saraswati was once a great river as described in the Rig-Veda. It was the life blood of the civilization there. These archaeological finds have now been confirmed by photographs taken by the American Earth sensing satellite Landsat and more recently by the French satellite SPOT. 17

These discoveries show that the Saraswati River had completely dried up in 1900 BC. This raises questions about the invasion of the Aryans. When the Saraswati dried up completely in about 1900 BC, it proves that the Rig Veda is the knowledge of before 1900 BC, in which the river Saraswati Mention is found in the form of a full river.

Evidence from Harappan sites includes the famous discovery of a metal relic known as the head of Vashishtha. During a trip to BHARAT in 1958, a young American collector named Harry Hicks found a beautiful metal head near Delhi, which he coincidentally saved from being melted down as scrap. Attempts were made to determine its date after scientific tests at nuclear physics laboratories in the US and Switzerland. It was found that it was cast around 3700 BC. The head was found according to the description of the famous sage Vashishtha given in the Rig-Veda. Vasishatha was the chief priest and advisor to the Vedic kings. This proves the Rig-Veda to be a book of before 3700 BC.

Thus, on the basis of evidence from archaeology, mathematics, astronomy and metallurgy, it is now clear that the Aryans were living in BHARAT before 4004 BC also. The age of the Rig-Veda was the civilization before the rise of ancient Egypt, Mesopotamia and the Indus Valley Civilization.

The reason we were presented with a wrong history was that most Europeans from the seventeenth to the nineteenth centuries did not know the present science and technology at all, as we have seen in the case of Max Müller. Another fundamental reason was that it was never the intention of the colonial authorities to discover the truth about history. They were interested in using all the things like tool kit for the fulfilment of their own political, commercial and missionary work.

The word "Arya" in Sanskrit means superior person and does not mean any caste. The Sanskrit dictionary Amarkosh gives the following definition "An Arya is one who is from a noble family who is of gentle behaviour and good nature and good conduct". All of us living in undivided BHARAT no matter what kind of worship system we have adopted, are actually Aryans. The word Arya is also used thirty-six times in the Rig-Veda, but it does not mean any caste. It is the cultural designation of people who built a great civilization.

Ancient BHARATIYE sources can be divided into three types of literature – Vedic, mythological and historical epics. But the Europeans cultivated the Aryan invasion theory and misinterpretation of the Vedas into a record of an invading Aryan race. From my point of view, I think that due to malice, inferiority complex feelings, blame and superstition of our society in BHARAT western people easily put their thoughts upon us. Society in ancient BHARAT was divided into sects and castes may be by some people. Later Muslims came to the central power, Europeans entered BHARAT and ruled BHARAT. After the weakening of the Mughal kings, the Britisher's became powerful. So taking advantage of the many weaknesses and divisions in the BHARATIYE society, the Europeans were able to impose their theories on BHARAT and further divided BHARAT in religion base and adopted divide and rule policy.

The description of the course of the river Saraswati as flowing from the mountain to the sea also points to the same date. Upon Careful analysis of data from the French satellite SPOT shows that the geography of northern BHARAT described in the Rig-Veda, the course of rivers, hydrology, mathematics, astronomy, archaeology and metallurgy have been related for many centuries, we can safely conclude it is believed that the Rig Vedic era was much earlier than 3700 BC.

A BHARATIYE emperor known as Mandhata led several campaigns against peoples in the northwest of BHARAT and there was a large-scale migration to the west as far as Central Asia and Europe. Based on linguistic similarities as well as similarities in myths and beliefs, it is possible to show that ancient BHARATIYE and Europeans have been in close contact at one time. (ZAMBODEEP comes into picture) Through a detailed linguistic and cultural analysis, Shrikant Talgeri has shown that many ancient European civilizations were part of this migration wave following Mandhata's campaign against the Druhyus. The Druhyus became known as Druids (Celtic) in ancient Europe.

BHARAT has been a powerful region since the beginning of all civilizations may be long before lakhs and thousands years ago. Long after Mandhata's campaign against the Druhyus, Sudas is again mentioned in the seventh book of the Rig-Veda. The famous Battle of the Ten Kings recorded by Vashishtha in the book was fought with a confederacy formed under the leadership of the Druhyus and others.

It is considered one of the major events of ancient history. Among those defeated and driven out by Sudas were Prithu-Parthava, Paras, Alina and many others who are mentioned in the Rig-Veda. They are related to many ancient peoples of Europe and West Asia.

The Prithu-Parthavs are certainly known as the Parthians, the Parthians actually called themselves Parthavas. The Parsas became the Persians and the Hellenes are the Hellenes of the ancient Greeks. Other opponents of Sudas included Paktha and Balahan. Their descendants are today known as the Pathans (or Pakhtuns) and the Baluchis of the Bolan Pass. And Srikanth Talageri notes many others in his excellent study. Thus many Indo-European peoples of the ancient world can be traced back to BHARAT in very ancient times. This also explains why people from BHARAT to Ireland speak similar languages to each other. They were the original Indo Europeans.

During a Sanskrit Meet at Delhi University September 27, 2015. Brainstorming on the dates of ancient texts at a conference organized by the Sanskrit Department of Delhi University, Sanskrit scholars said that the Vedas date back to 6000 BC. In his keynote address, Department Head Ramesh Bhardwaj said, "Vedas can be dated back to before 6000 BC and they prove to be more ancient than the Indus Valley Civilization." Apart from scholars from Delhi, Varanasi and Gorakhpur, archaeologist K.N. Dixit and B.R. Mani attended the meeting. 18

Saraswati is the Goddess and the river who is often worshipped, it is invoked about 75 times in the Rig-Veda Samhita.

"O best mother! O best of rivers! Oh best of ladies! Saraswati! We are without any accomplishment or knowledge, please Mother, make us skilful and wise! RV 1.3.10:

"Goddess Saraswati, full of energy and wealth, protector of wisdom, may she protect us." At the same time, Saraswati is also described as a mighty river: RV 6.61.2:

"She breaks the rocks on her sides with her mighty and mighty waves, like a trowel digging mud for the roots of a lotus. She destroys things quickly from a great distance (i.e. because of her mighty and immense flow) to that Saraswati, we offer our prayers and beautiful words for protection and prosperity." RV 1.13.9:

The Saraswati was the largest and most important river for the early Vedic people, as depicted in the Rig-Veda Samhita. In fact, the sixth mandala refers only to the river Saraswati and no other river west of it. The sixth mandala is universally accepted as the oldest part of the extant Rig-Veda Samhita, even by Western Ideologists such as Oldenburg. This fact has been brilliantly incorporated by Shrikant Talgeri to demonstrate indisputably, that the earliest original place of the Vedic people was on the eastern bank of the Saraswati and there is no evidence of their migration from the northwest out of BHARAT. The river Ganga is mentioned only 4 times in the entire Rig-Veda Samhita. In the Nadi Sukta (10.75) and once as a derivative (Gāngyaḥ गांग्यः) in RV 6.45.31, and twice as Jāhnavi (जह्नवी) (3.58.6, 1.116.19). The Sixth Mandala, the oldest part of the Rig-Veda Samhita knows the Ganges as well as the Saraswati, but none of the rivers to the west such as the Shutudri, Vipat, Asikni, Sindhu, etc. If the Aryan invasion/ migration had actually taken place, they would have had to cross all those rivers before meeting either the Saraswati or the Ganges, and one of them being more familiar would have been more sacred. Since the oldest part of the Rig-Veda Samhita only knows of these two rivers, it is clear that the earliest core of the Vedic people centred on the eastern bank of the Saraswati around Kurukshetra, and probably extended to all parts of the Ganges plains. The Rig-Veda is the only collection of the oldest songs or hymns. The oldest of these songs dates back more than 25000 years, to the time of the Grand Saraswati, when both the Sutlej and the Yamuna were its tributaries. The river began to dry up at the end of the Ice Age [11000 BCE] and completely dried up about 1900 BC.

The Rig-Veda is an exploration into the spiritual roots of human behaviour, leading to the subtle "source of all energy" in the universe, that is, the "ultimate truth" about the nature of all reality. Vedas have been in existence since time immemorial. Many believe that the sage Veda Vyasa began writing them around 3100 BCE. Vyasa classified the original single Veda into four. He was therefore called Veda Vyasa, or "the splitter of the Vedas", the division being an achievement that facilitated people to understand the divine wisdom of the Vedas.

Vedas have not been composed in the present era, so at least one cycle of the first half of the equinoxes must have been completed.

There are 27 Nakshatras in BHARATIYE astrology. The rate of evolution is 960 years per Nakshatra. Thus in 25920 years there would have been progress in 27 Nakshatras. So the Rig-Veda is at least 25920 years old (if we assume that only one preponderance has passed since then). By subtracting the current 2000 AD, the date is 23920 BC.

Another research has come that the world's first human literature Rig the Vedas date back to around 50000 BCE. It refers to the river Saraswati, which flowed through BHARAT and fell into the Arabian Sea. Satellite images have confirmed that the Saraswati River existed and there are research papers which suggest that a civilization flourished on the banks of the Saraswati River. Where there were urban settlements, whose number was about 800! In this research, it has also been said that Rig-Veda has also been talking about this land culture.

Such a river that flows from the Himalayan Mountains into the Arabian Sea is not there today. But what is quite interesting happened few years ago, archaeologists in BHARAT started studying satellite images. American satellites like Landsat are providing this. According to the images obtained, there is a dry river which starts in the Himalayas and fell into the Gulf of Khambhat in the form of a huge river. He found that there were 800 to 1000 urban sites on the banks of that river. So it appears that what Rig-Veda was talking about was a mighty river more than thousands and thousands years ago.

In Kashmir, the valley of Kashmir it looks like it was a lake many thousand years ago. There is an ancient Sanskrit manuscript which tells about a lake that existed in that area in ancient times. Now, according to modern geological reporting, about 40000 -42000 years ago the entire valley of northern Kashmir was a great lake. At a certain point, some natural change happened and the lake opened up and the water overflowed. That incident happened about 40000 to 42000 years ago.

I think this incident must have happened 42000 years ago due to the reversal of the pole. Due to the reversal of the pole there was a change in the water and air, due to which it seems that the water would have started flowing towards the south.

Forbidden Archaeology: Michael A. Cremo and Richard L. The Hidden History of Mankind by Thompson became a best-selling underground classic, selling over 200000 copies and being translated into over 13 languages. This massive work caused waves of resistance and surprise among the scientific community. More than 900 pages of well-documented evidence suggests that modern man did not evolve from ape man, but over millions of years co-existed together. 20, 21

Book History of Vedic Literature by Dr. Karan Singh of Meerut College, Meerut P. No. 43 It has been said that the oldest form of BHARATIYE religion is available from Rig-Veda only. This is considered the basic basis of BHARATIYE religion. According to the Rig-Veda, the work of reaching the deities given in Yagya is done by fire. Yagya word in Hindi YAG यज्ञ it is made up of three letters - य, ज and न. "Y" 'य' means gathering. "J" 'ज' means producing something, people meet and produce, then "na" 'न' means donate i.e. distribution. Production is not for possession but for Charity, is the source of emotion, non-possessiveness and sacrifice. Gives to a friend or needy. This is not a favour, but is a debt repayment. The debt which we carry since birth by taking all types of benefits from God and people, surroundings and environment.

Polytheism in Rig-Veda

On the basis of the large number of deities that have been praised in the Rig-Veda, it can be said that the religion of the Rig-Veda is polytheism. 33 koti Meaning (33 specialty / quality) of God.

Monotheism in Rig-Veda

According to Acharya Yasak, the same one soul is praised in many ways in the Rig-Veda for being opulent. Based on this opinion of Yasak, scholars have accepted that along with the praise of same God in many ways in Rig-Veda, the spirit of monotheism is also available. In the Rig-Veda, Agni is also called Varuna, Mitra and Indra and it is expressed that all the Gods are centred in him.

Pantheism in the Rig-Veda

Along with polytheism and monotheism, the existence of pantheistic ideology is also available in Rig-Veda. This ideology is represented by the creations in which the same deity is called all deities. Represents. In Rig-Veda 1 1 8 6 1 10 everything is attributed to the deity Aditi. That is, Aditi is the God, Aditi is the space, Aditi is the mother, Aditi is the father, and Aditi is the son. Aditi is the form of all the Gods.

Henotheism pantheism in the Rig-Veda

At many places in the Rig-Veda, the same deity is praised as the supreme deity. In this form, if at one place Indra is called the supreme deity (Rig 5 1 30 1 5), then in another place Agni and in the third place To Varun. The same has happened in the case of other Gods as well.

Thus we find that polytheism, monotheism, sarvatheism and pantheism, all mentioned in the Rig-Veda. In fact, the word Veda "Vid" is derived from the root, on the basis of which a person can worship that God in different ways depending on his mental state.

All the scholars know that there is a lot of similarity between the ancient Avestan language of Iran and the Vedic language. Due to the difference in their pronunciation, these different visions are visible. Like the language, the Iranian Gods and there is a great deal of similarity between the Vedic deities as well. The Iranian deities Mithra and Im bear a resemblance to the Vedic deities Mitra and Yama. 22

One important thing is that ALLAH is known by 99 names in Quran in Arabic language. So in other language ALLAH can be called by many other names.

Reference

1. https://www.britannica.com/science/missing-link

2. https://www.usatoday.com/story/news/nation/2019/01/21/study-south-african-fossils-missing-link-human-evolution/2636837002/

3. https://www.flynote.com/blog/dwarka-holiest-underwater-city-of-BHARAT -dwarka/

4. http://mahabharataresearch.com

5. https://www.cityofshamballa.net/profiles/blogs/32000-year-old-alien-city-found-in-BHARAT -dwarka-dwarka-BHARAT -12

6. https://archaeology-world.com/BHARAT-archaeologists-found-9000-years-old-city-beneath-the-surface-of-modern-day-Davaraka

7. https://www.basiraeducation.org/blog/was-Noahs-flood-global-or-local

8. https://www.fodors.com/news/photos/forget-atlantis-14-real-cities-that-are-completely-underwater

9. https://www.peakingtree.in/allslides/the-story-of-manu

10. https://en.satyavedapusthakan.net/2013/05/31/how-mankind-continued-on-lessons-from-the-account-of-manu-or-Noah/

11. https://en.wikipedia.org/wiki/Flood_myth

12. https://www.booksfact.com/puranas/ramayana-composed-2-million-years-ago.html

13. https://en.wikipedia.org/wiki/Yuga_Cycle

14. https://www.britannica.com/topic/chronology/Eras-based-on-astronomical-speculation

15. https://www.firstpost.com/tech/science/earths-magnetic-field-flipped-42000-years-ago-extinctions-and-upheaval-followed-study-9331021.html

16. Book New Light on Vedic BHARAT and Ancient Civilization by Dr. N S Rajaram. page number 7

17. Page number 12 of the book Vedic BHARAT on Nav Prakash

18. https://www.thehindu.com/news/national/du-sanskrit-meet-pushes-back-period-of-vedas-to-6000-bc/article7692864.ece

19. https://www.booksfact.com/vedas/rig-veda/rig-veda-is-composed-ateast-in-23720-bce.html

20. https://ramanan50.wordpress.com/2013/08/16/rig-veda-date-components-details/

21. https://ramanisblog.in/2014/04/28/hinduism-fifty-thousand-years-old-rig-veda/

22. Book History of Vedic Literature, Dr. Karan Singh. Meerut College, Meerut P. No. 43 -44

Chapter 5
Religion

One of the prestigious and all-time useful book for all people shrimad "Bhagavad Gita" begins with the word "Dharmakshetre". Vedic religion is based on "Veda". The word "Veda" is derived from Vid which means "knowledge". So a question come, what is "Dharma" (Religion)? Vid i.e. Knowledge is endless, vast, limitless, everlasting for everyone. Knowledge cannot be confined. The first word of Quran which was revealed to Prophet Mohammad by the angel Zibraiel was "IQRA" which means to read. So all the religion lay stress upon proper knowledge. Proper knowledge is the door to success in all sphear of life.

Shri Mohan Lal Mahato Viyogi in "**Arya Jeevan Darshan**" on page no. 194 - 209 it is written about "Dharma" (Religion) that there is a kind of unceasing impermanence in this world that is before us. Within this impermanence there is also such an element which is always stable. The wheel rotates, but the axle remains fixed. The axle that holds that wheel is "Dhri" and the word religion is made from its metal. The synonyms of religion in Rig-Veda Samhita are - Rit, Brahan, Vrat and Sav. "Rit" it basically means straight law. "Brahan" means brah – to grow, grow vast. And the word "vrat" is vri which means to surround, cover or like. The word "sav" means to generate. If the synonyms of religion are kept together, then the definition of the word "religion" is made. Religion is a simple straight rule for living a good life, there is no crookedness in it, and it is virtuous. All-encompassing, all-pervading, likable, procreative, productive power are in religion there is no sense of any rituals.

Then from where and how did different rituals, habits or specific worship practices etc. got added into religion, due to which the present religious differences arose? From my point of view religion is just like knowledge which cannot be confined.

In "Geeta Darpan" Swami Ramsukh Das wrote in page no. 70 – "There is a difference in the rituals and rules of all religions, but the great messengers of GOD & thinkers of Sanatan Dharma, Buddhist, Jain, Zoroastrian, Jewish, Christian, Islam and many other realized and gave the same principle of Love and Peace.

Then why is the difference? It is clear that this difference is in the rituals that are born out of Yug (era) dharma. The rituals associated with Dharma i.e. religion, which become dominant and the original element inspired by God is covered by it. It is understood only by the subtle intellect, it is suppressed and the religion of the era which is accepted by the external senses becomes dominant.

"Gita Rahasya" written by Lokmanya Tilak in page no. 65 it is written - When we ask someone what is your religion? Then we mean that which path do you follow for the entry into the other upper world - Sanatan, Buddhist, Jain, Parsis, Christian, Islamic, Jewish or any other way?

Apart from the religion names such as Sanatan, Buddhist, Jain, Parsis, Christian, Islam, Jewish or any other and the External rituals associated with them have no purposes than to fulfil the eternal rituals. The main eternal religions are Raj dharma (Ruler Religion), Prajadharma (Citizen Religion), Desh Dharma (Country Religion), Parivar Dharma (Family Religion), Dost Dharma (Friend Religion),

Patni Dharma (Wife Religion), Pati Dharma (Husband Religion), Bhai Dharma (Brother Religion), Pita Dharma (Father Religion), Mata Dharma (Mother Religion), Baccha Dharma (Child Religion), karya Dharma (Work Religion), Malik Dharma (Owner Religion), Employee and Employer Religion, Padosi Dharma (Neighbour Religion), Travellers religion, Co-workers religion, Co-passenger religion, Student Religion, Residence Religion etc etc. If one do not perform these eternal religious rituals then one cannot be a true human.

So it can be said that religion is the set of organized humanity beliefs, practices, performances, duties, responsibilities, roles, rituals and all works of humanity. It is the worship of a controlling supreme power known as God (Parmatma). Religion is also defined as a socio-cultural system of specified behaviours and practices, ethics, beliefs, worldview, texts, sacred places, prophecies, sermons, rituals, prayers, meditations, sacred places, symbols, feasts, organizations. All connects to the supernatural, transcendental and spiritual elements.

There is a difference in the religious belief of the properly and rightly educated and uneducated people. Because educated people can visualize abstract ideas and explain general principles while uneducated people do not go beyond what is perceived by external senses. The problem with closed minded people is that their mouth is always open.

Dharma i.e. religion is the simple act and practices of humanity which purifies human and makes healthy environment for happy and peaceful co-existence. It separates human from animal's behaviour, keeps away from evils and corruptions. The great works that separate us from other species. It involves the process in the form of actions to achieve the highest level of purity. All Religious activities help in making and maintaining a healthy environment. Thus we can say that Religion is a constitution in which the work and practice of humanity has been described. Religion is only one that is eternal and is for all.

There are many different sects which are branches of a big tree i.e. RELIGION.

There are many reasons why people need religion and sects. It is a moral reminder for performing good behaviour, it is a spiritual idea, it gives us confidence that we are not alone to struggle through life, there is someone to help and listen in our troubles. Its purpose is that for our existence there is a higher purpose. All sects serve a wide range of purposes and the ultimate goal is one. Dharma i.e. religion is a source of peace and gives right guidance. It give us a basis for ethical beliefs and practices based on humanity. It also provides a sense of belonging to society, community and tradition. It has a positive effect on health and surroundings. The practices and activities of Dharma (religion) help to keep us healthy, clean and pure. It has a direct and indirect effect on health and surroundings.

There are many aspects of religion and human. There are three aspects of the human mind. The first aspect (dimension) is the innate tendency (instinct) under which every living being, including human beings, has to fulfil their inborn natural needs, such as happiness, food, fear, sleep, enjoyment, etc. Under fear, they imagine a supremely powerful invisible power, and try to please it. In this state of mind, one fears God, not loves God.

There is another dimension of the human brain, the intellectual nature (intelligence) when it is developed, by being endowed with the power of reasoning, man finds the cover of the nature around him and the solutions to the natural events. The state of fear is diminished. He identifies the outer identity, that is, the outer-personality at the level of logical intelligence, but he is unable to identify his inner personality at the level of logic-based intelligence.

To identify our inner personality, one has to resort to the third dimension of the mind which is called wisdom or insight.

This dimension of the mind is beyond logic and is subject to emotion. It awakens not in scholars, but in true sages. In this state man not only knows his true nature, but he also understand and knows God and his relationship with God becomes not the one of fear but of love. At the individual level, religion helps man achieve this pure state. It is only a small goal to know the relationship between oneself and God and to connect with it, the big goal is to know the relationship between God and the world and to **see God in this world**. It is the path to other worldly well-being or the state of salvation at the individual level. It is the ultimate limit of individual achievement.

But at the individual level, attaining moksha is just a small goal that is knowing the relationship between yourself and God and connecting with it. To see the light of God in every speck, to see God, Shiva Shankar in all pebbles. To achieve this state, one has to take the support of another aspect of religion – the social aspect.

The moral expression of religion is in the form of purity and its social expression is in the form of love. Maharishi Kanad says – Yato amayudaya ni:shcheya sa siddhi: sa dharma:" That is, the medium through which both physical and spiritual progress is achieved is called **Religion**. Here physical progress means social progress that is the development of an egalitarian society in which everyone lives with love and supports each other. The meaning of spiritual progress is the looking (darshan) of the divine soul sitting within all human. This was the only message which was the soul concept of the great prophet Mohammad pbuh. But these days his teachings and the true spirit has been diluted by the followers.

According to Islam Allah has sent about 124000 messengers from time to time in different parts of the world to guide people of different societies to be on the right path. The messengers used to come in different places, at different times to eradicate evils and purify the societies. God used to send his messages for guidance which are available in the form of religious texts. Those texts guide man in every aspect of life. The Books of God act as a holistic guide. The question arises why 124000? If God is one his message can be one, then why 124000 messengers or Avatars?

The eternal religious scripture "Bhagavad Gita" has the answer to this question. It is said in Gita Adhyay 4 Shlok 7-8 – "Yada hi Dharmastha Glanirabhavati Bharat, Abhyutthanam Dharmastha Tadatman Sarjamyham", **"that is, whenever dharma (religion) i.e. humanity weakens, when unrighteousness increases, then I reveal myself"**. In other words it can be said that "Whenever there is a loss of religion that is unrighteousness increases, then God in every age for the protection of the good i.e. humanity and the destruction of the wicked i.e. evil and for the re-establishment of religion i.e. nothing but humanity, he manifests himself". Sanatan Dharma believes that God does not take birth, but manifests. The God who is present in every particle, is omnipresent, that is all-timely and all-local how can he take birth? It simply becomes manifest from the unmanifest that is why it is said to manifest. Now the next question is? How God gives his message. Hindus believe that God either incarnates himself, or he gives the message through his Vibhutis.

Many religious groups including Islam believe in God messengers. Hindus also believe in divine personalities and believe that (Mahajano yena gat: SA: panth :). That is, the path walked by noble men is the right path. Bhagavata Vibhutis or God-inspired messengers are externally bound by natural laws and its binding qualities, but internally they embody divine divinity. Avatars or messengers who preached the teachings to humanity and set a live example through their lives Installed. The followers of that avatar or messenger gave the name of a religion to the teachings of the avatars. Thus the teachings of holy incarnations and messengers provided the basis of humanity i.e. religion. Since different languages developed in different parts of the world, people call the God by different names.

The difficulty is that when the messengers or avatars as subject to the law of nature left the world, their followers distorted their teachings according to their convenience and gradually divided into many sects and sub sects. This happened in all the sects. Real religious teachings become secondary but the man-made local customs, culture, religious rituals become dominant. When religion is linked to rule or dynasty then more distortion comes. Religious power coupled with royal power always gives birth to religious atrocities. **Since ancient times when a powerful ruler used to conquer another state or society by brute force, they forcefully imposed their religious beliefs, customs and practices upon the conquered state and society.** Sometimes success was also achieved, but mostly the **insult done by the winner caste used to sit in the conscience of the conquered caste, that lead to revenge and hatred**. And the eternal chain of malice. To put it simply, during the rule of the kingdom in the olden times, when the powerful kings won the war, they used to make the losers follow him either willingly or forcefully. The amount of blood shed and atrocities committed in the name of religious supremacy in this world is the highest than for any other reason.

Some pray to the God facing west and some facing east, some wearing lungi and some wearing dhoti. Have we started beheading each other for such a small thing? Two, three or four. Two brothers who changed their method of worship a generation ago have become two nations. Can this be right?

Are Muslims a Nation? Are Hindus, Sikhs, Jains, Christians, Parsis or other religious followers are separate nations? Recent history has proved this wrong. BHARAT was partitioned in the year 1947 on the basis of religious practices, hence a separate nations took birth. But within just 25 years, this notion proved wrong and the Muslim nation

Pakistan was divided into two parts by making an incision on BHARAT chest, and as a result an independent nation named Bangladesh emerged.

Then what is nation? Is it a piece of land? Perhaps this is true! In the eternal religious text "Bhagvad Gita" Arjuna talks about the destruction of the whole religion as a result of the war. (A.1 / Shlok 38-44) Pitamah Bhishma the great hero of Raj dharma – Moksha dharma – Aapdadharma, the great knower of all, fought on the side of Kauravas despite knowing that the side of Pandavas was just. This happened because the concept of nation was not clear at that time. It was ancient tribal concept that clan religion was the prestige of religion and the central idea of the nation. Whenever dynastic power is recognized in a society, the bandage gets tied on the eyes. In the time of Gautama Buddha there were 16 Mahajanapadas in BHARAT that is there were 16 types of nationalities. The hundreds of kings who participated in the Mahabharata war, each came from different states. Before the invasion of Alexander BHARAT was divided into many nations, whose rulers were descendants of different clans? Kautilya Chanakya the son of Acharya Chanak, freed BHARAT from this illusion or say from fascination, and established an organized central authority. There was an external invasion and the BHARATIYE dynastic state - divided into different Kshatriya states in the fascination of power, they were defeated.

"A holy land called Bharat is a nation and all the people living on the land are BHARATIYE's", this idea was first propounded by Chanakya. Vishnu Purana Part-2 Chapter 3 Verse 1 states – " Uttar yat Samudrasya Himadre Shrauchav Dakshinam. Varsh Tad BHARATIYEAMA Bharati Yantr Santati: "That is, "The region north of the sea and south of Himadri is named Bharat and the progeny of Bharat is called Bharati." There is no mention of Varna or caste. Various religions existed in BHARAT since ancient times and all the followers of the different faith live side by side but were sanatanis. Buddha was not a Buddhist and Mahavira was not a Jain. They were the reformer of the then Sanatani society. Their followers gave the name of religion. "Ramakrishna Paramhansa" the great pioneer of Hindu renaissance in BHARAT, says – "Yato Mat Tato Path".

If Hindus and Muslims were two nations, there would have been no **Kabir** in BHARAT, no Sai Baba, no Raskhan, Rahim and even Vaishnav Poonja Bhai Meghji Thakkar, a devotee of Shri Nathji, of Paneli Moti village (Kathiawar) in Rajkot district. His son Jenna Bhai Poonja Bhai Meghji Thakkar who accepted Islamic religion under Khoja leader Aga Khan as a follower and his son Muhammad Ali Jinnah would not have been there. Then Maulana would not have been Azad, Khan would not have been Abdul Ghaffar Khan, BHARAT would not have had a President like Kalam Saheb and the grandson of Sapru Brahmin of Kashmir Poet-thinker Iqbal would not have been the one who gave ideological basis. Azim Prem ji would have been in Pakistan. If Hindu and Christian were two nations, BHARAT would not have had Sister Nivedita, Mrs. Annie Besant, Deen brothers Andrews, Mother Teresa. Father Kamil Bulke would not have even existed. If Hindus and Parsis were two nations, there would have been no Dada Bhai Naoroji in BHARAT, no Ferozeshah Mehta and Madame Cama, no Jamsetji Tata and so on and so on. Parsi wife Ratna Bai Jinnah would also not have been there. Jinnah's daughter and Wadia family would have been in Pakistan not in BHARAT. If Hindus and Sikhs were two nations, BHARAT would not have had Guru Tegh Bahadur, Sardar Udham Singh and Bhagat Singh.

BHARAT definitely had a religious identity but that was of Dharma, It is derived from Sanskrit word "Dhriti i.e. patience, i.e. doing favour, i.e. restraining the senses, Asteya i.e. not stealing, Sawach i.e. purity of the inner and outer, Indriya-Nigraha i.e. control of the senses Inspire towards, Dhi i.e. making Budhi wise, Vidya i.e. acquiring knowledge,

Satyam i.e. righteous conduct and Akrodha i.e. maintaining peace leaving anger.

The same teachings has been given by approximately 124000 Prophets or messengers or Avatars. Ultimately we all are eternal on this earth because we are all descended from a common ancestor. It is fact that Homo sapiens human civilization has originated from the BHARATIYE subcontinent. Vedic religious people named their religion as Sanatan Dharma. Sanatan means ever-present i.e. unchanging. The word Sanatan Dharma is not used for class, caste or sect, it the religious form of "eternal" duties, is an "eternal" or absolute set of duties or religiously ordained practices.

In the 19th century, researchers proposed various theories regarding the origin of religion. Early theorists such as Edward Burnett Tyler (1832–1917) and Herbert Spencer (1820–1903) emphasized the concept of animism, while archaeologist John Lubbock (1834–1913) used the term "fetishism". Meanwhile, the religious scholar Max Müller (1823–1900) theorized that religion began in hedonism, and Wilhelm Manhardt (1831–1880) suggested that religion began in "naturalism", by which he meant mythological explanations for natural phenomena. All these theories have been widely criticized; because there is no widespread agreement regarding the origin of religion. 1

According to few people it could be: in ancient times people seeing the devastation caused by nature, they must have become afraid. The thought must have come about something that there is someone, who runs everything and controls. There is life and death etc. During this thought they saw who is harmed and who is benefited. Due to this the worship of nature must have started. At that time food was very difficult. People get strength and happiness only by food. That is why they must have started praising and worshiping. Means worship system started out of fear and happiness both. Gradually this system established rules and regulations in the group and society.

Time passed and when the population increased, various means of luxury were invented. Slowly vices and corruption entered the society. Humanity would have been in stake, all unwanted and unacceptable things would have had happened. Then God sent his avatars or messengers to eradicate the evil practices and enforce the law of humanity. They used to teach the path of humanity and leave this world after doing their work. Their followers named their teachings as religion. Gradually after the origin of religion in almost every region the followers included extraneous practices like sects, caste, rituals, habits etc. Eventually added things became dominant and the original meaning of religion was suppressed. Whenever the teachings of the Lord were distorted and evils prevail in the society, the morality of humanity is lost, then God repeatedly takes new incarnations or sends new messengers. Through incarnations and messengers God purifies our society. According to Islam, Prophet Muhammad (pbuh) is the last Prophet and messenger of God. Other religion believe that as long as corruption and sorrow exist in the world, when unrighteousness increases in the society, God himself will incarnate or give the world saints and sages. Shasvat Dharma is re-established by sending in. Here eternal Dharma means truth. Yuga Dharma changes with place and time but eternal Dharma never changes.

Today in the age of science and technology fast progress is going on and the world is shrinking rapidly. Today, religion is an intrinsic element of human nature. The only question is, what should be the form of religion? Those religions which are not sensitive to human evils and social crimes, they do not embrace the modern man. Religion is not spiritual science, it is work and it is spiritual practice. One of the Great saint has said don't accept anything just because you respect me use your mind before accepting. Today the clash between different religions has raised the question, can they all live together? Or will one of them gain supremacy over the other? No religious element, however big it may be can be bigger than truth. Truth is always bigger and wider than any theology. The goal of religion is to make human purify thier soul and establish contact with truth. Truth can be described in many ways and there are many ways to reach it. But once the truth is attained, the path in itself has no importance. One should not insist that his path is the only one way to reach the truth i.e. God.

Prophet Mohammad pbuh has said, love your neighbours as you love yourself. The Prophet did not say to love only Muslim. God's consciousness resides within us? If the message of religions is to be understood clearly in the context of the problems of our age, we must abandon the notion that only one religion contains the ultimate, absolute and complete truth. BHARATIYE religions do not claim that they alone know the secret of human life. They are willing to accept that there may be other ways to reach this truth i.e. God.

There is a big problem before us today and that is, whenever there is any injustice, the religious leaders close their mouths. They do not have the courage to resist the injustices. It is a pity that today instead of helping each other and establish religion, people are hating each other in the name of religion.

Religion is an inner transformation, a spiritual transformation, an adjustment to the discordant voices of our own nature – and it has been found in this form since the beginning of history, it is original form. What is important about our moral life? The point is not whether we are Hindu or Muslim, Jew or Christian, but the important thing is whether we are good or bad. With the spread of scientific knowledge there is a liberalism in religions, but there are still some sects which are stick with narrow mind set. In the era, few are sticking to the external pomp and conventions of religions.

The goal of all religions is to change the vindictive nature of man. Prophet Muhammad (pbuh) has said that even if you have to go too far to get knowledge you should go. Contemporary knowledge keeps changing according to time, that means new things keep coming. That is, the circle of knowledge keeps increasing. **Darkness can be dispelled only by the light of knowledge.** There are two aspects of human. There is an external personality according to which we are Hindu or Muslim, poor or rich, officer or peon, child or youth, black or white, female or male. This personality separates us from each other. This personality is always changing. But we also have an inner identity or personality, which is the same in all of us. Hindus call it Atma. Muslims call it Ruh. He is one in all. When we live in the outer personality, then the devil easily misleads. By living with Dharma there is a possibility of change in our distorted nature, we can change ourselves and become a human.

A beautiful story goes about the understanding of Religion in which an elephant is placed in front of few blind men and they are asked to touch the elephant and tell how is the elephant? When a blind man caught hold of his ear, he said it is flat. When another blind man caught hold of his leg, he said that it is like a strong column. One blind man who touched the tail said it is like a rope. Their hand felt only partial truth. They felt the partial truth. Different aspects of a thing may appear opposite when seen from outside. Different Yuga religions seem to be opposed to each other but their main objective is to establish eternal truth.

The basic philosophy of religion is the search of truth, not a specific one path. "Truth is one; the wise call it by different names". God is one and is called by different names in different languages by different people.

Reference

1. Religion Encyclopaedia Universal Illustrada Europen-Americana 70 vols. Madrid 1907–1930.

2. https://www.worldhistory.org/religion/

3. https://en.wikipedia.org/wiki/Henotheism

4. https://scroll.in/article/936872/two-new-genetic-studies-upheld-aryan-migration-theory-so-why-did-BHARATIYE-media-report-the-opposite

5. https://www.worldhistory.org/The_Vedas

6. https://en.wikipedia.org/wiki/Indus_Valley_Civilisation

7. Manuel, Mark (2010). "Chronology and Culture-History in the Indus Valley". In Gunawardhan, P.; Adhikari, G.; Conningham, RAE Sirinimal Lakdusinghe Felicitation Vol. p. 145-15

8. https://english.newstracklive.com/news/bholenath-birth-story-news-hindi-me-birth-story-of-lord-shiva-and-secrets-sc93-nu-1024465-1.html

9. https://www.academia.edu/243477

10. https://ui.adsabs.harvard.edu/abs/2006AGUFM.T51D1553G/abstract

11. https://www.researchgate.net/publication/283831911_Earthquakes_and_civilizations_of_the_Indus_Valley_A_challenge_for_archaeoseismology

12. book Hamari Sanskriti by Dr. Sarvapalli Radhakrishnan

13. https://en.wikipedia.org/wiki/History_of_religion#cite_note-9

14. https://thesiscereseeker.medium.com/belief-in-the-past-scriptures-divine-books

Chapter 6

History of Religion in This Era

According to the written information that we have in the present era Yuga and which was written in the 17th and 18th century, the available records of the religion are as follows: -

- The oldest recorded Egyptian myths date back to 3500 BC.

- The first written evidence of religion in the world has been found recorded on Sumerian tablets dating back to 3500 BC.

- 3500 – 3200 BC First written evidence of religion in Sumerian cuneiform.

- 3000 BC Hathor, known as the mistress of Dendera, flourished as a cult centre in the city of Dendera.

- Osiris appears in the Pyramid Texts from 2500 BC as the dying and reviving God and the God of the dead.

- 2100 BC First ziggurats at Ur, Eridu, Uruk and Nippur.

- 1500 BC - 1100 BC Rig-Veda was rewritten which were orally transmitted from generation to generations.

- 1500 BC - 500 BC The Vedas, presented in written form, are found to have established the basic principles of Sanatana Dharma.

- 1120 BC The existing copy of the Sumerian Enuma Elish is made from a much older text.

- Rise of Yahwism before 1000 BC. To install Yahwism.

- 700 BC Greek poet Hesiod wrote his Theogony and Works and Days.

- Development of Charvaka philosophy in BHARAT before 600 BC.

- 599 BC - 527 BC Traditional dating of Vardhamana's life according to Jain tradition.

- 563 BC - 483 BC Life of Siddhartha Gautama according to modern scholarly consensus.

- 515 BCE - 70 CE Second Temple Period; Judaism is revised, the scriptures are canonized, Yahweh becomes the only God, monotheism is re-established.

- 6 BCE - 30 CE approximately Life of Jesus Christ.

- 1 CE - 100 CE Mithraism spread in the Roman Empire.

- 1 CE - 100 CE the Mahayana movement begins in BHARAT with its belief in the Bodhisattva.

- 42 CE - 62 CE Paul the Apostle goes on missionary journeys to Asia Minor, Greece and Rome.

- 64 CE Unofficial persecution of Christians in Rome.

- 65 CE - 100 CE Composed the stories of the life and work of Jesus (the Gospels).

- 132 CE Septuagint (Greek translation of the Bible) composed in Alexandria.

- 224 CE Zoroastrianism became the Persian state religion under the Sasanian Empire.

- 312 – 313 CE after cruel assasinations Roman Emperor Constantine adopts and tolerates Christianity.

- 570 CE Prophet Muhammad pbuh is born in Mecca.

- 610 CE Prophet Muhammad pbuh received his first revelation on Mount Hira.

- 622 CE Prophet Muhammad pbuh initiates Islamic calendar, migration from Mecca to Medina, Hijra (Hijra).

- 628 CE Treaty of Hudaybiyyah: A peace agreement is signed between the Muslims of Prophet Muhammad pbuh and the people of Mecca.

- 629 CE First pilgrimage to Mecca (the "lesser" pilgrimage or "umrah") by the Prophet Muhammad pbuh and his Muslims following their migration to Medina.

- 630 CE Nonviolent Conquest of Mecca: The Quraysh realize that the Muslims now outnumber them and allow the Muslims to capture their city, Mecca, and rule it as they wish.

- 632 CE "Farewell Haj Pilgrimage": This is the only Haj pilgrimage in which Prophet Muhammad pbuh participates.

- 632 CE Prophet Muhammad pbuh dies in Medina, not explicitly naming a successor to lead the Muslim people.

- 712 CE Kojiki is written, a collection of oral myths that form the basis of Shintoism.

- 720 CE The Nihon Shoki is a collection of written, oral myths that form the basis of the Shinto religion.

- 807 CE Imibe-no-hironari writes the Kogoshui, a collection of oral myths that form the basis of Shinto. 2

These details as above is only from this era (yug) i.e. from 3500 BC onwards. This history was written in 17th century. At that time science was not much developed and no one even tried to find what the true history of human is? As slowly now science and technology is developing, the correct history is coming before us. Research shows that Sanatan Dharma is the oldest religion and believed to be the 'Eternal Order' for living peaceful life.

Although Hinduism is often seen as a polytheistic faith, but Sanatan Dharm is also monotheistic and henotheistic. In Sanatan Dharma there is only one supreme power, "Brahma". The word "Brahma" is derived from the Sanskrit word Vri dhatu, which means to increase, braha (huge) and aprameya (immeasurable) and reflections. The Hindu belief system includes many avatars and these range from those who are highly known to lesser-known local deities. 3

There is a mantra in Yajurveda (32/3) - Na Tasya Pratima Asti Yasya Nama Mahaddash: Hiranyagarbha Ityesh Ma Hi Sidityesha Yasmann Jat Ityesh:

The word pratima in the mantra means that there is no similar to almighty God. *The making of idols of deities in BHARAT started after the making of idols in Buddhism and Jainism.* Here the meaning is **similar**. No one is similar to the one Almighty. Here describes his great fame. The meaning is that God is amavaram means incomparable.

Agni is the same, Aditya, the deities, Vayu, Chandra and Shukra are the same which is pervaded by Prajapati. All has appeared from the same Lightning-like Purusha. Purusha can be perceived above, here and there or anywhere in the middle. That means it cannot be seen from the surface. There is no idol of that man. His name is very great and the greatest. This great deity is present in all directions and everywhere.

Sanatan Dharma is considered to be the oldest religion in the world. It is important to note that Sanatana Dharma does not have a particular founder or a single text, but instead combines many ancient rich traditions and beliefs.

We can understand the history of Sanatana Dharma through Vedic literature developed in BHARAT: -

- Shruti ("that which is heard") - the revelation of the nature of existence recorded by the scribes who experienced it and recorded it in the Vedas.

- Smriti ("that which is remembered") - the way of living in different situations by the great heroes of the past or constitution which is compatible with the eternal Dharma.

In short, the introduction of the entire Vedic literature can be given in the present outline.

a) Four Samhitas (four Vedas) Samhitas come under creative literature. There is predominance of poetry in them. Their number is four.

   1. Rig-Veda – This is the most ancient and important of the codes. Most of its hymns are praiseworthy. The oldest of the Vedas, a collection of hymns.

   2. Yajurveda – Prayers related to Yajna are compiled in this. It is available in two forms (I) Krishna Yajurveda (ii) Shukla Yajurveda. Ritual formulas, mantras.

   3. Samveda – All its mantras except 75 mantras are compiled from Rig-Veda. All mantras of Samveda are lyrical. Religious texts, mantras, and songs

   4. Atharvveda – Its size is as much as the 10th division of Rig-Veda. Relation to mantra, tantra, witchcraft etc. Tantra mantra, hymn, prayer.

b) Brahmins – Texts: These texts are called Brahmins because they are related to Brahma. It is more focused on the appropriation of Vedic mantras in the rituals of Yagya.

c) Aranyaka - Granth: The last part of Brahmin - Granth itself is Aranyaka.

d) Upanishads – Texts: – Upanishads – texts come on the fourth step in the development of Vedic literature. Just as Karma Kand has got priority in Brahmin – texts, in the same way Gyan Kand has got priority in Upanishads – texts.

From the Samhita to the Upanishads, all the texts are called Shruti.

e) Six Vedangas – Helpful in the study of Vedas – The book is called Vedad. These are six.

Education – The rules of pure recitation of this Veda are included.

Kalpa - Kalpa is related to the rituals of Vedic Yagya.

Grammar – The etymology of these words and terms has been given and their pure form has been explained.

Nirukta – Some difficult posts (words) in the Vedas have been interpreted.

Verses – In this, verses like Gayatri, Anushtup and Jagati etc. used in Vedic compositions have been discussed.

Jyotish – In this Yagyaldi Vedvihit – appropriate time to perform tasks – Muhurta etc. has been considered.

Apart from Shrutis, there are Smritis in Vedic literature.

The texts related to Smritis are:

- Puranas - Folktales and legends about figures from the ancient past

- Ramayana - the epic story of Prince Rama and his journey to self-realization

- Mahabharata - the epic tale of the five Pandavas and their war with the Kauravas

- Bhagavad Gita - popular story in which Krishna instructs Arjuna about Dharma

- Yoga Sutras - commentaries on various topics of yoga and self-liberation

Sanatan Dharma is the oldest religions of the world. It has complex roots and includes a wide range of practices and a host of deities. Its plethora of forms and beliefs reflect the tremendous diversity of BHARAT, where most of its one billion adherents reside. Sanatana Dharma means eternal faith, eternal truth. Sanatana Dharma is a deeply pluralistic tradition that fosters respect for other religions and accepts the possibility of truth in them also. Hindus view the different types of religions and philosophies as different ways of understanding God. This philosophy leads to pluralism within sanatans and outside it. The core philosophy of Sanatan is the search for truth, not a specific path, it can be through different paths. A quote from the Vedas that summarizes the Sanatan view is, **"Truth is one; the wise call it by different names"**. It is God and is called by different names in different languages.

Prehistoric and Neolithic culture, which left material evidence, including abundant rock and cave paintings of bulls and cows, indicates an early interest in the sacred nature of these animals in one form or another. This is because these animals provided milk for the people in those difficult times. Mother milk for child when dry up then mother cow gave the milk for the humans for survival. Food is a basic necessity for survival. Milk was the first source of energy i.e. food in prehistoric times.

We are taught at the will of historians who were biased in writing the history during the seventeen century. The fact is that long back in history the whole earth was following Sanatana Dharma and the whole earth was full of Vedas. Fire is considered sacred in all religions. Even after the great flood, Noah sacrificed animals in the fire in front of considering God's altar. 6, 7

Till now there are many theories regarding the life span of Adam and Eve according to various researches. But no one has given the exact date of existence of ADAM and EVE on this earth. Big question mark? According to various researches it is established that Adam existed about 209000 years ago as mentioned in earlier chapter in this book also. Same is the case with Lord Shiva. Lord Shiva has no father or mother. He is Swayambhu i.e., He is anadi (unborn) and ananta (no end). He is the father of Vishva or the universe, hence he is called Vishveshwara. The word Shiva is used as an adjective in Rig-Veda. 8

Years ago during Lord Shri Krishna time also Shiva was worshipped. It is said that during the Lord Shri Ram time Shiva was worshiped as well. Emperor Yayati is said to be mentioned in Vedas and Puranas and it is estimated that he lived before 7200 BC. Brahma, Vishnu and Shiva were worshiped during his time also.

Its many sacred texts in Sanskrit and local languages served as a vehicle for spreading the religion to other parts of the world, although rituals and the visual and performing arts also played an important role in its transmission. Sanatan Dharma has had a major presence in Southeast Asia. The basic term or word of Hinduism is Sanatan Dharma (meaning eternal law).

Veda means "knowledge". From the book of Dara Sikho "Sir-I-Akbar" we learn that Dara Shukoh tried to uncover a common mystical language between Islam and Sanatana Dharma, boldly saying about the Kitab al-Maknoon or the "Hidden Book ", which is mentioned in the Quran.

This confirms that the Vedas must have been recited orally through Noah/Manu and his family, passed down from generation to generations by "hearing, reciting" and memorizing any form of communication until and unless it was written by the people of the Indus Valley Civilization. God must have chosen Noah to transmit the Vedas to his generations because he knew that the Vedas would guide people to lead a good life. The Vedas have been around since the time civilizations were flourishing all over the world.

Reference

1. Religion Encyclopaedia Universal Illustrada Europen-Americana 70 vols. Madrid 1907–1930.

2. https://www.worldhistory.org/religion/

3. https://en.wikipedia.org/wiki/Henotheism

4. https://scroll.in/article/936872/two-new-genetic-studies-upheld-aryan-migration-theory-so-why-did-BHARATIYE-media-report-the-opposite

5. https://www.worldhistory.org/The_Vedas

6. https://en.wikipedia.org/wiki/Indus_Valley_Civilisation

7. Manuel, Mark (2010). "Chronology and Culture-History in the Indus Valley". In Gunawardhan, P.; Adhikari, G.; Conningham, RAE Sirinimal Lakdusinghe Felicitation Vol. p. 145-15

8. https://english.newstracklive.com/news/bholenath-birth-story-news-hindi-me-birth-story-of-lord-shiva-and-secrets-sc93-nu-1024465-1.html

9. https://www.academia.edu/243477

10. https://ui.adsabs.harvard.edu/abs/2006AGUFM.T51D1553G/abstract

11. https://www.researchgate.net/publication/283831911_Earthquakes_and_civilizations_of_the_Indus_Valley_A_challenge_for_archaeoseismology

12. book Hamari Sanskriti by Dr. Sarvapalli Radhakrishnan

13. https://en.wikipedia.org/wiki/History_of_religion#cite_note-9

14. https://thesiscereseeker.medium.com/belief-in-the-past-scriptures-divine-books

Chapter 7
Concept of God and his Messenger

In the history of civilization, we find the development of God in the following forms.

1. Making God of the natural forces of our environment.

2. Deification of miracles that happened in our life or in nature; worship of volcano, worship of that stone when meteorite falls, worship of hot water spring, worship of sun or moon etc which is a source of energy.

3. Where there is freedom from disease or relief from major suffering, the power that makes that action happen was worshipped.

4. Divinization of a fearful thing or creature greater than oneself with reverence.

5. Divinization of Shasta, king, emperor or heroic man.

6. Tending to regard great religious leader as a God.

7. An abstract idea of Devadhidev – the feeling of considering him as Brahaya Rit or Paramatma.

GOD is the supreme power. When there was nothing there was God, if there was nothing there would have been God. God is light, omnipotent, omnipresent, omniscient, creator, destroyer and supreme judge. The body of a human is the temple of God. As many souls that many can be the path or way to the God.

The following are some examples of the concept of God in different civilizations with different names as per different languages. In Uganda, the Baganda tribe called Mukasa Namak, believe in a prosperous Mahadev. In China he is called Shang-ti, in Sikhism he is called the true emperor. In the beginning it was common for every tribes to have a family deity. According to Herodotus, the ancient Iranians used to stand on the mountain and by the name of "Zeus" worshiped the home spheres of the sky. The Iranians also worshiped fire and water. The Iranians later called Agni. The worship of Mazda is found before 2000 BC.

GOD is an English word. God is called as ISHWAR in Hindi. In Arabic he is called Allah. In Japanese he is called Kami. In Chinese he is called Shangri, Tinzhu. In Judaism he is called Jehovah. In South America he is called Viracocha. Vietnamese God is called Son Tinh – the Mountain Spirit, Thanh Giong. Chotanagpur Tribals call God as Bonga, Marang Buru, etc. Native Americans say Navajo. Many other natives call God by different names. In African traditional religions, God is called Serer in Senegal, Yoruba in Nigeria and Akan in Ghana and Bono in Ivory Coast. The religion of the GBE people (mostly Ewe and Fon) of Benin, Togo and Ghana is called Vodun. It is similarly named religions in the Diaspora such as Louisiana Voodoo, Haitian Voodoo, Cuban Voodoo, Dominican Voodoo and Brazilian Voodoo. Names of God in the Old Testament El Shadda (Lord Almighty), El Elon (Most High God), Adonai (Lord Master), Jehovah (Lord Jehovah), Jehovah Nissi (Lord My Banner), Jehovah Rah (The Lord My Shepherd), Jehova Rapha and many more are described. 2

It means that everyone takes the name of the Lord in their own language, who is the Supreme Being, the Creator and the head of the faith. As we speak different languages in different parts of the world, similarly we take the name of GOD in different languages. God has innumerable divine powers. The unique understanding in religion is that God is not far away, but is inside every soul, in the heart and consciousness, waiting to be discovered. 1

20 year old Ghanim Al Muftah specially abled person who was the brand ambassador of FIFA World Cup 2022. During the opening ceremony in Qatar Oscar Winner Morgan Freeman (of African descent) asked a question about the diversity in this world and in response, Ghanim al-Muftah recited a verse from the Quran (Quran 49:13 Surah Al-Hujurat) "O mankind, verily we have created you from male and female and among you different people and different tribes so that you may know and learn from each other". Different tribes make different culture and a beautiful world. The Quran clearly states that there are different types of human beings, as well as different types of languages. Here it can be concluded that world is like a big garden and just like in garden many different types of plants and flowers makes the garden beautiful likewise different tribes, people, languages and names make this world a beautiful world.

The idea of the development of the concept of God in BHARAT begins with the Vedas, when it was called ZAMBODEEP in the beginning Yug. The Vedic deity merciful & auspicious. In latter texts the worship of the deities was elaborated with great details. The institution of priests became predominant and the emphasis was on the purity of the method of worship. Coming to the Upanishads, the philosophical interpretation of God was carried out on a very high scale and at a higher level. According to Sikhism, God is self-existent . He is infinite, timeless and nirankar, as well as God is the supreme judge.

Sanatana Dharma is both polytheistic and monotheistic. But henotheism (literally "one God") better defines the eternal view. It means worship of one Supreme God without denying the existence of same God in different names. Sanatans believe in one omnipresent God, who animates the entire universe. Sanatani believe that God encourages all people to reach the ultimate truth or reality.

Sanatan Dharma gives freedom to approach God in one's own way. It allows people to believe in and pray to their own concepts of God, whomever they choose. There is a single omnipotent, omnipresent and omniscient deity who demands no allegiance. He does not punish anyone, yet gives wisdom, comfort, compassion and freedom to his loved ones. According to Ramdas Lamb, an associate professor at the University of Hawaii specializing in religious studies, mysticism, the interface between BHARATIYE religions and society, area studies, one needs only to look within oneself to find God. The reality is that God who is supreme present partially within each individual is changeless and divine.

Hindus refer to the formless absolute Reality as Brahma. Brahma means infinite in all respects. Brahma is not relative to anyone, it is the unchanging being. When Brahma is seen in the mirror of nature, it is given a form and people add more qualities with it and he is called God. Now a question comes in front of us, what is the form of God? In response to this it can be said that the form of water becomes the same as the vessel in which it is kept, in the same way the form of God becomes according to the state of mind of its devotee. Shri Vishnu appears in the incarnations of Kachhapa, Varaha, Narasimha, Vamana, Parashurama, Rama, Krishna, Buddha and Kalki respectively. Some people think of form and quality according to mathematical rules and consider four form of God as possible. It is (1) Nirguna – Nirakar can be formless, (2) Nirguna – Sakar can be corporeal, (3) Saguna – Nirakar can be formless and (4) Saguna – Sakar can be corporeal. Since form is a quality in itself therefore Nirguna – Nirakar there is no possibility of becoming corporeal. Out of the remaining three types, Muslims believe that God is Saguna – Nirakar formless. But Hindus accept God as Saguna – Nirakar formless and Saguna – sakar corporeal – in these forms. Sanatan is also unique in saying that Nirguna – formless God i.e. Brahma can only be felt, but Saguna – corporeal God can be seen. God is present in all forms with all qualities available in the universe.

In the Quran Allah has 99 names. Those 99 names are only in Arabic language. Then if we speak other languages then obviously the name of Allah will be used in that language also. That's why we know the supreme power as Bhagavan, Bonga, Jehovah, Kami etc. and the number of languages in this world are endless. Truth is one; the wise call it by different names.

Al Biruni's book Bharat is translated by Qayamuddin Ahmed in the book page no. 7. It is written that - **"There is a difference in religious belief between the educated and the uneducated people in every religion and caste, because the educated people conceive abstract ideas and explain general principles while the uneducated people do not go beyond what is perceptible by the senses"** and they are satisfied with secondary principles. They are not interested in their details and especially in questions of religion and law in respect of which people have different opinions and their interests. Believing that he is Eternal, Infinite, Willingly doing whatever he wills, Almighty, All-Knowing, Alive, Life-giver, Controller, Protector: He whose sovereignty is unique, he is Beyond Similarity. Neither does he resemble anything, nor does anything resemble him. But Albiruni also believes that the common people, who are often then uneducated people, do not understand their GOD/Allah as abstract.

How and when did the word GOD come? It is a big question? No one has the answer to this. Colin Wells wrote in a journal that God began with Abraham. But from my point of view I think he wrote only from the perspective of building Kaaba. And as we have already read, the Prophet Noah built an altar and offered animal sacrifices after surviving the great flood. This clearly shows that the word GOD have been in use and practice even before the great flood. Which has been mentioned in the books of almost all religions in different forms and with different names.

Here I would also like to mention that just as there are different food cultures in different parts of a big country or different parts of the world, similarly there are differences in religious practices and rituals from place to place. God has created only two classes' man and woman. From time to time Allah has sent his message through his messengers in every part of the earth and among different communities. Allah had given only one planet earth but humans have divided it in the name of country, religion, region, race etc.

A Prophet is a person whom God has sent to earth to deliver his message. When a Prophet speaks, it is as if God is speaking. According to Abrahamic beliefs, Prophets are humans chosen by God to be the bearers of revelation for other humans. BHARATIYE believe in the incarnation and Vibhuti of God. But they also believe that great Guru or Saint is human from outside but God from inside.

God has sent Prophets among men to all civilizations and countries with messages in their own languages. God has not created any religion. According to Islamic belief we know and accept that Adam is the first and Prophet Muhammad is the last messenger of God. Between these two great Prophets there came approximately 123998 Prophets in different parts of the world, among different communities, among different tribes, in different regions, at different times. Various Prophets have come through the ages to spread the message of goodness, kindness and humanity. Around 124000 messengers of God came to eradicate evils and wrong practices. They only preached humanity and guided to live a good discipline life. They did not created any religion. The followers named the teachings as a religion. And as time passed, the followers started misusing the religion for their own benefit and gradually started replacing the teachings and guidance given by the Prophets. The result is that the original book of the Lord are kept aside. The instructions in them are not followed in the true sense. 4

Vedas are the books of the Lord which were sent in the world even before the flood (Noah/Manu) incident. After the incident of Noah, according to Islamic belief, there is information about God sending more books through his messengers which are the Scroll (Abraham), Taurat (Torah or Law) Moses, Zabur Dawood (David), Injil Isa (Jesus) and the Quran is given to (Prophet Muhammad pbuh).

God is one all these holy books have conveyed only one message of God to humans that is humanity. All have to live their daily life on the ground of humanity i.e. religion. The Quran mentions that the revelation was also given to the Prophet Dawood (David). Not much is known about this revelation, but Islam confirms that the Suktas were recited as poetry or hymns. The Arabic word "zabur" comes from a root word meaning song or music. All of Allah's Prophets came with the same message, so hymns also include praise of God, teachings about monotheism and guidance for a righteous life. The Quran mentions a revelation called the Suhuf Ibrahim or the Scroll of Ibrahim. They were allegedly written by Ibrahim himself as well as his scribes and followers. Although this holy book is believed to be lost forever. The Quran mentions the scrolls of Abraham several times.

But the above books came after the Noah/Manu incident. Probably according to the reading and understanding of the Vedas, they were books of Allah / God before the occurrence of the great flood. Because it is clear in Islam that God has sent many Prophets to eradicate evil and spread humanity in different parts of the world and in different communities. Of the many, only few Prophets Names are mentioned by name in the Quran. Whose names : Adam, Idris (Enoch), Nuh (Noah), Hud (Heber), Saleh (Methuselah), Lut (Lot), Ibrahim (Abraham), Ismail (Ishmael), Ishaq (Isaac), Yakub (Jacob),

Yusuf (Joseph), Shuaib (Jethro), Ayyub (Job), Dhulkifl (Ezekiel), Musa (Moses), Haroon (Aaron), Dawood (David), Sulaiman (Solomon), Ilyas (Elias), Elisa (Elisha), Yunus (Jonah), Zakariya (Zakariya), Yahiya (John the Baptist), Isa (Jesus) and Muhammad (Ahmad). All or most of them were great men from the Jewish clan then who were the messengers sent in the civilizations? Aurangzeb brother Dara Shikoh, who was brutally murdered by the Mughal emperor tried to get the Upanishads translated into Persian and called them "Kitabin Maknun" (The Greatest Secret book) (lohe-Mahfuz) referred to in Quran Sharif (56:78). Philosophical thoughts of many sages are stored in the Upanishads.

It is said in Surah Al Momin verse 78, "We have sent many messengers before you, some of whom we have narrated to you and there are some of whom we have not narrated to you." In addition, Surah Yunus 10 verse it is said in 47 – There is a messenger for every Ummah (community). Then when their messenger comes, a just decision is given between them and there is no oppression on them.

Islam clearly states that everyone should respect all messengers and Prophets. That is, all sages, incarnations etc. in all sects and countries should be respected according to the words of GOD. And the one who refuses they are not a true Muslim. Prophets have come in different places of this world and at different times. 6

Sanatan Dharma developed in BHARAT and Islam dharma developed in Arabia, both emphasize on the purpose of divine guidance to humans. Sanatana Dharma believes that Almighty God comes to earth in some physical form to protect humans and humanity and to set an example and set rules to live by. Whereas Islam highlights that Allah chooses a person from among men to deliver his message and communicates with him at a higher level through his revelations. To such chosen people the messengers of God and he is called the Prophet. To such persons God makes known his revelations.

Reference

1. https://www.mycentraljersey.com/story/life/faith/2014/08/20/hinduism-many-Gods/14247795/

2. https://books.google.co.in/books?id=wikG_iOhSc8C&pg=PA64&lpg=PA64&dq=who+books+mention+about+124000+messenger+of+God&source

3. BHARATIYE Religions Series-2 The Faith and Philosophy of Islam by Shamim Akhtar published in 2009

4. https://en.wikipedia.org/wiki/List_of_Founds_of_religious_traditions

Chapter 8

Religion After Noah's Flood/Ark Noah Arc Event

According to the Abrahamic religions, when the world was full of sins and evils, corruption was common among humans the earth was corrupted and filled with violence. Then God instructed Noah to build a large ark. In that ark Noah entered with his sons and their wives, each male and female pair of many living creatures. And they all passed through the flood escaped destruction. (Quran Sharif Surah Hud 11 verse 36-44)

There is a story about Manu in the eternal religious book Arthavaveda and in Shatapatha Brahmana related to Shukla Yajurveda, that a fish came to him. Fish is considered as an incarnation of Lord Vishnu. The fish saved Manu's boat from the flood. According to the story described in the Mahabharata Shanti Parva / A-347, once after the deluge of the earth, Brahma revealed the Vedas again, then the TamoGuni demon Madhu and the Rajoguni demon Kaitabh read the Vedas. Then Lord Vishnu incarnated as the Hayagriva supported those deities and brought back the Vedas and handed them over to Brahma. The description of the destruction of the world by flood is found in all religions and cultures. Most flood stories involve a saving God and a catastrophic deluge that destroys the entire world.

It is clearly explained by many scientists that many civilizations refer to the occurrence of the deluge or flood. Geologists have identified the possibility of a great flood that occurred around 5000 BC. Until then, the Black Sea was a freshwater lake surrounded by farmland.

After the great destruction by God that happened at the time of Noah, everything was destroyed and the new world order came into existence and gradually the world flourished again from the creatures saved by Noah. The descendants of Noah may have initially been nomadic tribes and as the population grew they spread to almost all parts of the world.

In the course of development of civilizations, humans started doing bad things out of selfishness and corrupted the society again. Whenever that happened, God continued to send his avatars or messengers to purify humans and to eradicate evils. The followers of those avatars or messengers followed the teachings of the avatars and they started giving the name of "Dharma" i.e. religion to those teachings. The avatar or messenger assumed the body. After eradicating the evils and preaching humanity to the humans, those avatars and messengers used to give up the body according to the law of the world. Latter the followers made many changes in the teachings of the avatars or messengers according to their convenience and benefit. Thus lost the originality and value of the teaching and religion of those incarnations.

We see that Abrahamic religion is spread all over the world and is estimated to be 60% of the world's population. The reason is that since the beginning of civilizations in this present era "Kalyug" after Noah's incident the three civilizations Egyptian civilization, Mesopotamian civilization and Sumerian civilization first flourished and they had the most evils and corruptions in society. Due to the goodness, truth and love the religion originated from Abraham and his generations spread all over the world. To eradicate the evils in Abrahamic religion, God continued to send many Prophets, whose few names are mentioned in Quran Sharif.

The teaching and preaching of all religions is the same that is to lead a good life by doing good deeds. We see that the avatars or messengers spoke of eternal life, humanity, the right way to live peacefully, purification of the soul etc. All Avatars set examples through their conduct. But later on the followers as earlier distorted the teachings of the Avatar or messenger.

Many new religions came into existence in other parts of the world as well. Because in every part of the world there was need of service to mankind, right life, right conduct and education of eternal life because in those areas also some kind of malpractices or some kind of illegal activities prevailed. According to climatic conditions, food habits, cultural reasons, traditions etc. those evils or corruption were of different types which were harmful to the human beings living in that particular area and during that particular period.

All the messengers or incarnations who came in this world in different times gave humanity teachings according to that time and for the specific society. For salvation eating at night is a clear prohibited in Jainism because Jainism emphasizes on non-violence in all form. There are two reasons for not eating at night, first non-violence and second for better health. Scientific researchers have made it clear that germs which we cannot see directly spread rapidly at night, so proper and clean food does not enter the stomach after sunset. That's why eating at night is prohibited in Jainism and even in Ayurveda. 5

Jains believe that all animals and plants have living souls. Each of these souls is equal and should be treated with respect and compassion. This is also proven by science. Jains are vegetarian and **live in a way that minimizes the use of the world's resources**. Jains believe in reincarnation and seek to attain ultimate liberation – which means escaping the continuous cycle of birth, death and rebirth so that the immortal soul remains in a state of bliss forever. The three guiding principles of Jainism. The three gems' are right faith, right knowledge and right conduct. It is one of the 5 Mahavratas. Other mahavratas are non-attachment to property, not lying, not stealing, and sexual abstinence (with brahmacharya as the ideal). Mahavira is considered to be the person who gave Jainism its present form. That religion was re-established by Lord Mahavira (599-527 BC). Jainism, which originated in the BHARATIYE subcontinent is one of the oldest religions and its origins date back to 3000 BCE. They have the holy book Tatvartha Sutra. Jains are divided into two major sects; The Digambara (meaning "sky-clad") sect and the Svetambara (meaning "white-clad") sect. There is no priest in Jainism. Its religious people are monks and nuns, who lead a strict and ascetic life. 4

We know that electricity did not existed in ancient times. Everything used to become very dark after evening and when people ate in the dark they did not see what they were eating. In some places, due to wrong eating habits, many types of diseases must have erupted and man must have suffered. So the Lord send his avatar or messenger for the purification of the society and for spreading the teachings and the correct practices applicable to that time period for the cause of humanity applicable for all humans. Taught the right way to live life according to the need of that time. The followers named the teachings and practices of that avatar or messenger as the new religion. There must have been some changes in those religions with time, that's why we see two sects in that religion.

So it is very clear that messengers were born in different parts of the world at different times to solve problems prevailing in different communities. The teachings of those messengers were called religion by their followers. Religion has come only to serve man for right deeds and right practices. No religion teaches hatred or anything that is harmful to humanity.

With the increase in population in all parts of the world different Prophets came and so different followers formed different religions. In the same way we come to know from the history that in the particular period/time in the Middle East women were considered as a curse in the family and society. When a girl child was born, she was buried alive. Girls were considered only as objects of enjoyment. That's why God sent Prophet Muhammad pbuh to eradicate those evils and show people the right path. From time to time we find all kinds of evils in history. God send his avatars or messengers from time to time to eradicate the evils and purify the society and spread the right way of living.

From the above facts we can understand that just as various messengers of God came to the countries of the Middle East, similarly many incarnations and messengers of the Lord have been sent to different parts of the world in different times. All religions teaches humanity, love, human service, the right way to live life. They talk about eternal life.

Now the time has come for all of us to open our eyes. Looking deeply, we can say that the base and basic elements of all religions are same, only the path is different. There are many languages, many Prophets have come and that's why there are many religions. Due to the different languages GOD is known by different names. The followers latter distorted the religions and the originality is lost somewhere, due to which the basic meaning and purpose of the religion is lost. The misguided followers feel that they are superior to others. They try to show others that they are right and others are wrong, which result in conflicts. They pretends to be the supreme human being. When the followers of any religion start thinking that their own belief system is correct then there is bound to be a conflict. Mistaking the religious beliefs of others is religious deviation. Every religion in the world has some misguided followers. It is our duty to bring those misguided followers on the right path and make them follow the true teachings of the religion or sects. If we understand properly what is dharma then we will never quarrel. There will be peace in the whole world.

Reference

1. https://www.pbs.org/inentiallens/blog/a-flood-of-myths-and-stories/

2. https://www.pewforum.org/2012/12/18/global-religious-landscape-exec/

3. https://english.newstracklive.com/news/jain-religion-dinner-before-sunset

4. https://www.bbc.co.uk/religion/religions/jainism/atagance/glance.shtml

Chapter 9

Abrahamic religions and Judaism

The religions of Abraham's descendants are known as Abrahamicism. It is a group of monotheistic belief which are Judaism, Christianity, Islam, Baha'i faith and many other small religion. The group is named after the Prophet Abraham. Abraham was a resident of Mesopotamia Ur Sahar City, present-day Iraq. He lived around 2000 BC.

All Abrahamic religions accept that God himself appeared in the vision of the patriarch Abraham, spoke to Abraham and tested him. In that test Abraham lived up to God's expectation. His descendants are all monotheistic and believe in God as a supreme creator and source of moral law. In all his religious texts there are many figures, histories and places of the same personality. However they often present them with different roles, perspectives and meanings. Believers who agree on these similarities and a common Abrahamic origin tend to be more positive toward other Abrahamic groups.

All Abrahamic religions affirm an eternal God who created the universe. The one who rules the world, the one who sends Prophets, angels, messengers. They reveal the divine will of the Supreme Lord. Worship, ceremonies and rituals related to religion differ greatly among the Abrahamic religions. Some parallels include the concept of a seven-day (youm) cycle in which one day(youm) is usually reserved for prayer or other religious activities—Shabbat, Sabbath, Jummah, and Sunday. This custom is related to the Biblical story of Genesis, where God created the universe in six days(youm) and rested in the seventh. In the next volume of this book we will come to know exactly what is the meaning of youm.

Judaism mandates that males be circumcised when they are 8 days old, as is the Sunnah in Islam. Western Christianity replaced the practice of male circumcision with the rites of baptism. Jewish Encyclopaedia: Baptism "According to the rabbinical teachings, which dominated even during the existence of the Temple of Jerusalem (at c. viii. 8), next to baptism, circumcision and sacrifice, to be accomplished by a convert to Judaism circumcision was an absolutely necessary condition. Circumcision, however, was more important and like baptism was called the "sealing". But circumcision was discarded by Christianity.

All the Abrahamic religions originated in the Middle East. As time passed the enthusiasm and innovation of all the Abrahamic religions faded away one by one. That's why we see that so many Prophets, avatars or messengers came to that part of the world and one after the other tried to revive the same message of the God. But humans knowingly or unknowingly brought many changes in the teachings of their Prophets. Ultimately we see that one after the other all the religions got perverted. One by one all the Prophets of the Middle East tried to establish the law of humanity. In the beginning they were successful but after the death of the Prophets, the law of humanity was not followed resulting in corruption and evils in the society. So today we see that all the old religions of the Middle East distorted their original identity.

The main ABRAHAMINIC religions are: - Moses - Judaism - Yahwist, Akhenaten - Atenism - Egypt, Zoroastrianism - Iran, Ezra - Second Temple Judaism - Levite Judean, Jesus and the Twelve Apostles

- Pauline Christianity - Judaism, James. Just-Jewish Christianity-Judea, Judah Prince-Rabinic Judaism-Jewish Davidic Line, Montanus-Montanism-Phrygian, Sinope-Marsianism-Marsian of Pontic Greek, Man i-Manicheism-Western Persia, Arius-Arianism-Libya, Nestorius-Nestorianism -Romaniote, Eutykes-Monophysitism -Constantinople, Mazdak-Mazdakism-Iran, Mohammed-Islam-Arab, Ibn Nuser-Nuserism-Persian, Ibn Ahmad-Druzer-Nuserism-Persian -Persia, Sheikh Adi Ibn Musafir-Yazidism-Yezidi, Nai Fazlu La Astar Abadi-Hurufism-Iran, Mahmud Pasikhani-Nuqtism-Iran, Mormonism, Ali Muhammad Shirazi-Bayani-Iran, Baha'u'llah-Bahá'í Faith-Iran, Rastafari, Sabian Faith, Samaritanism etc.

Even before Moses, there were many tribal religions in the Middle East, but their followers do not exist today and all those religions have become extinct. Followers used to merge one after the other into the new religions of those days. The most important point here is that all Abrahamic religions trace themselves back to the great Abraham. But the irony is that today there is no harmony among the people of Abrahamic religions. The followers brought many changes in their religions.

Judaism

Western civilization has been related to Judaism in one way or the other. Many words in the Declaration of Independence of America have been taken from the ancient book of Jews. God is called Yahweh by the Jews. In the English translation of the time of King James, Jehovah was misspelled. Judaism in this era is the oldest monotheistic religion in the world, believed to be about 4,000 years old. Followers of Judaism believe in one God, who revealed himself through ancient Prophets. To understand Judaism, it is necessary to understand the history of Judaism, which has a rich heritage of law, culture, and tradition. Most Jews (with the exception of some groups) believe that their Messiah hasn't come yet - but will one day.

The Jewish people worship in holy places known as synagogues and their priests are called Rabbis. The six-pointed star of King David is a symbol of Judaism. Today there are approximately 15 million Jews worldwide. Most of them live in the United States and Israel. Traditionally a person is considered to be Jewish if his or her mother is Jewish. The Jewish sacred text is called the Tanakh or "Hebrew Bible". It contains the same books as the Old Testament in the Christian Bible, but they are placed in a slightly different order. The Torah – the first five books of the Tanakh – outlines the laws for Jews to follow. God first revealed himself to a Hebrew man named Abraham, who became known as the founder of Judaism. Later around 1000 BCE, King David the Great became the ruler of the Jewish people. His son Solomon built the First Holy Temple in Jerusalem, which became the central place of worship for the Jews. Around 587 BCE, the Babylonians destroyed the First Temple and sent many Jews into exile. Second temple was built in 516 BCE. But was finally destroyed by the Romans in 70 AD.

Tanakh (also known as Torah or Taurat) is considered the sacred text of Judaism. Later, the Talmud, a collection of teachings and commentaries on Jewish law, was created. It contains interpretations by thousands of rabbis and outlines the importance of the 613 commandments of Jewish law. For a Jew, his own small country has become God. The holy country has become a part of a religion. It is written in the holy book "Talmud", whenever you eat food or drink anything, thank God. If you live and eat without remembering him is like stealing God things. Enjoy the good things in life but at the same time always remember God because all good things are available because of God. Torah Keeping God as a witness, the world should be enjoyed sacrificially that is considering it only as God's Prasad. The resources available in this world do not belong to anyone, they are God's wealth, it is not right to be greedy for them.

In the history, we find that Prophet Hazrat "Yusuf" (Yuhana) was pushed into the well by his own brothers because of jealousy, but he did not die, so after a few days he was brought out of the well and his brothers sold him to traveling merchants. Who eventually sold Yusuf as a slave to the king of Egypt? When he grew up and handsome, the then queen wanted something from him when he refused the queen accused Yusuf and imprisoned him. A few months later, the Prophet Yusuf interpreted the king's dream and Egypt was saved from big draught and famine. Seeing this miracle, King Pharaoh and his wife apologized to him and King Pharaoh released the Prophet from prison. The queen also accepted her mistake. Moving on, the king of Egypt made Yusuf to be his advisor. During the famine, Yusuf brothers reached Egypt to get grain. Yusuf saw his brothers and then after a small incident he called his father and all his brothers and they all settled in Egypt.

After many centuries passed Yusuf family generation grew and became a large community. They were all given respect and involved in the running rule of Egypt kingdom. Much latter when the population grew, then some evil Egyptians started saying that Yusuf had come as a slave and all his descendants are ruling. The then King Pharaoh at that time again enslaved all the descendants of Prophet Yusuf and his brothers and they were forced to work as slaves in Egypt. The name of Yusuf eldest brother was Yehuda. Yehuda cleverly made all the descendants to be known as "yahudi". A few centuries later in Egypt, the king of that time was told by a priest that a child would be born among the Jewish people and that child would destroy the king and his dynasty. King Pharaoh of that time started to kill every child born in the "Jewish" (yahudi) community. A child was born in the same community. The mother of that child put the child in a basket and floated it on the river Nile. He reached the Egyptian queen's bathing place. The Egyptian queen had no child of her own, so she picked up the child from the basket and raised it like her own son. The king and queen named him Moses. Moses grew up. Out of jealousy, the queen's maid told the king everything about Moses. The king became very angry. Moses was sent among the slaves. King Pharaoh Tourchered the whole community a lot. When the pain increased among the Jews a lot, then God appeared in front of Moses and told him to take all the Jewish people out of Egypt. God brought them all to the promised land of Israel.

The escape from Pharaoh's slavery and return to home land of the Jews was by the grace of God. By God's grace the people of Israel were saved from persecution and death and freed from the oppression of the Egyptians. (Exodus 12.50) God destroyed the mighty empire of Egypt. "O people of Israel, you are happy. You are a special human being created by Yahweh" which will continue through inheritance. This God has given it for his chosen people i.e. for the Jews. Many messengers of God came among the Jews community.

The modern state of Israel was re-established in 1948. This small nation has grown tremendously in a short period of time. The Jewish race has been a force to be reckoned with in the history of Western civilization, turning history and becoming a world power. Small in number but great in strength and vitality.

Most Jews observe Shabbat (Friday eve to Saturday eve) by reading or discussing the Torah, attending a synagogue, or attending a Shabbat meal with other Jews. Yom Kippur 'the Day of Repentance' is the holiest day of the year in Judaism. Its central themes are atonement and repentance. Jews traditionally observe this holy day with a day of fasting and intense prayer and often spend most of the day in synagogue services. 8

Abraham, Moses, David and Solomon were the main Prophets who taught the Jews to follow the laws of humanity. As usual the Prophets left this world, then their followers changed the laws, evils and corruption started among them. The Lord tried to restore the faith of Judaism but the followers continued to disobey the Lord. God continued to send the same command through Abraham, Moses, David, Jesus, Muhammad and others. All the other Prophets also preached the same thing during that time.

Moses was one of the greatest Prophets of God. He was the only one who spoke directly to God. No other Prophet spoke directly to the Lord. God has given his best mind to the followers of Moses i.e. the Jewish community only because of Moses. From time to time between Abraham and Jesus, many Prophets came in the community of Jews to purify the society. Even Jesus was born as a Jewish man. And most of the present Muslims of Middle East were once upon a time a Jew.

Reference

1. https://en.wikipedia.org/wiki/Abrahamic_religions

2. Fiaz Fazli, Crescent Magazine, Srinagar, September 2009, p. 42. "Many Muslim scholars refuse to use the crescent moon as a symbol of Islam. Historically, the faith of Islam had no symbol, and many Muslims refuse to accept it.

3. JSTOR 10.1525/nr.2006.9.4.034.

4. Peters Francis E, Esposito John L (2006). Children of Abraham, Judaism, Christianity, Islam. p

5. Kunst, J.; Thomson, L.; Sam, d. (2014). "Late Abrahamic reunion? Does religious fundamentalism negatively predict dual Abrahamic group classification among Muslims and Christians". European Journal of Social Psychology. 44(4): 337-348.

6. Samuel P. Huntington: Der Kampf der Kultern. Die Neugestaltung der Weltpolitik im 21. Jahrhundert, Frankfurt 1997, p. 337.

7. Leonard Swidler, Khalid Duran, Reuven Firestone, Trilogy: Jews, Christians, and Muslims in Dialogue

Chapter 10
Christianity

Christianity is an Abrahamic, monotheistic religion based on the life and teachings of Jesus of Nazareth. It is the largest religion in the world. This religion reached from zero to peak.

Jesus was a Jewish carpenter, born in a stable in Bethlehem (Jerusalem). There is a difference of opinion about the date of his birth. It is believed to be about four years before AD started. He was crucified at the age of about 33. He never went on a long journey. He had no worldly possessions. He did not composed any book. He had no army. But today the whole world celebrates the birthday of such a simple man. He used to roam among the people of the poor, distributed the ray of hope among the depressed people, removed their troubles and taught the lessons of love and non-violence. His teachings and the works of Jesus convinced the public that Jesus is a human form of God.

Prophet Jesus Christ, the great messenger of God, in his time taught to eradicate evils and purify the society in the Middle East. His teaching was a continuation of the teachings of the earlier Prophets. The way in which Jesus taught, simply, comprehensively, balanced and decisively is unique. His words were the same as all the Prophets. Such as **"Love your neighbour as yourself"**, **"Do unto others as you would have wished unto you"**, "Know the truth and the truth shall set you free". Right Ways to Live, Christ preached about the value of life, love and peace, service to mankind, helping marginalized people, rights and duties of citizens, kings, human beings etc. He preached to stop slavery. In fact Jesus was against the prevailing evils at that time. But the words of Jesus were contrary to the interests of the influential elite people of the time. In an age of violence, Jesus raised the voice of non-violence. He talked about doing well to others instead of evil. He talked about forgiving others. He said forbade hatred of the sinner. Jesus words of love and service had created panic among the elite people of the society. Jesus asked man to surrender before God. Due to the teaching of Jesus the then ruling Rome saw many types of rebellions. The influential and elite people felt so threatened and insecure that they wanted to kill Jesus. Jesus influence was so widespread that the Jewish priests accused him of blasphemy and ultimately brutally executed Jesus on a cross. Jesus death increased their influence. Before being crucified, Jesus said to his disciples: I leave my joy with you. This joy was found in the early Christians. Saint Paul said that the influence of the Holy Spirit gave them such strength that even after being few in number and suffering the oppression of the rulers, the followers of Jesus did not stop and eventually they were victorious. The result of the agonizing death of Jesus was that suffering had become meaningless for the followers of Jesus.

After the death of Jesus, the misguided people tried to stop the teachings of Jesus and also punished the true followers of Jesus. The true followers of Jesus kept following the path shown by Jesus by remaining silent and hiding. As time passed after the death of Jesus, the noble people began to understand that the preaching of Prophet Jesus was not going to stop and neither was it going to end.

Roman religion was polytheistic from the beginning. There was a series of Gods and spirits. Rome included Greek Gods as well as many foreign pantheons in this collection. As the empire expanded, the Romans avoided imposing their own religious beliefs on those they conquered. 3

The acceptance of Christianity did not come quickly. Christians endured hatred and cruelty for almost 300 years. The Jews had established themselves firmly in the Roman Empire before Christianity. But they were often the target of the emperors, who were often blamed for any ills that befell the empire. Nero expelled them from Rome, Emperor Vespasian's son Titus continued his father's war against the Jews. Eventually the city of Jerusalem was destroyed and thousands of its citizens were killed. 4

Christianity was initially seen as a sect of Judaism and it was. Emperor Nero became more suspicious as this small sect began to grow. But as time went on, Christianity continued to spread throughout the empire, attracting intellectuals and illiterates along with women and slaves. Persecution increased as Christian churches were burned. But eventually Diocletian's successor Emperor Constantine, recognized Christianity in the Edict of Milan in 313 AD. Constantine's generosity to Christianity can be traced back to the Battle of Milan Bridge in 312 CE, where he saw a vision (a cross in the sky) and prayed that if he emerge victorious and become emperor of a united Roman Empire he will accept Christianity. He was victorious. Later, in 325 CE the differences between the various Christian sects were resolved. The Council of Nicaea was organized. He rebuilt the churches destroyed by Diocletian. After his death, Christianity continued to grow and eventually replaced traditional Roman religion. Rome became the new centre of Christianity.

Here comes the most interesting thing that Jesus Christ did not write any religious book. The original name of Jesus in Hebrew was "Isa". The Christian Bible has two sections, the Old Testament and the New Testament. The Old Testament is the original Hebrew Bible, a collection of the sacred texts of Judaism, written at various times between approximately 1200 and 165 BCE. Jesus reintroduced the message of the almighty GOD. The New Testament were written by Christians long after Jesus Christ had left this world. There are many differences between the Old Testament and the New Testament. For the convenience of the Romans, many changes were made according to their wishes. 6

The Bible text is available in two sections – the former and the later. The latter is called the New Testament.

Old Testament Law: The Hebrew Bible consists of 39 books, written over a long period of time. It is the literary corpus of the ancient nation of Israel. The Hebrew word for law ('Torah') means 'guidance' or 'instruction', and includes stories that offer everyday examples.

New Testament: The New Testament consists of 27 books, written after the end of the 1st century AD, which fall into two sections: The Gospels, which tells the story of Jesus (Matthew, Mark, Luke, and John). There are additional letters written by various Christian leaders to provide guidance to early church communities.

In 1604, King James I of England authorized a new translation of the Bible with the aim of settling some of the religious differences in his kingdom and consolidating his power. But in an attempt to prove his supremacy, King James democratized the Bible instead.

Martin Luther actually deleted many things from the book. They are called Protestants who believe in the Bible revised by Martin Luther to adapt the Bible to their theology.

Birth of Christ: In history we find references of two dates that were widely recognized - and are still celebrated - as the birthday of Christ: 25 December in the Western Roman Empire and 6 January in the East (especially in Egypt and Asia Minor). December 25 is not the date mentioned in the Bible as the day of Christ's birth; The Bible is actually silent on the day or time of year when Mary is said to have given birth to him in Bethlehem. By most accounts, the birthday was first celebrated - in about 200 AD - on January 6th. Why? No one knows for sure. By the middle of the 4th century, the birthday celebration had been moved to December 25. Who made the decision? It is not clear. 1 1

Thus it is very clear that the originality of the true teaching of Jesus Christ has been lost during the translation and writing of the New Testament. So it is clear from the history that present day Christianity is different from its original form. Later on all kinds of evils and corruption started in the name of religion and the society of Middle East kept getting corrupted. The original teaching of Jesus Christ disappeared. So this is a big question for today's preacher and people engaged in the mission of spreading Christianity? What exactly are they spreading? Are they spreading the true message of Jesus Christ or the message of kings who changed the original Bible? The people of the kings wrote the New Testament according to their wish and comfort and just to get benefitted in the name of Jesus Christ and religion. Jesus never used the word "Christianity".

In 313 AD, Emperor Constantine issued the Edict of Milan legalizing the Christianity. In 380 AD with the Edict of Thessalonica under Theodosius, the Roman Empire officially adopted Christianity as its state religion and Christianity itself was established primarily as the Roman religion in the state church of the Roman Empire.

Now there is a big question for those who are professing themselves to be Christians. Why are they leaving any religion or their ancestral religion and going to a religion which has distorted the message of its own Prophet and following the message of few kings. If any flaws has entered in your religion then try to rectify it and follow that. All religion has truth within itself and all religion is for humanity. Man is man after all and we know that so called religious leaders have made some small changes in every religion, but people can remove every evil if they want. Jesus never called himself God. The fact is that "there is only one God".

One very good thing about Christian Missionaries is the service of humans and works for mankind. We all have great regards and respects for Christian missionaries and all should, but latter the complaint is that they try to convert people from one religion to another sects. If they continue to do human service without converting people, they will be the most respected people in the world. Otherwise, there is no use of service in the way for conversion. In such a way even GOD might not accept the service.

Reference

1. https://en.wikipedia.org/wiki/Christianity

2. https://www.worldhistory.org

3. https://www.bbc.co.uk

4. https://askinglot.com/why-did-martin-luther-remove-7-books-from-the-bible

5. https://www.washingtonpost.com/news/answer-sheet/wp/2014/12/24/

6. https://owlcation.com/humanities/Comparing-the-Gospels-Matthew-Mark-Luke-and-John

7. https://www.history.com/topics/religion/bible

Chapter 11
Islam

Islam "is an Abrahamic religion. It is the second largest religion in the world. The religion of Islam was initiated by the Prophet Muhammad (pbuh) in the beginning of the seventh century.

In medieval time all kinds of evil and corruption prevailed all over the world, maximum in the Middle East countries. God and religion had become a source of income. Girls were considered a curse in the family and society. Girls were buried alive. Females were considered as a means of enjoyment. All illegal things were prevalent in the society. People hated each other, one tribe used to kill other tribes as a hobby for enjoyment. The Baqqa (Kaaba) was a place of business and worship of many idols of Gods and as a centre of trade rather than a religious centre. Nomadic Bedouin tribes dominated the Arabian Peninsula. War and killing were considered hobbies among all the tribes. There was turbulence everywhere, darkness was everywhere in the world, so those periods and times are called dark age in our history, maximum in the middle east countries and in that darkness Prophet Muhammad pbuh came with a light i.e. the light of humanity. God sent Prophet Muhammad pbuh to eradicate darkness, evils and corruption and to establish humanity.

Arab society before Islam

- The old name of Mecca was Bakka.

- Pre-Islamic religion in Arabia included indigenous polytheistic beliefs.

- Before the rise of the monotheistic religions of Judaism, Christianity and Islam, most Bedouin tribes believed in polytheism in the form of animism and idolatry.

- 360 idols were placed in and around Bakka before Islam came in existence. Ibrahim (Abraham) laid the foundation of the Bakka (Kaaba) with his son Ismail, around 2000 BC. It is believed that the Kaaba is the first place where Prophet Adam first prayed to God on this earth, when he met Eve at the same place after 300 years of separation.

- The main moon God in pre-Islamic Arabia was **Hubal,** the Syrian deity. Hubal's three daughters were the principal Goddesses of Bakka in Arab mythology: **Allat, Al-Uzza and Manat.** Allat was the Goddess associated with the world. Al-Uza, "The Most Powerful" or "The Strong", was a fertility Goddess, and Manat was a Goddess of fortune.

- Women were treated as objects under the customary tribal law that existed in Arabia before the rise of Islam. There were no law; the father used to sell his daughters in marriage for a price, the husband could end the marriage at his will, the women had no property or inheritance rights.

- In pre-Islamic Arab culture women had little control over their marriages. They were not allowed to divorce their husbands. Marriage was usually an agreement.

- Political life was absent in Arabia before Islam. With the exception of Yemen in the southwest, there was no government in any part of the Arabian Peninsula.

- Since there was no government in Arabia and since Arabs were anarchists by nature, they were in constant war. War was a hobby in Arab society.

- To them, war was a game or a species of drama, performed by professionals, to the delight of "spectators".

- War gave them an opportunity to display their skills in archery, swordsmanship and horse riding as well as bring pride and honour to their tribes through victory in battle.

- Slavery was an economic institution of the Arabs. Male and female slaves were sold and bought like animals.

- Before Prophet Muhammad PBUH, there were different types of marriages in Arabian Society. Due to which women were abused and their life became miserable.

- The social condition in the Arab society was very bad. Drinking, gambling and all illegal works was a part of Arab society. They lived in heavy debt because usury was very common. 4

As we have already seen in earlier chapters that God sends his messengers in such a society, where there were a lots of evil and corruption. The Lord sends his messenger in all the societies where humanity goes out of control. So God send one of his greatest messenger Prophet Muhammad pbuh to eradicate evils in Arab society.

Prophet Muhammad (pbuh) was born in 570 AD in the then most powerful tribe of Arabia. He was an orphan. When he was about 40 years old, he started preaching about the right practices and actions of humanity and declared himself to be the Prophet sent by God. He had to face many problems due to his teachings. In 622 AD he was forced to flee Mecca and went to Medina where the practice of any religion was allowed. The Arabic Hijri (Islamic calendar) begins from that year. Gradually after resistance his teachings were accepted by all and he returned to Mecca in the year 630 AD with a large number of his followers. They entered the city and eventually all the citizens of Mecca accepted Islam without any war or protest. The Prophet removed idols from the Kaaba and allowed the worship of only one supreme power. Prophet Muhammad pbuh died in 633 AD. 5

The old name of **Medina was Yasrib.** Allah chosed an Ummi as his Prophet so that no one should say that an educated person is writing something of his own free will. He was made a special man by Allah from a simple shepherd. Widow Khadija was a 40-year-old widow played an important role in shaping Prophet Mohammad pbuh as a Prophet. Mother Khadija was so impressed by the honesty and ability of the Prophet (who was then 25 years old) that Mother Khadija send a marriage proposal to the Prophet. The Prophet was scared because he was very poor and mother Khadija was 15 years older than him and she was very rich. But mother Khadija persuaded the Prophet to marry him. In that era when girls and women were considered as a material or goods, there was no respect for the widow, at that time the Prophet presented an example to the whole world by marrying elder widow. Prophet Mohammad pbuh married many but except one all were widows. The other marriages was to support her and her children with respect.

Prophet Mohammad (pbuh) established the rule of humanity by eradicating evils and corruptions from Arabia with his new teachings and philosophies. People named it as ISLAM religion. Soon after the death of the Prophet Muhammad pbuh there were military campaigns to establish Islamic rule, called "futuhat" or literally "openings", which also took place in Egypt and other parts of North Africa. In other parts of the world, Islam also spread through the trade and commerce routes. 6

The important point in the spread of Islam was that Islam introduced a system of political affiliation of the Arabs. Earlier the Arabs had no social or political affiliation. The new religion established the political system in the country. People started feeling the power and kingship. Since the Arabs were tribal warriors and they enjoyed warfare for centuries and centuries earlier, so the much later Muslim Caliphs took advantage of this and started wars in the name of religion and expanded their kingdoms. The Caliphs latter the early Rashidun Caliphate replaced the simple life of Muhammad with a life of luxury. Gradually after the death of Prophet Muhammad pbuh the followers slowly drifted away from the original teachings of Prophet Muhammad pbuh.

Prophet Muhammad himself fought wars, but all type of studies show that Prophet (peace and blessings of Allah be upon him) battles and wars were based on various legitimate causes. All wars were based on legitimate causes; therefore, it can be concluded that none of the Prophet's wars or interventions were unjust. The Prophet did not unjustly attack any tribe or kingdom. He did not commit any act of terrorism and at the same time set and followed all the proper rules and regulations of war so that humanity prevails. 7

The principles of Islam are based on the Quran and Sunnah taken into account, it is seen that the relations between individuals and states are based on the principle of peace. War is an unwanted obligation which is temporary; it can only be in the form of a struggle for existence. 8

Truthfulness, authority, simplicity, equality and ease of living were among the most important factors in the spread of Islam in the early period. Prophet Muhammad pbuh and his companions lived a life of truthfulness and simplicity which impressed everyone. But as time passed, many unwanted practices and evils entered inside Islam. As Islam spread away from Arabia, the Arabic practice inside Islam started facing opposition in other places. When Islam spread outside Arabia, many difficulties started coming in front of Islamic Caliphs. Rashiddun Caliphates (632–661), the Umayyad Caliphates (661–750), the Abbasid Caliphate (750–1258), the Mamluk Abbasid Caliphate Dynasty (1261–1517), the Ottoman Caliphate (1517–1924) tried to find a solution in their own way in which some were just and some were based on personal interests or may be something was only for that time being. Among all these only the Rashiddun Caliphs in the beginning have been considered correct and true.

As the religion of Islam spread outside Arabia in different countries and among different languages the customs of different places mixed with Arabic civilization and culture. Prophet Muhammad pbuh had tried to end the old and wrong practices that were present in Arabia, but after his passing some Muslims For their benefit started using the old bad practices by tilting and breaking them according to their wishes. Prophet Mohammad Sahab pbuh did not choose his successor, that's why there were many differences among Muslims on making of Caliph.

The first Abbasid Caliphate shifted the capital to Damascus, then shifted in the city of Baghdad and made it the capital. The caliphate moved away from the Arab environment and went to another environment. External influence was beginning to fall inside Islam. Initially Islam was taught from the Quran as well as attention was paid to education, learning and great respect was given to scholars. Philosophy developed in Islam and Islamic philosophers studied all the philosophical teachings of the world and included them in their philosophies. According to the saying of the Prophet in the early days people used to go even far off places to get proper knowledge. The

Muslims of that time progressed a lot by getting knowledge and took Islam to the height of prestige and golden age. Those were the golden periods of Islam. It prevailed up to mid of 13th century.

During the lifetime of the Prophet, the Quran and the words of the Prophet Mohammad pbuh were enough to solve every question. But after the departure of the Prophet and after the passage of almost a century, when Islam had spread in different directions, there were many discussions on wisdom and Sunnah. From all those discussion the differences started.

There are were four different sects or sub sects in Islam:

1.   "Hanafi" of Imam Abu Hanifa (767).

2.   Imam Malik (715-65) "Maliki" of Medina.

3.   "Shafai" of Imam Shafai (737 – 820).

4.   "Hambaliyya" of Imam Ahmad ibn Hambal.

The four sects are considered correct by the Muslims. They follow religious beliefs according to their own interpretations.

Then from there the speculations and probability started coming in conclusions. Then came the era of following the majority (Ijmaa). It is clear that as Islam started spreading in different countries whose cultures and languages were different so according to the people of those places to run the kingdom Laws were made. Slowly difference of opinion started to start. After the year 1000 AD, the huge Islamic state was fragmented and resulted in different sultanates. In 1258 AD, the main city of the huge Islamic state was captured and destroyed by the Mongols in a very ugly manner, which is not worth describing. The result was Abbasid Caliphate ended there. The world's largest university and library at that time was completely destroyed in Baghdad. With that the Golden Age of Islam came to an end. And this was the result of the wrong deed done by Muslim king in BHARAT in the NALANDA

UNIVERSITY. Allah who is for all gives the rewards and punishment as per the deeds of the people. Bhaktiyar Khilzi was very proud of Islamic things which was given by the Baghdad University, and when he was cured by Nalanda University unexpectedly he became jealous and due to the jealousy he burnt the whole university. He wanted that no university shall become great than Bhagdad university. In return the Islamic university was destroyed within one century. A big lesson is in this for all. The lesson is if one harms other due to any inhumanity reason then that deeds will take its revenge. It is happening with everyone but people are not realising. Because of the revenge progressiveness of Islamic society vanished and then the interpreted teachings was brought forward as per the influencers. Gradually, Islam was no longer a friend of the poor. The rulers themselves had produced feudal lords and priests. Slowly the imams became paymasters of the rich. The true spirit of ISLAM started diluting.

The most important word of Prophet Muhammad (pbuh) was **"God has send about 124000 messengers in different places of the earth and among every community"**. Muslims consider all Prophets like Adam, Noah, Abraham, Moses, David, Solomon, Jesus etc. to be the messengers of God. Then if this is true, then the missing link between Adam and Noah is also true that there were other Prophets, messengers, avatars whom we have to find and include in the list according to Prophet Muhammad pbuh. Those Prophets must have been born in different countries. In BHARAT, China, Africa or America and everywhere else in the world. All Prophets or incarnations have taught the same eternal Dharma, that is the service to mankind, love, charity and peace. As well as being pious and doing the right things. 9, 10

Prophet Muhammad pbuh never taught to hate other people or other religions. Prophet Muhammad pbuh has offered all kinds of deliverance in his life. He stood for justice, love and peace, service of mankind. He established true salvation through his life. It is the duty of all Muslims to follow the path of Prophet Muhammad pbuh who spread education to all human beings. He said that if one's neighbour sleeps hungry then that person cannot be religious, that means he is not a human. Prophet Muhammad pbuh gave all the good teachings to the Arab people which gradually spread all over the world because at that time all the good teachings of Prophet Muhammad pbuh were followed by the followers. The main teachings of Prophet Muhammad pbuh are as follows,

1. Suicide, abortion and killing of innocent people are wrong and illegal.

2. Laws for protection of family, parents, women and children. Equal rights for women as well as men.

3. Alcohol and other intoxicants are illegal because they impair intelligence.

4. Protection of rights of all.

5. Law against theft, gambling, corruption and interest (usury).

6. Take proper education and become a wise person. (Note here that he did not use the word Muslim).

7. Help others for the sake of humanity.

8. **Do not take away the rights of brothers and sisters. Don't take away the rights of the poor. Don't break fidelity.**

9. Love your motherland and die for the motherland if required.

10. Islam is the religion of peace and mercy. It does not allow any act of terrorism. The Messenger of God lists that murder is the second major sin and warns that: "The first cases to be judged between people on the Day of Judgment will be bloodshed.

11. "The best among you are those who are best to their wives" Support and empower.

12. Prophet Muhammad (Sallallahu Alaihi Wasallam) forbade soldiers to kill women and children.

13. Jihad means fighting against evils inside oneself, one's weaknesses, being virtuous and moral, making sincere efforts to do good deeds and helping to improve society. When everything fails then war is the last option. Even as Islamic law sets clear guidelines for the conduct of war and forbids acts of terrorism, the Quran provides detailed guidelines and rules regarding war: whom to fight (48:17, 9:91), when the fighting should end (2:192), how to deal with the prisoners (47:4). It also emphasizes proportionality in warfare.

14. Committing suicide and killing innocent people is not Jihad in Islam. In fact it is a heinous crime and a sin. Islamic law sets clear guidelines for the conduct of war and condemns acts of terrorism.

15. Donate without delay.

16. "Whoever believes in God and the Day of Judgment, should not harm his neighbour, whoever believes in God and the Day of Judgment should welcome his guest with open heart and say only what is good."

17. "A sadaqah is to be given for every joint of the human body, and every day when the sun rises there is a reward of a sadaqah (charitable gift) for one who establishes justice between people."

18. "When if someone gets angry while standing, then he should sit down. If the anger leaves him then it is good, otherwise he should lie down or sleep.

19. "Do not indulge in overeating as it will extinguish the light of faith in your hearts."

20. Learn to think carefully before speaking.

21. The Prophet stressed the importance of thinking and believing.

22. The lifestyle of Prophet Muhammad pbuh was remarkably simple and full of simplicity. He had no luxuries and the gifts he received were often distributed among others or donated to charity.

23. The most important lesson is never to do anything that hurts others. 11

The list of good teachings and sermons that Prophet Muhammad pbuh has given in every sphere of life is endless. But as time and centuries passed people changed and distorted the real teachings of Prophet Muhammad pbuh, and the true spirit of Islam was lost over time. Now a days Muslims are not following the real teachings of Prophet Muhammad (pbuh). These days Muslims are just for the name shake living with the ISLAMIC name without following the Islam.

For the first few centuries of the formation of Islam, all the Muslims were properly following the teachings of Prophet Muhammad pbuh, so Islam was considered as a good religion and it was widely accepted by all and it spread almost everywhere. The Muslims lead a simple life. Muslims used to stand for the rights and justice. Those were the days of Islam and world power was in the hands of Muslims. As time passed, the Muslims weakened the true spirit of Islam. So gradually Allah has withdrawn his blessings from the Muslims due to bad deeds.

I am a BHARATIYE first so first I will talk about my country. After independence, we Muslims in BHARAT have completely changed the teaching and spirit of Islam. There are many reasons for this. Quran and Hadith were first written in Arabic language. In the BHARATIYE subcontinent, we do not understand the Arabic language properly. So Arabic was translated into Urdu. We read Quran in Arabic but we read all Hadith in Urdu which are translated by Maulanas. This is because the Quran is the book of God and it cannot be changed. All Muslims have to pray and perform all holy rituals in Arabic. Quran is translated into all the languages of the world for better understanding. But it is recited in Arabic only.

As time passed during the translation, there were many changes in the Hadith and some followers have changed the true spirit of Islam. The dogma in BHARAT is that we think whatever the religious leader says is right. We listen only to what Maulana speaks. We know that there are many types of Hadith, we will read about them in the another chapter in this book only. Few Muslims in BHARAT have converted the Islam of the great Prophet Muhammad pbuh into the new Islam of Mullahs. Not all Maulanas are bad but there are some due to which the bad names are coming.

The five pillars of Islam are

- Shahada: Declaration of one's faith in God and belief in Prophet Muhammad pbuh.

- Salat (namaz): Praying five times a day (before sunrise, noon, afternoon, sunset and night)

- Zakat: Giving monetary help to the needy

- Roza: fasting during Ramadan

- Hajj: making the pilgrimage to Mecca at least once, whoever is able, in a lifetime.

- A central idea in Islam is "jihad", which means "struggle", i.e. "struggle with oneself against evils ". While the term is used negatively in mainstream culture, it is in fact a defence of one's faith. For refers to internal and external efforts. However, this may include military jihad if "just war" is required, which is the last option. 12

When Muhammad pbuh died, there was a debate about who would be his successor. This gradually led to a split in Islam and two major sects emerged: Sunni and Shia. Sunnis make up about 90 percent of Muslims worldwide. They accept that the first four caliphs were the true successors of Muhammad. Shia Muslims believe that only Caliph Ali and his descendants are the true successors of Muhammad.

The Quran contains some of the basic information found in the Hebrew Bible. The text is considered the sacred word of God. Muhammad's friends and scribes wrote down his words, which became the Quran. The Islamic calendar, also known as the Hijri calendar, is a lunar calendar used in Islamic religious worship. The calendar year began in 622 CE, which is the date of Muhammad's journey from Mecca to Medina. The legal system of Islam is known as Sharia law. This faith-based code of conduct instructs Muslims on how they should live in almost every aspect of their lives.

Chapter 12

How Islam came to BHARAT?

I slam in BHARAT first came to present-day Gujarat and around the same time it entered present-day Kerala (then Malabar), during the life period of Prophet Muhammad (pbuh) through traders by winning the hearts of people with the practices of actual islam.

The people of the Middle East had trade relations with BHARAT through the sea route since ages. After the rise of Islam in the Middle East, Muslim Arab traders came to Ghogha (Bhavnagar, Gujarat) in the early seventh century and built a small mosque there with the permission of the then king of Bhavnagar. This was the time when the Kiblah (the direction one faces when one performs Namaz) of Muslims was towards Masjid AQSA in Jerusalem instead of Mecca. For a short period of 16 to 17 months between 622 and 624 AD after Hizrat (migration) to Medina, Prophet Muhammad (pbuh) and his followers faced Jerusalem during Namaz. This is the oldest mosque locally known as Barwada Masjid or Juni Masjid. Later Prophet Muhammad (pbuh) received revelation and he was ordered to change the orientation point from Jerusalem to Mecca. Islam came into existence in South BHARAT peacefully long before the arrival of Muslims in the BHARATIYE subcontinent from the North West part.

The arrival of Muslims from North West BHARAT was through the war in Sindh much later. Initially, the main reason for invading

Sindh was for the sentiment of retaliation, not the desire for expansion of the state. In the BHARATIYE subcontinent in the beginning of the 8th century some Arab ships were abducted by pirates including Hajis, women and children near the port city of Dabel in Sindh the present city of Kranchi. The ships and people were plundered by the pirates. This message reached Damascus, the capital of the Umayyad Empire like fire. The then king of the world's richest Umayyad Empire sent a letter to King Dahir of Sindh, but Dahir did not responded. As a result the Umayyad Caliph declared war for the release of the Hajis. Raza Dahir had used many things and tantoms and inhumane things as per the advice of his astrologers to avoid the war but all went in vein. King Al-Hajjaj send a 17-year-old Iranian youth military commander Mohammad bin Qasim to attack Sindh in 711 AD. Mohammed bin Qasim captured the port city and freed the kidnapped Muslims. This was the first attack by Muslims in the BHARATIYE subcontinent. Dahir was killed in the battle. In the war the rebellious and disgruntled people of Dahir also fought on behalf of Qasim's army against Dahir.

There are mentions about Dahir's bravery in the book titled 'Grand Old Man' of Sindh and 'Independent Sindh'. According to him, earlier Dahir also granted to give refuge to Hussain, the grandson of Muhammad pbuh. It is mentioned in one place that Hussain was on his way to Sindh when he was intercepted and brutally killed in Karbala, Iraq. (Sindh Story Chapter the Truth about Dahir Sen) we will learn more in next volume of this book.

Muhammad bin Qasim's army had captured Sindh province, Multan and Brahmanabad province. He stayed in Sindh region for three years. After the death of Al-Hajjaj, the new caliph recalled Muhammad bin Qasim and arrested him, and Muhammad bin Qasim was executed in Mosul in 715 AD.

Similar to the zakat obligatory for Muslims, Jizya was originally a contribution donation for non-Muslims in 632, which is believed to be first mentioned in a document sent by Prophet Muhammad pbuh to Yemen. W. Montgomery Watt has argued that the document was tampered with by early Muslim historians to reflect later practice, while Norman Stillman regards it as authentic.

Jizya is described as a tax in Quran 9:29. During the lifetime of the Prophet Muhammad, non-Muslim tribes were not consistently taxed. The Nubians of North Africa, despite being non-Muslims, were exempted; instead he entered into a trade agreement with the Muslims. In the period following the death of Prophet Muhammad pbuh, Jizya was imposed on non-Muslim Arab tribes in lieu of military service, performance of military service earned an exemption; For example, under the second caliph, Umar ibn Al-Khab, the Jarajima tribe were exempted when they agreed to serve in the army. The non-Muslim poor, the elderly, women, serfs, religious workers and the mentally ill generally paid no tax. Early sources state that under the first caliphs, poor Christians and Jews were given stipends from the state treasury, which was largely funded by zakat, a compulsory tax paid by Muslim men and women of financial means and from jizya.

After the death of Muhammad bin Qasim, the Arabs or Turks were not able to enter the mainland BHARAT for almost 300 years. BHARATIYE kings were strong enough to defeat the invaders. Muslim rulers were confined up to Sindh. But Islam was prevalent and grew in different parts of BHARAT. It was present in BHARAT as many BHARATIYE accepted Islam because of ISLAM virtues, actions and good practices. Also Hindu kings were not preventing BHARATIYE people from practicing Islam. History is the witness that from the very beginning, BHARATIYE people were free to follow any religion or sects. BHARATIYE Muslims also used to go for Haj. Later on, different Muslim leaders continued to grow in other parts of the world. Mahmud, the Turkish conqueror of Ghazni in 998 AD, succeeded his father and established a vast empire in Central Asia with its capital at Ghazni present-day south of Kabul. He was then 27 years old and was the first ruler to receive the title "Sultan", which means authority, indicating his power. He invaded BHARAT 17 times between 1000 and 1027 AD, which was a significant event in the history of BHARAT. Its main aim was only to plunder the wealth of BHARAT. It had nothing to do with religion, humanity or Islam. The reuins of the attack by GHAZNI in Bharat has been like a thrown in the eyes of Bhartiye people till today.

Then after about 150 years, other Muslim leaders of Central Asia did not attack BHARAT on a large scale.

After this came Mohammad Ghori, who invaded BHARAT in 1175 AD. After the conquest of Multan and Punjab, he advanced towards Delhi. The Rajput chiefs of North BHARAT under the leadership of Prithvi Raj Chauhan defeated him several times in battle. Year after year, Muhammad Ghori came again and again to avenge his defeat. In 1192 AD again a fierce battle took place in which the Rajput king was defeated and Prithvi Raj Chauhan was captured and killed. But he was also not interested in BHARAT, only he wanted BHARAT wealth. So he went back to his place. He installed his slave Qutb-ud-din Aibak as the king of Delhi and asked him to make an annual payment in return for the kingdom. From that time the Muslim rule established itself in BHARAT. Then kings from different parts of the world came and plundered Delhi several times one after the other and it continued till 1947 AD.

On the other hand, some Maulanas started establishing themselves as God man. Maulanas translated different Hadith in different languages. Happy with the word of equality in Islam, many non-Muslims even converted themselves in the hope of a better life. Many converted willingly and some changed their religion due to many other reasons. But the converted Muslims were left to live at the mercy of the landlords. Even today, many Muslims come under the category of backward class due to poverty. Islam does not allow upper and lower classes, but then how did this class category entered? The invaders were only interested in the wealth of BHARAT. Religion had nothing to do with it. Muslim rulers converted people to Islam in the BHARATIYE subcontinent just to make their work easy. They had a thought that they have done their work and will go to heaven as Promoted by some. It is as if you sow a seed and do not water it and move away from the place and think that the seed will grow into a tree and bear fruit and benefit others, whereas the seed dies due to lack of water.

Most of the converted Muslims were left to do whatever they wished. This is the reason why we also see many similarities in the rituals and practices of Hindus and Muslims across BHARAT today which is totally different from Middle east. The customs and traditions of Muslims and Hindus are very similar in every part of BHARAT which can be easily observed. The names differ according to the language. When Muslims go to Hajj in Arabia, they are called "Hind ka Musalman" or Hindi Muslim so it is clear that all are basically Sanatani Muslims.

Islam in South BHARAT

According to Sumerian records, Kerala has been a major spice exporter since ages before 3000 BCE and is still referred to as the "Garden of Spices" or "Spice Garden of BHARAT". The spices of Kerala also attracted the ancient Arabs, Babylonians, Assyrians and Egyptians to the Malabar Coast in the 3rd and 2nd centuries BCE. The Phoenicians established trade with Kerala during this period. Arabs and Phoenicians first entered the Malabar Coast to trade spices. The Greek historian Herodotus (5th century BCE) recorded that the cinnamon spice industry was monopolized by the Egyptians and Phoenicians in his time. It was spices that also attracted Arabs, Assyrians, Babylonians, Phoenicians, Israelites, Greeks, Bomans and

Chinese. Various coins from different civilizations of the world have been found in some parts of Kerala.

There were considerable trade links between the Middle East and the Malabar Coast even before the time of Prophet Muhammad (570 - 632 AD). Muslim tombs with ancient dates, short inscriptions in medieval mosques and rare Arab coin collections are the major sources of the early Muslim presence on the Malabar Coast. Islam reached Kerala through spice traders from the Middle East.

Everything was good in the early Islamic era. In the beginning of Islam during the life time of Prophet Muhammad pbuh there were many kings all over the world and also in BHARAT who got influenced by the good philosophy, acts and practices in Islam and converted themselves. In those days there were various small states in the BHARATIYE subcontinent. BHARAT was not a country but was divided into many small states/countries. The first person in the BHARATIYE subcontinent who converted himself was a Chera dynasty king from Kodungallur in Kerala named Cheraman Peramul. He had witnessed the splitting of the moon, a supernatural phenomenon done by Prophet Muhammad (pbuh). This incident aroused curiosity in the king, due to which he started inquiring here and there. The bewildered king confirmed by his astrologers that the event had happened, but did not know what it meant. Arab merchants had arrived at the Malabar port on their way to Ceylon (today's Sri Lanka). A group of Muslim merchants led by Zaheeruddin came there from Arabia. He visited Kodungallur and met the Chera king. When the king asked him, he told the story of Prophet Muhammad pbuh, who had splitted the moon into two pieces through the prayer to Allah at the behest of the unbeliever. The Chera king was taken aback by this miracle. And the Cheraman king told the Arabs that he would like to meet Prophet Muhammad pbuh. With the group of merchants the king went to Arabia. There he landed at Shahr from where he went to Jeddah and met Prophet Muhammad pbuh. Then he accepted Islam of his own free will in front of the Prophet. He settled there and changed his name to Abdul Rahman Sumuri Tajuddin and married the sister of Habibuddin, an Arab king and lived there for about five years. He then started his journey back to Kerala but died on the way at Shahr Mukulla. Perumal has a tomb in Dhofar, a province of Oman. The king's companions and Syed Malik ibn Dinar (companion of the Prophet) returned to BHARAT.

One of BHARAT first mosque in Kerala, was built on the orders of King Cheraman by a companion of Prophet Muhammad pbuh. The mosque is named Cheraman Jumma Masjid after the king and was built in 629 AD at Kodungalloor, making it one of the oldest mosque in the BHARATIYE subcontinent and is still in use. It was built by Malik Dinar, a companion of the Prophet Muhammad. Islamic scholars consider the Cheramun Jumma Mosque to be the second in the world to offer Jumma prayers after the mosque in Medina, Saudi Arabia. The Barvadda Mosque in Ghogha, Gujarat was the first mosque built in 623 CE, the Cheraman Jumma Masjid in Kerala (629 CE) and the Palaiya Jumma Palli (or Old Jumma Masjid 628 - 630 CE) in Kilakarai, Tamil Nadu are three of the first mosques. In BHARAT, which were made by Arab traders and local people.

Mappilas in Malabar are the first BHARATIYE community to be converted to Islam. At the same time and a little before that, some Sanatani people had accepted Islam in Bhavnagar, Gujarat. At that time Muslims had set an example of good and true humanity and at that time many natives across world accepted Islam due to the right teaching, philosophies and goodness of Islam which are in line to the main teachings of different religions and sects.

The Sufis played an important role in the spread of Islam in BHARAT. His success in spreading Islam was paralleled in Sufi belief systems and practices by BHARATIYE philosophical literature, specially non-violence and monism. Sufism had a lot of tolerance which used to influence people.

In the beginning of the seventh century we find that people accepted Islam of their own free will with sincerity and purity in Islam. Many Sanatan and other kings also accepted Islam in different places around the world. Islam spread by winning the hearts of people in its early days. But later, after about 200 years, the kings of Central Asia hijacked the Islam religion and started expanding the kingdom in the name of religion and sects. They started using the religion and sects as a tool kit.

So the conclusion comes to the fact that 99.9% of BHARAT Muslims are of BHARATIYE origin and once upon a time we all were Sanatani. Initially many people had accepted Islam because of the correct teaching and good message of Islam, later may be some had also accepted it out of compulsion. If the DNA of Indian Muslims is tested, the DNA will match with the DNA of all BHARATIYE people, the DNA of Turks or Arabs will not match. That means we all are Sanatani Muslims.

A bitter truth is that Muhammad Ghori made Qutb-Ud-Din Aibak the king of Delhi. Qutb-Ud-Din Aibak was a slave and became the first Muslim king of BHARAT. But Muslims had been living in BHARAT three hundreds of years before that under Hindu kings peacefully. Islam existed in different states of BHARAT from the seventh century onwards and Sanatani Muslims were living comfortably and co-existing in BHARAT. Hindu kings used to give Muslims their full rights and respects.Muslims used to perform their duties. Sanatani people gave a lot of respect. When the Caliphate shifted from Arabia to the Turks and from there to Central Asia, the expansion of the kingdom started forcibly. The kings of Central Asia expanded their kingdom by using religion as a weapon and Islam continued to spread, new kings were born in new territories and they started expansion using religion.

When Babar came to BHARAT, then the king of BHARAT was Ibrahim Lodi and he was a Muslim king.

Reference

1. Ahmed Prof. Dr. Nazir: Conquest of Sindh.

2. The advent of Islam in BHARAT with special reference to the contribution of the Turk Abdullah al-Ma'mun.

3. a. Sridhar Menon: A 3 b r m pai atrali plafferty, Ottayam (1967), p. 9.

4. a. Sridhar Menon: The Kerala District Gazetteer: Volume 4 Superintendent of Kerala (BHARAT), Govt. press pages 179-183

5. A. Sridhar Menon: The Cultural Heritage of Kerala - - Google Books. 9788126419036. 2012-11-16.

6. Asani, Ali (2006), "Muhammad ibn al-Qasim", in Mary, Joseph W. (eds.), Medieval Islamic Civilization: L-Z, Taylor and Francis, pp. 524-525,

7. Crawford, Peter (2013). The War of the Three Gods: Roman, Persian, and the Rise of Islam. Barnsley, Great Britain: Par Na and Sword Books. P. 216. ISBN 978-1-84884-612-8.

8. "India oldest mosque and the growing irrelevance of the Muslim vote in Gujarat | Ahmedabad News". The Times of India. 8 December 2017. Retrieved 28 July 2019.

9. K.S. Lai. Early Muslims in India, New Delhi, 1984, p-13.

10. Masudul Hasan, History of Islam, Volume-I, Delhi, 1995, page-169.

11. Mehrdad Shokuhi, Muslim Architecture of South India p 139-142

12. Malkani K R: The Sindh Story, Chapter Truth about Dahir Sen

13. Mahajan Vidyadhar, Muslim Rule in BHARAT, New Delhi, 1970.p.l7.

14. Logan, William. 1951. The Malabar Manual. Vol. I Government Press. Madras. Page no. 192-194

15. "Oldest BHARATIYE Mosque: Trail Leads to Gujarat". The Times of India. 5 November 2016. Retrieved 28 July 2019.

16. Sharma, Indu (22 March 2018). "Top 11 famous Muslim religious places in Gujarat". Gujarat Travel Blog. Retrieved 28 July 2019.

17. Stillman 1979, pp. 17–18.

18. Vink, André (1996) [first published 1990], Al-Hind: The Making of the Indo-Islamic World, Volume 1: Early Medieval INDIA and the Expansion of Islam (3rd ed.), Brill, ISBN 0391041738

19. Contribution of the conquest of Sindh. Performed by Dr. Nazir Ahmed.

20. https://www.siasat.com/perumal-is-first-king-to-accept-islam-at-the-hands-of-Prophet-muhammad

Chapter 13
Quran

The Quran is a heavenly book of GOD. The Quran contains message sent by Allah. Allah has sent the Quran through Prophet Muhammad pbuh, which is in the form of a holy book. Quran can never be changed, because the message of Allah is preserved in the glorious holy book.

It is he who created you out of a single being and appointed for each of you a time-limit and a resting place. He explains his signs for those who understand. (Quran 6:98)

The Quran is the central religious text of Islam. It is widely considered to be the finest work in classical Arabic literature. It is organized into 114 chapters (surah's), consisting of 6236 verses (ayats).1

Allah Himself says in Surah al-Hijr 15 verse 9 – I have sent down this Quran and I am its custodians.

Here's another thing to remember, that when the Quran was revealed, the scribes Prophet's Companions wrote down the exact revelation and memorized the exact words accordingly. The original script in which the Quran was written is called **the Kufi script** (similar to Arabic), and this script did not have zabar/zer etc. Many years after the Quran was compiled in book form, the words zabar, zer, etc., were added to make it easier for people who do not have Arabic as their first language. 2

Muhammad pbuh received his first revelation in the cave of Hira near the Kaaba during his isolation. After this Allah sent down the complete Quran gradually over a period of 23 years. 3

After the death of Prophet Muhammad pbuh in 632 CE, many of his companions who had memorized the Quran were killed in the Battle of Yamama. So the first caliph, Abu Bakr decided to collect the book into one volume so that it could be preserved. Zayd ibn Thabit was the person who collected and compiled the Quran into a single book. Muslims believe that the Quran is the final revelation of Allah to humanity, a work of divine guidance revealed to Prophet Muhammad pbuh through the angel Gabriel. 4

All good things are mentioned in the holy book and it speaks about all religions and all human beings. No one can deny this. Quran shows the complete right way to lead a good life and be loyal to family, society, community and mother land i.e. country. The revelation of the Quran began in 610 CE when the angel Gabriel (an angel sent by God) appeared to Prophet Muhammad pbuh in the Hira Cave near Mecca to convey the divine message. When the angel Gabriel went to Prophet Muhammad pbuh and asked him to read, Muhammad (peace and blessings of Allah be upon him) replied that he did not know how to read or write. Actually Prophet Mohammad (Sallallahu Alaihi Wasallam) did not take any formal education. He was an orphan and poor. Then Gabriel said to him, 'Read! Read in the name of Allah who created humans! Read! The one who nurtures you is the most beautiful, the best of all. Thereafter the Prophet Muhammad (pbuh) continued to make revelations until shortly before his death in 632 AD.

Gabriel brought the word of God verbatim through Muhammad pbuh. The Quran has remained unchanged since then. The Quran emphasizes that Muhammad was only there to receive the sacred text and had no right to change it. After Muhammad received the revelation, he narrated it to his companions, who also memorized it and wrote it down. Before the Quran became commonly available in written form, reciting it from memory was prevalent as a mode of teaching it to others. The practice of memorizing the entire Quran is still prevalent among Muslims. They are called Hafiz. Millions of people have memorized the entire Quran in Arabic without any changes. Translators have also translated into languages other than Arabic. The original Quran has survived to this day.

But the question here is that memorizing the Quran, understanding and practicing the Quran are completely different. Memorizing the Quran is like memorizing anything, which does not give the benefit of understanding and practicing. If Quran is properly understood and followed then it is 100% sure that all the evils and corruption prevailing in the Muslim society will come to an end. It is easy to call yourself a Muslim, but it is the duty of a Muslim to bring the true spirit of the Quran into his heart and into his conduct.

Now a day's people in BHARAT read the Holy Quran just for the name sake. Very few people understand the Quran properly and even very few out of them follow it. But even those who understand the Quran rarely apply the message of the Quran in their lives. Everyone quotes Hadith which is a man-made book. There is uniformity in Quran that's why Quran is read in Arabic only in every part of this world, but Hadith is read in different languages.

Islam is a natural and scientific way of life, in which special attention has also been given to social aspects. Islam has protected the rights of relatives, neighbours and women, the same on human equality, moral life, non-violence, drug abuse, environmental protection and cleanliness. In his last sermon, Prophet Muhammad gave a clear explanation of human rights and equality, he also exhorted to treat parents better, relatives, poor, orphans, relatives and neighbours with whom there is no relation. Quran made strong remarks against female slaughter. Even the fruit tree has been warned not to be harmed during the war. It is worth noting here that Prophet Mohammad did not take the name of Muslims, in his last speech he spoke about the human race i.e. about all humans.

The importance of education is repeatedly emphasized in the Quran with injunctions such as "God bless those of you who have believe in GOD. Quran (20:114) so high is Allah the sovereign, the truth, And O Mohammad do not hasten with (recitation of) the Quran before its revelation is completed to you and say "My Lord, increase me in Knowledge". It is only by His will that man can do anything. Do not say that I will do it tomorrow, rather say that as Allah wills.

Renowned Islamic scholar Maulana Waheeduddin Khan writes in his Hindi translation of the Holy Quran that each book has a theme and the theme of the Quran is the Divine Creation Plan. Who is God? Why did he create this world? Why was man created? And what kind of behaviour a man should conduct in his life time so that God's plan is fulfilled. This is the purpose of the Quran, this is the subject matter of the Quran's talk.

Sri Ramakrishna Paramhansa Dev, the Guru of Swami Vivekananda, the great father of spiritual renaissance in modern BHARAT sings – "Aami Yantra – Tumi Yantra" O God or Allah, let us become the instrument in your hands. It is not my will, but your plan will be fulfilled and how will it happen. To guide him is the basic purpose of Quran Sharif along with all religious books.

It is the fault of all Muslims that they think that it is the job of Maulanas only to decide about Islam. Everyone should understand the Holy Quran and try to live according to the message of Prophet Muhammad (pbuh). Why blame only the Maulanas? All Muslims are guilty because Allah has given everyone the right to education, so why don't everyone study Quran properly and understand its true meaning and follow it. The first word of Quran that came in this world is "iqra" means read. So why Muslims are of different opinions towards educations?

Chapter 14

Hadith

Hadith is a type of book believed to be a descriptive record of the sayings and practices of the Prophet Muhammad pbuh and his companions. Some Muslims consider it a record of the Prophet Muhammad pbuh words, actions and "tacit acceptance" of Islam. Here this word tacit acceptance is a word with a double meaning, which nowadays Muslims are misusing.

Hardliner Muslims believe that only Muslims will go to heaven and everyone else will go to hell. In fact, we all know and believe that only those people will go to heaven, who are righteous. This means that every Muslim should be pure in all ways and should stay away from all evil and corruption. But a question arises? Because it is often found that some Muslims in BHARAT are involved in all types of bad deeds and some non-Muslims are in good deeds. Then who will go to heaven and who will go to hell?

The reason for this confusion is that people have made Hadith the backbone of Islamic civilization. Prophet Muhammad (Sallallahu Alaihi Wasallam) pbuh never used the word Hadith. But today people consider it to be the second most powerful book after Quran. The number of verses related to law in the Quran is relatively small. The Hadith gives instructions on everything in the description of religious obligations, but the Hadith did not existed during the lifetime of the

Prophet Muhammad (pbuh). The Hadith was actually written in the 9th century.

In its classic form, Hadith consists of two parts – the chain of statements that have transmitted the report (isnad) and the main text of the report (matan). Individual Hadith are classified by Muslim clerics and jurists into categories such as Sahih ("authentic"), Hasan ("good") and Daif ("weak"). Different groups and different scholars classify Hadith differently. This has become the cause of disagreement in many places. Due to which sectarianism has started and Muslims have been divided, which resulted in hating other sects.

Islam is a holistic religion integrating all aspects of life. But the true spirit of Islam has been lost by Muslims only. So today there is a need for a reformation. Which will reflect the social, economic and political realities of society. To act responsibly and properly, in which human develops. 2, 3

Hadith were not written by the followers of Prophet Muhammad (pbuh) during the Prophet's life or immediately after his death. The Hadith was written about 200 years after the death of Prophet Muhammad pbuh so there were several generations gap. Just as happened in the case of the New Testament, Bible.

Hadith is in four major classes Sahih, Hasan, Daif and Maudo. There are six canonical books of Hadith.

- Sahih al-Bukhari. • Sahih Muslim. • Sunan Abu Dawood. • Sunan al-Tirmidhi. • Sunan al-Nasai.

- Sunan ibn Majah.

Apart from the above 6 main Hadiths, there are many other books which are also in vogue. These books may have been written mainly to teach and guide the students according to the time and according to the need of that time. Secondary Hadith books are books that have been selected and compiled from primary Hadith books. They are not original collections. 5

Muhammad ibn Ismail al-Bukhari (810–70) was born in Bukhara, present-day Uzbekistan and died in Khartank near Samarkand. He is considered by Sunni Muslims to be the most authoritative collector of Hadith. Completed in 846 AD. This work is Al-Bukhari's most famous collection of reports of the sayings or actions of the Prophet Muhammad. It is the most authoritative which was written 200 years after Prophet Muhammad (pbuh). 6

Ismail al-Bukhari went to Mecca at the age of about 18 and stayed there for 16 years to collect Hadith. He visited Egypt and Syria twice, visited Basra four times and spent several years in Hijaz, then went to Kufa and Baghdad several times. He also travelled to other Islamic countries to collect Hadith. He collected about 600000 Hadiths from more than 1000 scholars, of which he accepted only 7275 as authentic and arranged them in 93 chapters. 7, 8

Although Imam Bukhari wrote many books, he gained prominence because of Tarikh al-Kabir, Adab al-Mufrad and Sahih al-Bukhari. Imam Bukhari had a very sharp memory.

In 250 Hijri he settled in Neshapur where he met Muslim ibn al-Hujjaj as his disciple, who compiled Sahih al-Muslim, considered second only to Bukhari in the Muslim world. The time of Imam Muslim ibn al-Hajjaj (817–875 CE]) initiated the discussion of the norms of Hadith.

There are four other classical collections in the tradition all within the 3rd century Hijri and partially interdependent. Abu Dad al-Sijistani ([817–889 CE]) produced his Kitab al-Sunan ("Book of Traditions"), which contains 4800 traditions related to matters of jurisprudence. Abu Isa Muhammad al-Tirmidhi (died AH 279) [892 CE]) edited Sunan al-Tirmidhi, which included notes on the specific interpretations of the schools of law. Abu Abd al-Rahman al-Nasa ([830–915 CE]) produced another book Sunn al-Nasai with a special concern for religious law concerning religious rites. Abu Abd Allah ibn Majah [824–886 CE], a disciple of Abu Daud compiled another with the same title. 9

Also Shia Hadith are collections of their religious leaders which differ from Sunni.

The traditions of the life of Prophet Muhammad (pbuh) and the early history of Islam were passed down mostly orally after the death of Prophet Muhammad pbuh in 632 AD. It was Abu Abdullah Muhammad ibn Idris al-Shafi'i (150–204 Hijri), known as al-Shafi'i, who insisted on the final authority of Muhammad's Hadith, in order to interpret the Quran "in the light of "traditions (i.e. Hadith), and not vice versa." While the Quran is traditionally considered above the Sunna in authority. 10, 11

The rationalistic Mutazila School declined in 851 CE during the Abbasid Caliphate.

Sunni and Shia Hadith collections differ because the credibility of the scholarly narrators and translators of the two traditions differed. Narrators who favour Abu Bakr and Umar instead of Ali in leadership disputes after the death of Prophet Muhammad pbuh are seen by Shias as unreliable; and the sayings written for Ali and Muhammad's family and their supporters are given priority. Sunni scholars rely on narrators such as Ayesha, whom the Shia reject.

In contrast, Quranists believe that if the Quran is silent on a matter, it is because Allah has not laid down its detail. 12

So it is clear that Quran and Hadith are completely different. The Quran is the book from Allah, compiled and documented by the Prophet Muhammad (pbuh) through his companions. Whereas Hadith is a book written about 200 years after the death of Prophet Muhammad pbuh. Hadith were written down by various religious leaders, transmitted orally from generation to generation. During the approximately 200 years of oral transmission of the Prophet Muhammad life, some of his teachings may be tweaked and some gaps may have been left between the original practices and sayings and the oral words transmissions through generations.

Here I am quoting a sentence that if someone write a book on poor people and poverty by traveling in AC first class train coach looking at rural areas and poor people through glass window. Then the book will not have the original feeling and essence of poverty because the author has not experienced poverty and hardship. The same happened with Hadith, the real life story of the Prophet and his actions and words were documented after 200 years of his life. So one can easily understand that many things must have been left out and many false things must have been included. That's why there are many different and difference in Hadith. But the Quran is only one. Nowadays Muslims rarely quote quotes from the Quran but often quotes from Hadith.

Now a day's people are getting misguided by few Hadiths because there are 6 different Hadiths and apart from 6 Hadiths many other books have been written with quotes from Hadiths. There are many different discussions and practices in all the six Hadiths, which seems to contradict the life of the Prophet Muhammad and Islam.

One thing to be noted here is that Ismail al-Bukhari (810-70), who started writing about Hadith himself considered only 7275 Hadiths to be authentic and he rejected the rest. The writer himself said that more non-authentic things have been found.

One thing should be noted here that Islam is the religion which gives the most importance to science. But because of some special people, we have gone away from it. Islam has always been open to critical scrutiny of reason. We are ordered to follow Sunnah and the important question is that we have to understand what the reason behind implementing it.

As time passed different Hadith were written and translated into many different languages. The question arises that why didn't Prophet Mohammad pbuh or his companions, who were called Rasidi Khalifas, get the Hadith written during their lifetime? Why his immediate successor Caliph did not wrote the Hadith? The gap of about 200 years between the death of Prophet Muhammad pbuh and the writing of the Hadith is a big question?

During few decades following the death of Prophet Muhammad pbuh people who knew him directly shared and collected quotes and stories related to the Prophet life. Within the first two centuries after the Prophet's death, scholars reviewed the stories, the origin of each quote, as well as the chain of narrators who attributed them. Traced, through whom the citation was passed. Those that were not verifiable were deemed "weak" or "fabricated", while others were deemed "authentic" (saheeh).

In the period of translations and interpretations of Hadith by the then leaders, Maulanas or translators, along with many interpretations and incorporation of many unwanted practices which have nothing to do with the life of Prophet Muhammad pbuh and Quran.

Many types of evils and corruption have entered due to false and fabricated translation. Different sects have emerged within Islam itself. Different types of wrong practices have entered the religion. Due to one wrong interpretation slowly many wrong interpretations have entered and gradually the wrong interpretation has gone to such an extent that few Muslims have gone astray. The result is that whole Muslim community is getting bad names.

Another big question is that we know that Ismail Al Bukhari had collected about 600000 Lakh Hadith but he authenticated only 7275

Hadith and said that only 7275 is correct. Why and on what basis did he do this? This is absolutely correct because he realised that more than 5 Lakhs Hadith is either fabricated or false.

We can see that because of the Hadith Muslims have divided themselves into many different sects. All sects hate each other. They call each other Kafir among themselves. People use different texts of Hadith for their own benefit and desire and if they feel necessary then some people also change the meaning of the Hadith.

As we have seen in the case of the Bible, the kings changed the Bible many times and thus the people and the kings through fabricated translations used religion to fulfil their desires and expand their territories etc.

Now the time has come for all Muslims to open their eyes, mind and heart and start thinking properly. Reform society and follow Quran properly and follow the right path shown by our great Prophet Mohammad (pbuh). Bring peace and harmony in the society and make our motherland the best country in this world. Muslims shall educate their children like Khan Abdul Ghaffar Khan, A P J Abdul Kalam Sahab, freedom fighters like Ashfaq Ullah Khan, Paramveer Chakr Abdul Hamid who sacrificed his life for the country. Just by name and dress one shall not become a Muslim but by character one shall be a Muslim.

Reference

1. https://en.wikipedia.org/wiki/Hadith

2. https://ibnusina.utm.my/Hadith/

3. Dr. Mohd. Al'Ikhsan Ghazali, for Scientific and Industrial Research, Universiti Teknugai, Malaysia.

4. https://books.google.co.in/books (Aboul Ella Hasanian - Mohd. F.Tolba -Khalid Shalan - Ahmed Taher Azar, Proceedings of the International Conference on Advanced Intelligent Systems of Informatics 2018. P253)

5. https://en.wikipedia.org/wiki/List_of_Hadith_collections

6. https://www.wdl.org/en/item/11227/

7. (Aboul Ela Hassanian - Mohammad F. Tolba -Khalid Shalan- Ahmed Taher Azar, Proceedings of the International Conference on Advanced Intelligent Systems of Informatics 2018. P253)

8. https://www.britannica.com/topic/Hadith/The-compilations

9. https://www.britannica.com/topic/Hadith/The-compilations

10. https://en.wikipedia.org/wiki/Hadith

11. Brown, Rethinking Tradition in Modern Islamic Thought, 1996: p.7

12. https://www.coursehero.com/file/52067560/importance-of-Hadithdocx/

Chapter 15
Inside Muslims

In BHARAT, non-Muslim people used to treat Islam and Muslim people with a lot of respect in earlier times because the Muslims of that time were a true Muslim by following the true spirit of Islam. But from the last centuries or few decades Muslims are not getting that respect because the true spirit of the Islam has been tampered by Muslims only.

The fore most important thing for Muslims is to have faith and to belief that whatever is happening in this world is happening according to the will of Allah. Not even a leaf moves without the will of Allah. This means that whatever is happening today is happening only and only by the will of Allah. This is the truth. The truth can be suppressed but it cannot be erased. Muslims are lagging behind, Muslims are being humiliated everywhere, Muslims themselves are responsible for that. Muslims have deviated from the path shown by Prophet Muhammad pbuh so Allah has withdrawn his blessing because of the deeds of Muslims.

Prophet Muhammad pbuh had once said if require then one should even go to China to get good education. That time the word China was used because China is very far from Arabia and the journey at that time was very difficult. The meaning of this was that the right education should be taken even after tolerating the adverse situation and difficulty. **Prophet Muhammad pbuh said that the light of the pen of the wise is more superior to the blood of the martyrs.** The right education makes a person a good human. And only good person can be religious. The house in which a human is born, he/she starts following the religion of his/her parents. If the first President of BHARAT Shri Rajendra Prasad was born in a Muslim house his name would have been different, and if Avul Pakir Jainulabdeen Abdul Kalam had been born in a Hindu family, his name would have been different.

Everyone knows that mosques, temples, churches or any religious place are meant for all people, irrespective of religion, caste or creed. People have seen some people display in writing at the entrance of the mosque that only Muslims of a particular sect are allowed inside the mosque. What all is this? Who are the people who can stop any people from prayers? That too in the house of Allah. What would you call such people?

Muslim talks about universal brotherhood. If Muslims are not able to make proper coordination and peace in their own home or in small society then what to talk about the whole world! Muslims have divided the religion of Islam into different parts and sects according to their wish and likes. Within the religion of Islam many times one sect calls other sects infidels. These are the people who are misleading the public. Many times the some Imams of mosque say that they should not offer Namaz behind other sect's imams. Muslims have divided Islam into many sects and sub sects, all say that others are bad and only they are right. Because of all this, the hatred has entered in Muslims and this hatred is increasing exponentially. This is the main reason for which Muslims have remained Muslims only for name shake. Muslims feel happy and proud to say that "Prophet Muhammad (pbuh) himself has said that Muslims will be divided into 73 sects and only one sect will go to Jannah". Every sect's claims that only their sects will go to Jannah and all other sects of Muslims will go to Jahannum. This attitude has ruined the whole Muslims society.

Imam al-Barbahri (died in 329 Hijri) said: "Know that the Messenger of Allah (peace and blessings of Allah be upon him) said: "My Ummah will be divided into 73 sects, and they will all be in the Fire except one" and that is Jamaat. **Jamaat refers to anyone who is on the truth, even if it is just one person.** "The gathering of a large number of people does not in itself indicate that they are on the truth." And most people will not believe – no matter how keen you are (Sur: Yusuf 12: 103))"l" We did not find most of them true to their covenant; indeed we found most of them transgressors. (" Surah Al-A'raaf 7: 102). Therefore numbers are not taken into account, but those who are on the truth, even if they are few in number in a given time or place. So even if only if there is one person, then he can be considered as Jamaat. It was said, "And who are they"? Allah's Apostle replied, "The ones that I and my companions are on today." So this is the right path: whoever is on that on which the Messenger and his companions were, then he is the right.

Everyone specially Muslims are fighting in the name of caste, creed, gender etc. They have pushed themselves into darkness and then talk of light. They indulge in all evils and illegal acts and claim that they are only the right ones. Now a days Muslims do not have fear of Allah, but they have fear of people. They hide all their evils and corruption from the people and think that if people have not seen the evils then they are very good people in the society. The meaning is clear who cares about the invisible God? People think that if their sins are not revealed to the people then they are good and superior. That's why everyone commit sins hiding from people. I ask one question if you are bad yourself, How can you speak ill of other people? With all the evil and corruption how can Muslims say they are good? Why won't Allah punish? At present Allah is angry with the deeds of Muslims. I am sorry to say that many Muslims these days are not following the teachings of Prophet Mohammad pbuh and are not following the Islam. Just for name shake they are Muslim. They have neither become true Muslims nor true citizens of country. Due to the bad deeds of some Muslims, the name of all Muslims is tarnished.

Here I want to make it clear that I am not against any religion or any people. I am a true human and a true human can only be a true Muslim. Allah took me on different paths, showed me the world, made me face, feel and experience different situations and introduced me to all aspects of life, so that I can honestly put all the facts in front of everyone with my knowledge and experience by giving live examples of evils. As we look at the mirror and put on makeup and beautify ourselves, same way I wish that we all assess ourselves by looking inside our self and change ourselves and become a true Muslim. Some Muslims have become destroyers of religion Islam, their actions have gone against Islam. Muslim faith means complete submission before God that is to destroy your external and internal ego and purify yourself and then live in the society as an instrument in the hand of God.

Today few Muslims do all such activities which are against the teachings of Islam. Many Muslims hurt their own brothers and sisters, even mother and father. They grab the rights of others. They just try to earn money regardless of halal or haram. As Muslims hate other sects and other religion and thus gradually hatred has entered in the nature of Muslims. Many times Muslims take pride in defying Sharia law or BHARATIYE law. Few Muslims have also changed the definition of Jihad. Knowingly or unknowingly commit all acts of terrorism. Some people have become such bad citizens that when Pakistan wins a cricket match, they burst crackers and because of these few people, the whole society gets bad name.

Some maulanas also give wrong fatwas, which is against Islam. If the amount of interest (usury) is haram in Sharia law, then how can the same amount of interest (usury) become halal in BHARAT? How did some Maulana give such a fatwa that Muslims can take interest amount in BHARAT? If this is true then why don't we follow BHARATIYE law in all aspect? Now-a-days if the interests and benefits of Muslims are not fulfilled according to Islamic law, then people go with Indian law. Whereas if the interests and benefits of the Muslims are not served by the Indian law then we go with Sharia law. Why use and misuse Sharia law only for benefits and profit? Where are we going?

Being a true Muslim and a true human being and a true BHARATIYE we shall say that either Muslims should follow Sharia law only or follow BHARATIYE law only. Some people mislead the Muslims of BHARAT. Some fatwas also tends to justify evils and corruptions. The moral value of Muslims are decreasing? Everyone has to find the solutions?

Many times we see that when there is a fight between Palestine and Israel, some BHARATIYE Muslims want to go and fight against the people of Israel. Some Muslims want to show universal brotherhood. Here I say that first look at your home and fight the evils within yourself and within your family and society. Most of the Muslim families in BHARAT indulge in hatred among brothers, sisters, father and mother, in-laws and relatives. Now-a-days Muslims have good relations with outsiders but Muslims do not have good relations with their own relatives and inside family. One member of the family keeps trying to usurp the rights of other members of the family. Some even go to the extent of killing own brother or sister to grab the property. Is this the character of a true Muslim??? Everyone will do bad things and wear white clothes to show that they are very good. If you don't have brotherhood ambience within a small family then how are you thinking of brotherhood for another country where you can't even reach. The only option with us is to pray for the peace. Our prayers can be listen by Allah only if we are a true Muslim.

To give a live quote, during the 2021 war between Israel and Palestine, in a what's app group, which has many learned people, a so-called Muslim social activist started speaking against Israel. Further he wrote that he wanted to go to Palestine and fight against Israel. I wrote in the WhatsApp group that just as you think that the people of Palestine are your brothers, then similarly the people of Israel are also your brothers because both communities are the generations of Prophet Abraham. At that time that person in that group abused me badly. Then I posted why are we talking about Palestine or Israeli? First think about our own people in BHARAT. If you want to fight then fight against the evils in our society. I wrote in that group that Jews and Muslims are fighting in the Middle East and if we talk about the religion of the Jews, they follow Prophet Moses, David and Solomon. Muslims consider all of them as Prophets sent by Allah. If Arab Muslims are our brothers, then we can accept that Jews are also our brothers, even if they have different opinions and religious path. That person said Jews are the Descendants of Pharaoh. That person has no knowledge of history and Islam and he was pretending to be a true Muslim. This is the irony. Going deep, history proves that all Abrahamic religions have originated from Judaism. Actually Jews are not descendants of Pharaoh but Jews are descendants of Prophet Yusuf and his 9 other brothers. Jews are the descendants of Abraham, Moses, David, Solomon and many other Prophets whom we respect. They belong to the same clan from where Prophet Muhammad pbuh came. Yes they may have some big issues, which needs to be solved. But who are we to go and fight in their internal affairs? Yes we can show our empathy and pray for peace. Why to talk about war and fight? Prophet Mohammad pbuh himself has given example of love of Jew. When a Jewish woman used to throw garbage upon the Prophet Mohammad pbuh, but when the same woman fell ill, the Prophet served that Jew woman by giving medicine and water.

Yes a good Muslim has to stand against all the evils and corruptions. Out of Israel and Palestine who is right and who is wrong is not the question? The question shall be how to resolve the problems? What are the solutions for peaceful living? At present what is in our hand is not to become aggressive as we Bhartiye cannot go out of Bharat without valid visa, but one most important weapon is in our hands that is prayers to Allah. We can pray not only for the peace in Middle East but we have to pray for the peace in all over the world. Further deep if we go then we find that all humans are the generations of ADAM and EVE. False brotherhood in the name of religion is just for name shake no one is going to help without any benefits. So along with sympathy one shall start praying to almighty "Allah" for peaceful solutions. The strength of co-existence of different faith people.

Hatred is propagated by few Muslims towards other religions and they are mainly responsible for hatred among own people as well. This is completely against the teachings of Prophet Muhammad (pbuh). If we start eradicating evils from home and locality, then automatically the whole society and the country will become evil free.

Today, Jews have the highest percentage of education in the world and Muslims have the least. One shall study for knowledge and not for degrees. You can take information from books, but knowledge will be achieved only and only when you acquire information and understand it. Degree is earned by hard work, but it is not that a person with a degree can do everything. A knowledgeable person can do a lot more even without a degree.

Before the revelation of the Quran, the Prophet Muhammad pbuh had seen in his life how the Arab tribes in the area were in fear due to evils, corruptions and looting at every step, despite the people living on the same land. They were engaged in all evils. The law of Islam, which literally means peace was implemented in the place of the law of the forest. What work Prophet Muhammad pbuh did in his place of birth in Arabia, we shall try to implement the same in our country by following the foot step of the Prophet.

In the prehistory and medieval time the role of a country was not so much important but after the start of Modern period the concept of Country and mother land has taken a major place in the mankind. This is the major development in this era. Prophet Mohammad pbuh knew all these things and that's why our beloved Prophet has told "HUBBUL WATAN MINAL IMMAN." To love ones motherland is a major part of ISLAM. So a Muslim cannot become a Muslim if he does not love his own country.

Reference

1. It-Haf al-Qari, Shaykh al-Fawzan's Interpretation of the Sharhus-Sunnah of Imam al-Barbahri, Vol. 1 pp. 419-423.

2. Tirmidhi, no. 2641; Ibn Nasr al-Marwazi in As-Sunnat, no. 59; In al-Hakim al-Mustadrak,

3. https://www.abukhadeejah.com/this-ummah-will-divide-into-73-sects-shaykh-al-fawzan-explains-what-it-means/

Chapter 16

Islam and Muslim. How, What and Why?

Prophet Muhammad (pbuh) united Arabia as a country, earlier there was no country or state in Arabia and the people were divided into tribes. Prophet Muhammad pbuh brought the concept of nation and administration. Means Prophet Mohammad pbuh had given the concept of country, which clearly means identification in terms of land marks that is as a country.

Prophet Mohammad pbuh has given a lot of encouragement for education and knowledge. This was the reason that in the early century of Islam Muslims made great progress in every field. The first word of the holy Quran that Allah sent to Prophet Muhammad (PBUH) through an angel was **"Iqra"** which means "Read", meaning clearly that education and knowledge are very important. The Quran urges mankind to think, ponder, reflect and acquire knowledge, which leads humans to Allah and bring closer to the creator. The word Allah is repeated 2,800 times in the Quran, Rab 950 times and Ilm (Knowledge) comes third with 750 mentions. Hazrat Ali the fourth Rashidi Khalifa once said "I would like to be the slave of the one who teaches me to write a letter". The importance of knowledge is emphasized here. A teacher is given high respect. Initially following these orders, Muslim rulers insisted that every Muslim receive education. They also gave great support to education in general. 1

Muslims are encouraged to seek knowledge from any part or any corner of this world. The Hadith is also full of references about the value of knowledge. Some sayings of the Prophet are as follows -

"Acquiring knowledge is obligatory for every Muslim (man or woman)".

"Seek knowledge, even if you have to go to as far as China"

"The ink of a scholar (a learned person) is purer than the blood of a martyr."

"If someone travels on a road in search of knowledge, Allah will make him travel on one of the roads of Paradise. The angels will lower their wings in great joy to accompany the seeker of knowledge."

At present time the education system and social environment of Muslims is not present in its original form as Prophet Mohammad pbuh had created and shown the right path. Many Muslims have distorted their mentality by limited education system, as a result of which Muslims in every field are lagging behind. Some Muslims are neither taking proper education, nor giving proper education to their generations. Children are considered to be the future of a family, community, society, state and the country. If we give limited education to them, then we are limiting the development of our generations. Everyone wants their child to become a good human. So if Muslims want to improve and do good and live good life then Muslims have to bring right education system in the society i.e. contemporary (modern) education along with the Islamic education. The education system should be adopted in such a way that a Muslim has a Quran in one hand and a computer in the other hand. We have to study the Quran properly and understand it not only from the point of view of religion, but from the point of view of humanity. Traditional education to the children is very important but along with the contemporary education as per the instructions of Prophet Mohammad pbuh for becoming a good Muslim. One fact of everyone's life is that our great grandfather used to live in a mud house, our father built a brick house there and we live in that house. Has he insulted our forefathers by getting the floor and tiles installed? Has he Erased ancestors sign? We are making progress by adopting new technology and high living standards as per time and requirements. We have to adopt the developments coming in every field, like from landline phone we have come to pager and small mobile and now came the android mobile. The world has become very small and everything is in our hand. We have to decide what we want to become an asset or a liability.

Due to various reasons, many unwanted things have entered in few madrasas. The unwanted thing that has entered has made the Muslims stand on margins. Have we seen any IAS officer taking education from Madrasa? There are only one or two who took basic education from madrasa but later they went to contemporary universities and got contemporary education then they became officer.

The fact is that the Golden Age of Islam was from the 7th century to the 12th century. The Abbasid Caliphate made Baghdad its capital in 762 AD. Caliph Al-Mansur laid great emphasis on education and made Baghdad the centre of knowledge. Once upon a time it was called the "house of wisdom" (Power house of knowledge). There were many different types of scientists, thinkers, mathematicians, chemists etc. in Islam those days. The early Abbasid caliphs had encouraged all kinds of knowledge. Knowledgeable men were given a lot of respects. At that time Baghdad had the largest university in the world. People from all over the world used to go to Baghdad to gain knowledge. But the caliphs after the Abbasid Caliphate became engrossed in luxury and became weak. Then in the mid of 13th century something happened that led to the end of the Golden Age of Islam. Genghis Khan, the Mongol king started brutally invading the whole world. After his death his next Mongol king Hulaku Khan launched a massive attack on the city of Baghdad, the capital of the Abbasid Caliphate in 1258. It was razed to the ground. The Mongols brutally destroyed the entire city in two weeks. Completely destroyed the irrigation system. All the buildings, the mosques, the hospitals, the schools, the libraries and the buildings were badly looted and ruined. Baghdad University books of the city's libraries were thrown into the Tigris River. There were so many books that the entire Tigris River became black with the ink from books and a bridge of books was formed above the Tigris River for the Halaku army's to cross the river. The world never knew it again that how many lakhs and lakhs of books and valuable knowledge were lost from that university. Along with the university more than one million people were brutally killed by the Mongols whose leader was Halaku Khan. The whole city of Baghdad was completely destroyed. Halaku Khan Soldiers fled the city because of the stench of rotting flesh of dead humans and animals. The whole city was deserted. The university and the scholars were brought to complete end. All the knowledge vanished in the river Tigris. The news of the complete destruction of Baghdad by the Mongols shook the entire Islamic world. The source of education and knowledge within Islam came to end. Due to the invasions of Mongols, the progress of Muslim stopped. As the house of wisdom was destroyed Muslims went far away from knowledge, then no one tried to bring that knowledge back.

Here I tell you one very important point to be noted, a proverb is **"history repeats itself"** and Allah gives the rewards and punishments as per the deeds of human in this world itself. But here I say **"ALLAH DOES NOT GIVE PUNISHMENT, IT IS THE PERSON DEEDS WHICH PUNISHES A PERSON"**. The pride and jealousy with which Bakhtiyar Khilji burnt BHARAT Nalanda University in the year 1193 and mercilessly killed countless people, destroyed the Nalanda

University completely. The pride and cruel deeds of Bakhtiyar Khilji took the revenge by destroying the University of Muslims in Baghdad In 1258. That is why it is said that one gets the fruits of one's deed in this world only. Allah rewarded the atrocities done by the invaders in this world only. Babur was also a Mongol. One of the special hobbies of the Mongols reign was to chop off the heads of the inhabitants of the conquered cities and build a minaret (kaalla-minar) from the chop off heads. Regrettably, some BHARATIYE Muslims consider it a matter of pride to call descendants of the Mughals. Actually the Mughals are the descendants of Ghengij Khan and Halaku Khan who destroyed the knowledge, education and progress in Islam. Latter their descendants adopted the religion of ISLAM and used it to expand their territory. Negligible Muslims in India are the descendant of Mughals. Also one of the most notable thing is that the Ghengij Khan and Halaku Khan was not a Muslim. They followed the tribal religion of Mangolia. Later on their few descendant became Muslims and few became Buddhists. When they destroyed everything of Islam in Baghdad then what led their successor to adopt Islam religion is a big point of discussion?

Contemporary education keeps changing with time, means new thing gets added, which should have been adopted by Muslims, but Muslims did not adopt it. It is our duty to bring improvement in the education system of Muslims by taking guidance from Quran. For example it is like using old mobile phone nokia 666 which is now outdated and traditional mobile phone has been replaced by ANAROID PHONE. Today, if we use Nokia 666 phone, then we will be called old-fashioned people and we will be left behind the modern society and information's. Android phone is the need of the hour, so that today we can sit in any corner of the world and be benefitted. One can talk, do video calling that too for free, you can get whatever information you want from the internet, adopting it is the need of the hour.

Now a days Muslims are lagging behind in every field. Due to limitation in education system, some Muslims are also becoming tyrants and traitors. There is a need to assess, re-think, and reform and modernization in Madrasa education system and there is a need to remove the loopholes. Muslims are already left far behind in the modern era and if Muslims do not improve now, they cannot stop their generations from falling into the ditch. Coming generations will not forgive us. Just like we all cannot forgive and forget the pains of the partition of united BHARAT.

The world has developed in every field and is continuously developing and growing. The world is changing according to time, time does not waits for any one. Time moves on and on according to its normal speed and Muslims have not walked with the time and so they are not left behind. Recently the world has changed from short hand writing to digital voice recorder. From telegram to land line and from land line to mobile phone, fax and e-mail, how fast the world has progressed. In earlier times, ISD calls had to be made to talk to our people in other countries, its charges was also charged according to the per second count, but today we all talk for free through whatsapp calls and many other options. Now humans are also doing space tourism. How fast are humans developing? And I confirm that the day is not far when we will have a time machine. We will be able to see the past as well as the future. There have been many changes since the beginning of civilization, and we have also seen that those who changed themselves with humanity values according to time flourished.

In the beginning of Islam many scientists of the Middle East invented many things and gave many theories and were progressive. But as the world entered the industrial age, contemporary education could not enter in Madrasa education. Later when people saw that the world had changed, and they were left behind. So people tried a lot but they faced a lot of limitations. So Muslims specially in BHARAT is wondering "who are we?"

In the earlier chapter we have read that people were unable to make changes in the Quran so they brought Hadith, Hadith also came in abundance. We have already read that Ismail Al Bukhari had collected 600000 Hadith, but Only 7275 Hadiths are considered authentic by him. Whatever evil or corruption exists in society these days, it is because of some selfish people who brought changes and misinterpreted old ones.

Few influencers are affected by the donations given by someone, as the Madrasa always passes through a severe monetary crunch. Some people have misinterpreted the Hadith and are also misleading the youth by saying that if a man dies fighting, he will get martyrdom i.e. the status of a martyr. After death they will go to heaven and they will get hoors. Here I ask a question? That if a woman dies while fighting, will she also go to heaven? If this is true, then if a man will get hoors, then what will the woman get.............?

But the main question is with whom to fight? Is it with our own countrymen? With own brother? The Prophet Mohammad pbuh had shown the way to live and let everyone live peacefully but today some are teaching the way to fight and die. It is very pathetic. Due to the poverty of Madrasa students, they start working at an early age. Some who get the higher education of Madrasa reach a place where they feel themselves in a no man island. And they are forced to live just to survive. Some clerics, moulanas and muftis are good and truthful who try to bring reforms and says to improve but no one listens to the good moulanas and muftis.

According to one Hadith, Muslims will be divided into sects. It is said that Muslims will be divided into 73 sects and out of this 72 will go to hell and only 1 will go to heaven that means almost 98% of

Muslims will go to hell. If it is true then Prophet Mohammad pbuh must have realised and knew that his Ummah will go astray and do all wrong things. Muslims will follow Islam just for show off. Very few will remain good and only those who follow humanity will go to heaven. Prophet Muhammad pbuh preaching was for all human beings. It is very simple that the humans who follow humanity will go to heaven. **There is no reservations in heaven**. Some had done partitioned of country in the name of religion and made a separate nation, will such people divide heaven also?

Religion is only for the betterment of mankind. The principle and instruction of Quran is very simple and peaceful so Muslims should focus only on Quran. Everyone shall start cleaning the impurities that have entered inside the Muslims. Not all Muslims are bad. Only a very few people are bad but because of the few, all Muslims are being defamed and are suffering. Muslims like cleanliness and keep themselves clean as per the instructions of Quran. But unfortunately they keep their surroundings very dirty, which can be easily seen in almost all Muslim localities of BHARAT. This is a big question WHY? That means something is missing. There is a need for a big reform here. Unknowingly the mind-set has become completely against the teachings of Prophet Muhammad pbuh. Islam was created for the values of humanity, love, peace, cleanliness, environment and cleanliness. Overall humanity. If Muslims do not accept the values of Islam, then they are not Muslims.

Everything is not bad among Muslims. Muslims are very hardworking by nature. Muslims have an inherent talent of patience and loyalty, an inherent nature of quick learning, an inherent quality of skills. These are the inherent qualities and resources which are to be used by all Muslims. But the uses of the qualities depends upon the Muslims only. Either use these qualities in a progressive and positive ways or negative ways. Now the time has come that Muslims should not allow themselves to become victims of negative forces and shall stop being used as a tool kit. Regarding education also all Muslims have to think and reconsider because proper education is the most important thing for the development of any society and country.

It is in the hands of every parent what they want to make of their children "Capable" or "Incompetent" "Asset" or "Liability". Think, decide and act. Yes............ There are many issues, some problems too. The most important and major issue for the contemporary education system is the financial issue. The economic condition of Muslims are very pathetic, but who is responsible for this? Since independence Muslims are just being used like a tool kit. If everything starts improving then I have a strong believe that the government will help in this and there will be better education system for Muslims also. Every government want its citizens to become the asset of the country. If civic responsibilities become a liability, the country will not develop. The government will again have to distribute free food and all free facilities to the underprivileged. And development of the country will be hindered and inflation will increase. On the other hand, if people are educated properly and made progressive, they will contribute to the development of the society and country. Look at the educated Muslims who go to gulf countries and then earn abroad and spend in BHARAT and contribute to the development of our country. I have worked in different big companies in different parts and places of BHARAT and I have found that top managements and executives of every companies likes educated Muslim works through dedications, because Muslims are loyal, hardworking and sincerely. They gives the good results. The main reason for loyalty is faith. Followers of Islam have faith in Prophet, so they are able to be faithful in their actions if Muslims uses their qualities in a positive way, as given by the great Prophet Mohammad pbuh.

After independence Muslims forefathers loved BHARAT and stayed in BHARAT, so it becomes our duty to respect the decisions and views of our forefathers who remained loyal to motherland BHARAT and Stayed here. Our freedom fighter forefathers opposed partition and loved brothers and sisters of our country, taught us to live and die for our motherland. There is no need to die for religion or sects because religion is just a positive thought process and rituals which purify our soul. Religion and sects has all the practices of humanity only. No one can destroy any Religion because it is not a tangible thing. Religion is true, eternal, it is within humans and is a way of living. One has to follow the religion completely with heart, mind and soul. No one is stopping Muslims from practicing Islam if they are according to the teachings of Prophet Muhammad pbuh i.e. for the sake of humanity. Everything in Islam is for humanity and a way to live peacefully. That is why famous writer George Bernard Shaw quoted "Islam is the best religion, but Muslims are the worst followers".

Muslims are misguided by few destructive people who are also spreading rumours that Hindus are against Muslims. Which is absolutely wrong because no true Sanatanis are against true Muslims. No one is stopping a Muslim from offering Namaz. No true sanatani person is forbidding Muslims from practicing true Islam. Yes it is true that few misguided people have harassed and harmed some Muslim people but that is taken care by law of BHARAT and also their bad deeds will punish them also. Here all Muslims will agree on one thing that whatever happens, it happens by the will of Allah. Not even a leaf moves without the will of Allah. It is because of the activities and it is happening only by the will of Allah because Muslims have gone astray so Allah has withdrawn his mercy from Muslims.

There are many examples of Prophet Muhammad (pbuh) that he respected even the enemy. An old woman used to throw garbage upon Prophet Mohammad pbuh daily. One day when Prophet Mohammad pbuh was passing that house, he did not find any garbage upon him. So Prophet Mohammad pbuh was surprised and he went inside the house to see the old lady, he found the old lady was ill, the Prophet brought all necessary things and served her. The old lady started crying and apologizing. I think all Muslims know this story, but do Muslims follow the actions of Prophet Muhammad pbuh? Enemy is far away, now a days Muslims hate their own parents, brothers and sisters. Many Muslims takes the rights of own brother and sisters. It is happening in almost all the Muslims family but due to many issues they are not coming in front. I am a live example of all these things.

Sometimes some imprudent Hindu people force a Muslim to say Jai Shri Ram after finding him alone. It is wrong to force someone for anything. But I say that Muslims do not become infidels by saying Jai Shri Ram. In schools and many places Muslims children says Jai Shree Ram that doesn't make the children infidel. Just like saying Allah Hu Akbar does not makes a Hindu a Muslim. As a true Muslim, it is the duty of all Muslims to respect all the 124000 Prophets. I am sorry to say that these days due to the activities of few Muslims it seems that Islam is only prevailing for name shake. The Muslims have weakened the spirit of Islam. Nowadays Muslims are doing atrocities. Islam spread during the lifetime of Prophet Muhammad (pbuh) because of the values of humanity.

The right education and awareness I have seen in an organization and many times I have met different people of that organization. Earlier as a normal Muslim I hated that organisation, but when I meet few people of that organisations then I found the members are doing the same work as Sahabaa (Prophet pbuh Companions) did. I was amazed and more than glad to see the simple life, way of working and all the acts of the members of that organization. The people of the organization lead a simple life, eat less food, do all the works of humanity in the society, give rights to everyone and talk with decency.

They don't have any human guru. They believe in supreme power knowingly or unknowingly they are doing all work like sahabas used to do. Many sacrifices have also been made. They suffered but kept patience, then why Allah will not shower blessing upon them? Who are we to defame them? They are doing the work for humanity and for country. May be some other groups are doing some unacceptable act by which majority is being blamed. This is the only point upon which they have to rethink. They are not against ISLAM and they are not against true Muslims. The most important thing for BHARAT to become a supreme power is that true Muslims has to be given responsibilities and misguided Muslims has to be brought back into the right track and all have to start contributing according to the teachings of Prophet Muhammad (pbuh).

Reference

1. Zahid Ashraf Wani and Tabassum Maqbool, University of Kashmir.

Chapter 17

Namaz

"Namaz" appears to be derived from the Persian word (nemhya) as well as the Sanskrit word (namati) (Namaste) (namaskara) (namah + yajna) words. It is coming from the Sanskrit word NAMAH + AAJ, Namah means to bend in front and Aaj means the supreme power. So Namaz means to bend down with respect in front of the lord. In Arabic it is known as Salah. It is a special request to Allah with actions of all the parts of the body just like yoga. It is to request Allah with sincerity. To make supplication or prayer as a religious act; specifically the supreme power is to be addressed with worship, confession, prayer and thanks giving. It is the complete surrender of oneself before the mighty Allah.

The word 'namaz (prayer)' is also coming from two Sanskrit words 'namah' and 'yajna' (nam+ yajna). Three meanings are wrapped in the Sanskrit word it is – ya "Y" means to gather. "J" means to give birth. To give birth to what? To give birth to knowledge & truth within yourself. "Na" means to distribute properly, that is to distribute that knowledge and truth. The physical posture used during Namaz prayer is similar to the Vajrasana posture in yoga. Allah is a combination of Al + Illah, Al in Arabic is male energy, and Illah is female energy of the Supreme Creator. Therefore no one can say ALLAH is male or female. Everything is in and from Allah and Allah is everything and everywhere. So it is the duty of human to respect everything either living or non-living things. Also AL is used for the praise for the beautiful things, it is also used as the conjunction word THE.

The Quran (29:45) says, "Surely prayer prevents from misdeeds, indecency and evils, the remembrance of Allah is a great thing".

Prayer is for seeking blessings from Allah. Islam teaches complete submission before Allah. It stands for Adjure, Appeal, Ask, Beseech, Brace, Crave, Entreat, Implore, Importune, Invoke, Petition, Recreate, Request, Say, Solicit, Sue, Supplicate, Urge, and Commune with Cry.

Outside the Arab world, the most widespread Persian word for prayer in Islam is namaz. It is used by speakers of Indo-Iranian languages (such as Persian and some languages of South Asia) as well as by speakers of Turkic and Slavic languages. In Lak and Avar, Chak and Kak are used, respectively. In Malaysia and Indonesia, the term SALOT is used, as well as a local term, sembahyang (meaning "act of worship", from the words semba - worship, and hyang - God or deity). 1

Prayer is offered by facing the direction of Qibla i.e. Kaaba. In the beginning Prophet Muhammad (pbuh) used to offer prayers in the direction of Masjid Aqsa (AQSA) in Jerusalem. Later, by Allah's command, Prophet Mohammad (pbuh) offer Namaz facing the Kaaba (KABBA). Muslims first pray standing and then kneel down and then sit to recite phrases from the Quran. They prostrate themselves in the middle and prostrate before Allah. Salah is made up of prescribed repetitive cycles of bowing and prostration called rakats. The number of rakats, known as units of prayer, varies from prayer to prayer. Religious purity and wadu are prerequisites for performing prayer.

"Salah" i.e. Namaz is an act of pleasing and connecting with the Supreme Creator Allah which is expressed in a specific and well defined physical action that purifies the soul. The prescribed five daily prayers are obligatory on all adults. Voluntary prayers are highly encouraged and recommended as a means of turning to divine help in times of personal sorrow and distress. Another form of worship is called Zikr which means meditation or a personal act of remembering Allah and being grateful for His mercy and benevolence. Through both these means the Muslim seeks closeness to his Lord and attains inner peace.

Different types of prayers have positive results in individuals. The psychotherapeutic science of prayer gives peace of mind and satisfaction and relieves symptoms like stress, anxiety, depression and antisocial tendencies. Advice when followed in right form and measure is the cure for mental distress. Salah is an act of pleasing Allah, the believer puts his unconditional faith in it and pleads for the acceptance of prayer. Islam is not only a religion but a complete way of living a healthy life.

Before each obligatory "salat", one performs ablutions and maintains a high degree of physical cleanliness and spiritual purity. The mind is given a rest from all worldly affairs and stress. Starting prayer with a clean body and clear intention allows the worshiper to enter a state of mind suitable for communicating with Allah. It is an act that is scientifically proven to help calm the mind and reduce stress levels. Spirituality, if performed properly, transcends any worldly concern. 4

"Salah" also has many physical benefits if done properly. Most of the muscles and joints of the body are exercised during Salah. In addition to the limb muscles, the muscles of the back and perineum are also repeatedly exercised in the most notable movement of prostration. The muscles of the neck in particular are strengthened in such a way that a person suffering from cervical spondylitis or myalgia's can be found in a person doing regular exercise several times a day. Snowing is unusual. "Sajdah" is the only position in which the head is in a lower position than the heart and hence the blood supply is increased. This surge in blood supply has a positive effect on memory, concentration, mood and other cognitive abilities. A recent study examining alpha brain activity during Muslim prayers reported increased amplitude in parietal and occipital regions, indicating parasympathetic innervation and thus indicating a state of relaxation. 2.3.4

Similarly Yoga is a set of physical, mental and spiritual practices that originated in ancient BHARAT and aims to recognize a detached witnessing-consciousness untouched by the mind and worldly suffering. The term "yoga" often refers to a form of body movement, posture-based physical fitness, and stress-relief and relaxation techniques through asana (body postures). The ultimate goals of yoga are to relax the mind and gain insight, rest in detached awareness and liberation (moksha) from samsara and suffering: a process that leads to oneness (ekyam) with the divine or with the self (atman). This goal varies by philosophical or religious system.

Yoga has been known for its scientific basis as a healthy lifestyle practice for thousands of years. It is older than our Namaz. Today, regardless of one's religious affiliation, yoga has become one of the most popular fitness exercises all over the world. Muslims are blessed with Salah i.e. Namaz which has become an integral part of their daily activities since fourteen hundred years with physical, psychological, social and spiritual benefits. Yoga can be considered not just as a set of 'asana' but as a lifestyle, which is completely related to the health, happiness and longevity of an individual.

Yoga means the union and integration of the whole human being with the inner soul to the outer nature or the Almighty. It is the path of self-discovery that brings balance and harmony in life. It is the science of strengthening the human mind and maximizing the level of consciousness. On the one hand, it helps normal people to lead a healthy and satisfied life and on the other hand, it provides relief, solace and peace of mind to persons with mental distress. The meaning and ultimate purpose of yoga appear to be fundamentally similar to the messages and its prayers of other religions of the world, including Islam, despite differences in their fundamental concepts according to the origin. 4

The physical similarities between Salah and yoga are in the body movements that are repeated in a set pattern. Salah finds associated movements called 'asana' in yoga along with its five major physical movements. When combined with physical activity alone—Hatha Yoga and Salah—have been found to achieve comparable healing benefits in all major organ systems. While in yoga the trainable 'asana' (but not all 'asana' but some of them) are found in Salah, where on the other hand the latter is a spiritual imperative duty. As mentioned earlier, Islam is a prescription for a complete and balanced lifestyle, so Salah becomes an addition to worship as an overall health tonic. 4, 5

Prophet Muhammad (pbuh) went to heaven during his lifetime. This happened through proper namaz. He attained the highest level of meditation and took his soul to heaven and again returned back to this earth. Meditation is practiced in different ways in all religions. Everyone has the same ultimate message or goal to command themselves and that person can go anywhere through meditation.

Yoga is also a kind of practice and action to keep oneself mentally and physically fit along with the body parts. Yoga has nothing to do with any particular religion. It is a good practice to do only special exercises. Islam only forbids the worship of polytheism as Islam believes in the worship of monotheism. And if yoga is taken into consideration then it is not any kind of worship it is basically a kind of exercise as far as we can do all kinds of activities and keeping ourselves in monotheism worship state which is good for health, environment and mankind.

So Namaz is a way of keeping oneself in a good healthy condition and attachment with Almighty God i.e. Allah.

As mentioned earlier, religion is a way of leading a good healthy life. No religion teaches violence. War is permitted only when it comes to violating a peace treaty or when a person's life is at stake. Like Prophet Mohammad (pbuh) fought war only for existence and for truth when the treaty was broken. At the same time lord Shri Ram and Shri Krishna fought a war for the existence of peace and truth. Similarly Prophet Mooses fought a war for peace, truth and existence.

Today in BHARAT, the practice of giving Azaan by installing loudspeakers in mosques is prevailing, there is no harm in it if the level of sound is within the permissible limit set by the government. But there were no loudspeaker at the time of the Prophet Mohammad pbuh. As the world is progressing everyone is adopting new technology. We are adopting and using new technology for calling people for Namaz then why we do not adopt new technology and contemporary education in Madrasa for making children wise and a true Muslim. The irony part in Muslims which we face today is that during Namaz instead of connecting with Allah, Muslims divert their mind and start thinking about worldly matters and affairs. During namaz times Muslims instead of complete surrender to Allah and connect with Allah, Muslims just seems to be doing acting behind the Imam Sahab. And it seems that Allah is not accepting these types of Namaz and that's why our prayers are going astray. Because of our activities and deeds Allah is not showering his blessing upon Muslims. Muslims are suffering because of own deeds and activities. I will say one thing here Muslims have to think now that how to become a true Muslim.

Reference

1. Yusuf, Ghulam-Sarwar (30 December 2015). One Hundred and One Things Malay. Partridge Publications Singapore.

2. Ayad A. In: Healing body and soul. Hakam J, editor. Riyadh: International Islamic Publishing House; 2008.

3. Integration of Islamic Prayer (Salah/Namaz) and Yoga in Mental Health by Shabbir Ahmed Sayeed and Anand Prakash

Chapter 18
WAJU/WADU

Wadu is a process of washing away the impurities from one's body with limited water.

One of the pillars of Islam is that Muslims offer prayers five times a day. Before those prayers, they are required to perform a purification ritual called wadu, which requires human to wash their face, hands and feet. Shuddhi is a ritual which is an Islamic procedure for cleansing the body parts with limited water. The 4 Farz (obligatory) acts of Wadu include washing the face, hands, then wiping the head and finally washing the feet with very less water. 2

In fact, the practice of WADU/WAJU gives the message of water conservation and cleanliness. There has been a scarcity of water in Saudi Arabia so Prophet Muhammad pbuh showed and started the practice of cleaning the body parts with very little water (one mug of water). He spread the message of judicious use of water and the message of water conservation. This is a message not to waste water, because water is a very valuable gift given by nature. Nowadays we see many advertisements on television and other media about judicious use of water. These days even government spends thousands and lakhs of rupees to spread the message that water should not be wasted, but still all of us do not understand the importance of water and spend or use water excessively. Everything about humanity and good life is present in the religion of Islam. It tells the easy way of living life and talks about conservation of everything for the coming generations. Today everyone talks about water conservation and it has been made mandatory in many places to do water harvestings. About which the Prophet had said 1400 years ago. It is a Sunnah to use less water, spend water judiciously and conserve water. But today are we Muslims really following the message of our great Prophet Mohammad pbuh?

All religions specially Islam teaches hygiene and cleanliness. All the practices and rituals teaches us to be a contributor and save for future generations. Religion teaches us to become a contributor not to be a consumer only. But it is very sad to say that instead of being useful and contributors, we all have become only consumers. The way we have to keep ourselves clean, in the same way it is the duty of all Muslims to keep their surroundings neat and clean. If any person passes through a dirty place and if that person becomes dirty or impure then the sin of becoming impure goes to the person who has made that place dirty.

Only the government cannot be blamed for the filth of any area. Every Muslim should keep their surroundings neat, clean and tidy just like we keep ourselves. There is every good thing in every religion, we just need to apply things judiciously. Prophet Muhammad pbuh never taught to be selfish. So it is the duty of all the Muslims to save and conserve water and all resources for the generations to come. Because there is a shortage of pure water everywhere. Pure water is gradually decreasing. The ground water level is slowly depleting. Today the government is spending lakhs and crores of rupees for pure and safe. JAL JEEVAN MISSION is a live example in front of us in which Government of India is spending millions and billions of rupees in India.

Religion teaches everyone to use all the resources judiciously. It teaches to save resources for the coming generations. The world is going mad to save water whereas Islam had showed about the values of water 1400 years ago and taught to save water. Muslims shall follow true Islam and spread the real message of Islam, i.e. "to live humanely and to save all the resources for the future". All aspects of Islam are for love, peace and humanity. But we have tarnished it. Islam does not teach any violence or war. There are traitors and oppressors inside Islam who have unnecessarily misinterpreted some Arabic words of Islam and misled the people whom Allah will never forgive.

Allah has made available every resource in this world in sufficient quantity for every human being to live happily. But even today after making so much progress, many people are forced to sleep hungry. Why? The answer is that today every human being is becoming a consumer instead of being contributor. Parent provides all facilities to their children and give good educations and gets their children married, the same children forget their parents in their old age. If I am wrong, then why there are so many Virdha Ashrams in my country? I understand that parents are also equally responsible for this. During the time of upbringing, parents do not teach moral values and humanity properly. The parents lay more stress upon the children to fulfil their wish and desire to become more and more successful in life. The parents calculate the success in terms of earnings and facilities. And this is the reasons why people are becoming more and more consumer instead of becoming contributor. The dream of becoming rich and richer has spoiled the society of the elite class people and made them selfish. The selfishness goes to such an extent that children leave their parents also.

I would like to give a living example of a man who for years and years fought with his own father, sisters and brothers for the property inheritance for his only one son. The case trials all happened and then one day he himself died due to his bad deeds under suffering. The boy for whom his father had quarrelled with his father, sisters and brothers, on the first year of the death anniversary neither he went to his father's tomb nor read the Quran, nor did any rituals for his father. That son did not did any religious rituals, but on that day itself he went about 150 km away to take the grandfather property. What would you call such a Muslim? The father who fought with all the relatives for his son, after his death his only son said hell to father and abused him in various ways. He was rewarded according to the upbringing given by his father. Then for whom do people cheat.

Today it is necessary that every parent should give moral and proper religious and contemporary education to their children so that in old age they do not have to go to Virdha Ashram and after death their children shall not abuse them. One should love and respect the elders, love the younger ones. That means to become capable and to make other capable. If you become capable then automatically everything will be all right.

In earlier times, we used to get enough water by just digging 30 feet well, but nowadays we all have to go more than 300-400 feet and even more than that for water. The question arises, why is this happening? The time has come that not only Muslims, but people who worship God in other ways also understand the basic principle of religion and behave accordingly. In every religion, giving water to someone is a pious act, then why water is being sold? It means that we all are going against religion. Why? Because pure water is available in very less quantity today. We all are responsible for this because everyone has become a consumer. No one wants to be a contributor.

Now it is a humble request for everyone to become a contributor and save all the resources for future generations. Minimise the luxury just only take as per your needs and requirements judiciously. Here I appreciate the tribal people of the world and specially of Bharat country as I have stayed with them also and have closely observed them like the BIRHORE tribes of Jharkhand who are very less in numbers but they think that the jungle is their home and they take only little from the jungle for their survival. They preserve the environment and does the worship of environment and only natural energy and powers.

FOR BECOMING A CONTRIBUTOR WE DON'T HAVE TO WORK HARD JUST WE HAVE TO CHANGE OUR THOUGHT PROCESS. WHEREAS FOR BECOMING A CONSUMER WE HAVE TO WORK HARD AND EXPLOIT THE RESOURCES WITHOUT JUSTIFICATION. LUXURY IN THE COST OF EXPLOITATION OF RESOURCES IS NOT JUSTIFIED.

Chapter 19
Sacrifice (Bakrid)

The meaning of qurbani is "sacrifice". Eid Al-Adha is 'festival of sacrifice'. It is based on the memory of the Prophet Abraham, who at the behest of God agreed to sacrifice his beloved son. God wanted to test Abraham's loyalty. The origin of this tradition among Muslims is believed to be from the story in which Prophet Abraham had a dream in which he is sacrificing his beloved son Ismail on the call of almighty Allah (Quran 37: 102-107).) But when Prophet Ibrahim was on the verge of sacrificing his son, Allah replaced Ismail with a dumba (goat). In memory of this surrender before Allah by Abraham, an animal is sacrificed in the month of Dhul Hijjah of every lunar year. One-third of the meat of the sacrificial animal is kept by the sacrificial family, one-third is given to relatives, while one-third is distributed among the poor and needy.

The meaning of Eid is happy festival. Celebrating Eid Al Adha in the memory of Prophet Abraham is a festival of sacrifice. The eternal meaning of Sacrifice is any act of giving one's belongings to others for the sake of goodness and humanity. It is also an act of overcoming selfish desires and evils. For increasing the happiness index of any country, peace is required. And to achieve peace sacrifice in different forms is very important. Sacrifice is not only to kill an animal in front of God. The true and eternal meaning of sacrifice is very eternal living.

Sacrifice can be of giving one's food to other, sacrifice can be of leaving one's own luxury for other, sacrifice is giving up own comfort for the cause of humanity, sacrifice can be of overcoming lust, sacrifice is any activities of leaving one's selfish desire and overcoming the evils and corruptions. It is to overcome wickedness.

Now coming to the most important part of our past history, the practice of human sacrifice existed in almost every primitive tribes in ancient time. Even in BHARAT this practice existed. According to a legend once Shunashepa was chosen for the sacrifice in a special religious ritual but he was saved after praying to the Rig Vedic Gods. The earliest extant text to mention this legend is the Aitareya Brahmana (7.13–18) of the Rig-Veda. The story is repeated with some changes in the Balakand (1.61) of Valmiki Ramayana. The way Allah protected the son of Abraham, in the same way Shunashepa is protected by Indra and Agni.

In ancient times in course of time we find that in all the primitive civilizations the practice of human sacrifice in the name of God was slowly converted into animal sacrifice. From Abraham incident of sacrificing his son we can reach to the conclusion that this was the first stage in the evolution of humanity in the Middle East when human sacrifice was replaced by the animal sacrifice? Why animal sacrifice? That was the time when humans were not in the food gathering state but they were in the state of cattle-grazing. The animals used to be in the form of money. And to save humans, GOD must have created such a situations among different tribes and different civilization that people shifts from the sacrificing of humans to the sacrificing of animals. Now again in this age further reformations are required in this also as it was done earlier.

Ramdhari Singh Dinkar, in his book named "Sanskriti ke char adhyay", has mentioned about words of the Vedas – the essence of Yajna was first in man, then it went into animals like horse, then into buffalo, then into heifer, then into sheep and so on and on and in Aja. When Aja was sacrificed, this essence merged into the earth, from which Yava and Tandul were born. The Purodash (bread or pithi) of Yava and Tandul is also the sacred offering of YAG. Fortunately, reformers like Videha Jana Krishna, Mohair and Buddha were born in BHARAT to intellectually support the development of humanity.

In Valmiki Ramayana Aranya Kand / Sarg 9 / Shlok 2-4 (pg. 488) there is a reference that Shri Ram vowed to kill the demons to protect the sages. Knowing this Sita, the daughter of Videha Janak, stopped him and said you will kill the demons of Dandakaranai without enmity. The link between violence and non-violent Buddha was Shri Krishna, who did not oppose YAG but expanded the meaning of YAG so much that the establishment of non-violence became easy.

The traditional practice of animal sacrifice in Eid Al Adha is still present among Muslims, but as it has been written above, only one third of the meat of the animal is ordered to be kept for themselves and the rest is to be distributed among the other needy people. This is a stage where we move towards the real meaning of Qurbani that is "Sacrifice". Meaning to say to give own things to other people. So it can be concluded that whatever Allah has given to you share it with relatives and other and by doing this the blessing of Allah will increase and happiness will come. So giving ones belongings or sharing ones belongings with other is a form of EID-AL-ADHA.

In this regard, there are verses in the Holy Quran, where it has been told that some verses of this book are Mahakam (clear), they are the core of the book. And other verses (sentences) are mutashabeh (similar). Those whose hearts are crooked, they follow the verses of Mutashabeh in search of nuisance and in search of its meaning. No one knows the meaning of those words except Allah.

Leaving some of the Jains and Hindus in BHARAT, almost the entire population of most countries around the world consumes meat in some form or the other. Food is a part of our culture which is difficult to change overnight. But the thought process can be developed and implemented so that in future we may try to implement it.

Eid Al-Adha is considered holy and is therefore called the 'Big Eid' while Eid Al-Fitr is known as the 'Small Eid'. Eid Al-Kabir means 'Greater Eid' and is used in Yemen, Syria and North Africa, while other translations of 'Big Eid' are used in Pashto, Kashmiri, Urdu and Hindi. The 'Big Eid' or Eid-ul-Azha, has the advantage of two major rituals, as both have prayer, but one has sacrifice. The 'Big Eid' brings all Muslims together in celebrating the Hajj, which itself commemorates the Abrahamic sacrifice, while the 'Choti Eid' merely commemorates the end of the fasting of Ramadan. 1

Eid is also considered as a festival of happiness and joy. It is sharing of happiness and greetings with relatives, friends and people. We can celebrate Bade Eid every day if we sacrifice our bad thoughts and bad deeds. If we help and distribute things (foods, clothes, happiness etc.) among needy people and relatives we can celebrate Bakrid every day. Just as we divide the sacrificial animal into three parts (1 for ourselves, 1 for our relatives, 1 for the poor), in the same way we should divide our happiness among relatives and the poor's. This is the true purpose and spirit of sacrifice.

The irony is that nowadays, during the festival of Bakrid, Muslims are not even dividing the sacrificed goat meat into three parts. They try to keep 100% of the sacrificed goat within the family only. Here also we are not following the words of Prophet Mohammad pbuh, then how we are calling ourselves Muslims. Rituals are being performed half-heartedly for their own benefit or just for show off. These days Muslims are not understanding the main objectives of Islamic rituals. Day by day they are pushing the society towards evil and that is why even Allah has turned away from Muslims. These days we can easily see in almost all Muslims family that one brother is stealing the rights of own brothers and sisters. These are against the ISLAM and against the true meaning of EID-AL-ADHA.

Prophet Mohammad (pbuh) told that the real meaning of Sacrifice (Bakrid) is to sacrifice lust, sacrifice of Nafs (nerve), giving good foods and cloth to others, Sacrificing our luxury, comfort and convenience for others. Less utilization of the resources. Now is the time to bring reformation in the society and start a new life by following the footsteps of Prophet Mohammad (Sallallahu Alaihi Wasallam) pbuh, having patience and being ready to sacrifice small happiness for the sake of humanity and peace. The word Sacrifice has a vast and deep meaning and it needs to be understand by all. Tolerance is also a part of Sacrifice. Giving rights of others is a kind of sacrifice. Muslims has to come out of the well so that one can understand the true concept of Islam and coexist happily with own brothers, sisters, relatives, colleagues, neighbours and country citizens.

Chapter 20

Prayer and Haji

Hajj is one of the five basic pillars of Islam. Haji people wear only two white clothes. One cloth down the waist and one up around the shoulders. The most important thing is that both the pieces of cloth should be unstitched. When Muslims go for Hajj, men have to wear unstitched clothes before performing the holy rituals. After bathing (ghusl) they have to wear a special white cloth called ihram, which consists of two unstitched cloths. Izar is a long sheet of cloth that goes around the waist and is tied with a belt or a strip of cloth torn from Ihram material. Rida, a second sheet of cloth, goes over one or both shoulders. Men are not allowed to wear underwear or socks, and have to keep their heads uncovered. Uniformity of dress shows that all men are equal before God whether rich or poor.

Hajj clothing for women is not as prescriptive as that of men. They can wear clothes of any colour as long as all the parts of the body except their hands and face are covered with clothes. In ihram many women wear black or white abaya and hijab.

Men have to shave their heads after performing all the Arkan (rituals) of Hajj or Umrah. Women only have to cut a piece of hair because it is forbidden for them to shave their heads in Islam. 1

In Vedic worship of Sanatana Dharm, men wear only two clothes. One dhoti below and one cloth above. Both the pieces of cloths are unstitched. There are many similarities in the method of worshiping the Supreme Being in both the religions. The eternal rituals and practices of fasting in all religions justify the treatment of many diseases. Different religion people path may be different but ultimately it heads towards the one supreme God.

When we follow the code of conduct related to the rituals of dress as described in Sanatana Dharma, such as a clean dhoti worn during worship, a shawl worn loosely over the shoulders or a small single piece of cloth, nine- yards (yards), jewellery, garlands of scented flowers in the hair, applying kumkum or tilak. Through these measures, we move forward on the path of sattvikta through our gross body.

The dhoti or lungi as the dress of the worshiper rests at different places. Its knot is tied at the navel. The navel area is called 'Panchak-Mandal'. The Panchapranas (five vital energies) concentrated around the centre of the navel area are activated due to continuous pressure from the knot. The folds of the dhoti or lungi are tied at the same place where the knot attached to the panchak-mandal is formed. It emits and transmits the frequencies associated with the universe and the Panchamahabhutas into the environment as per the requirement. After praying and attracting Chaitanya (divine consciousness) into it, clothes of any colour can be worn. 3

The science behind men wearing TOPI. Wearing a TOPI makes it possible for a person to use the stored energy (frequencies) concentrated in the hollow space of the hat for a long period of time. This is because the inherent nature of a human being is not Raja-predominant and as a result the sattva-predominant frequencies cannot be destroyed at the level of the physical body in a short period of time. The contact established due to the medium and concentration of the cap makes it possible for the individual to gradually absorb these waves.

Nowadays Muslims have changed the originality of TOPI also in style and appearance. Jaali dar TOPI of various styles have been adopted by Muslims. In fact most TOPI these days are made in such a way that hardly any air gets trapped inside the cap when wearing a mesh cap. This confirms that Muslims have adopted new style and false modernization for appearance. But don't know why Muslims are keeping themselves behind in adopting modern education. The things by which we will not be benefited, those things are being adopted by the Muslims while the things through which Muslims will benefit, that scientific education system is not being adopted.

Now there is a need to think deeply and understand each and every point to make life good and reap the scientific benefits of religious practices. A Muslim does not need to be a part of the crowd just for the sake of name and show orthodoxy.

Women covering the head with pallu (the free end of her saree):- A woman emit specific divine energy frequencies into the environment through the freely dangling end of the pallu of her saree or dupatta. Apart from this, it can also emit this power in the body by activating the Raja component. In this way woman is an imitator and spreads the Shakti element in the environment through her saree.

It is beneficial for the priest to wear white clothes. White colour has equal ability to absorb and emit Chai Tanya, thereby reducing Raja-Tama in the environment. White clothes have the ability to improve the sattva guna in the atmosphere which makes it conducive for worship. 2,3

In Islam, Muslims offer prayers. But nowadays the true spirit of Namaz is not present among the Muslims. During Namaz one has to surrender oneself completely to God but during Namaz nowadays Muslims only perform physical acts not the spiritual act. Nowadays, at the time of Namaz, the mind of a Muslim starts thinking about worldly matters. The soul of prayer (original sense) is lost and Allah does not accept this type of prayers. Because this type of prayers does not connect with Allah. Now a days some Muslims are selling Imaan just for small profit. The worshipers show themselves that they are the representatives of the Lord. People take the oath of prayer and take the name of Allah and Mohammad to show that they are the only right and righteous. The real meaning of prayer is to reach the higher level of spirituality and to meet or talk to God.

Today few Muslims themselves are far from the right path, so how can they blame others. I have mentioned earlier that Muslims are fighting within their own community in the name of sects and sub sects. During Jumma (Friday) prayers in mosques, each sect starts criticizing other sects rudely. Some people also display no entry posters for other sects Muslims inside mosque. What a foolish move! One Maulana blames other Maulanas and calls each other Kafir. What are the Muslims doing? Muslims have forgotten the teachings of great Prophet Muhammad pbuh and people are Muslims only for the name shake. Nowadays, especially in BHARAT all the evils has entered inside the Muslim society. That's why Allah has withdrawn his blessing from Muslims.

Earlier it was very difficult to perform Hajj and the Hajis were undoubtedly given very high status and respect in the society. Hajis were considered true Muslims and they never did any wrong thing. The hajis used to keep themselves away from the worldly affairs.

Earlier some Maulanas used to give fatwa against making of photographs of any living thing. Earlier people used to perform Haj without photographs. But in today's world can anyone think of going for Haj without photo ID card? Photography was considered as a sin before one century back because of few fatwas.

The irony part is that Haj has become a fashion these days. The most auspicious thing in Haj is that before the person go for HAJ, he or she has to visit all relatives and known people, and has to ask for forgiveness from all if they have hurt them knowingly or unknowingly. But this is missing these days. Some people takes Haj as a certificate. People perform Hajj regardless of Halal or Haram money and feel proud to be called Haji sahab. Even after Haj they get involved in wordly affairs and does all the evils and corruptions hence the word Haji also has lost its true spirit. Criticism against someone is considered as a great sin in Islam but nowadays all Muslims and even Hajis criticizes people. Earlier Hajj was considered spiritual and truly holy and the pilgrims were true pilgrims. After Hajj, Haji used to lead a simple life away from the material world. But today it is quite different. Another important thing in our childhood was that we used to observe and see that many sick people of different religion used to come to mosque at the time of namaz and used to stand in queues outside the mosque along with small children, in the belief that after performing namaz the namazis will blow air upon the sick children and with the power of Quranic verses through Hajis and Hafiz the diseases will be cured. But today no one comes to mosque, why? A true worshiper and a true Haji has the power to bring peace and harmony in the society.

Reference

1. https://hajjumrahplanner.com/clothing/

2. Sanatana's Holy Book 'Required Personal Preparation before Ritual Worship'

Chapter 21

Loyalty

The loyalty of Muslims in general was given as an example and proverb during the earlier times. Because during that time Muslims used to be a true Muslim and had real iman and strong faith. Loyalty is another name of iman. The contribution of Muslims in the freedom struggle of our country cannot be ignored or forgotten, as well as the contribution of Muslims in the development of BHARAT cannot be ignored. With love affection and respect we the people of BHARAT have lived together happily because all BHARATIYE are of the same origin. 99% people of BHARATIYE DNA are same. After the partition of our country, most of the Muslims remained in BHARAT because it is the motherland of all BHARATIYE Muslims. Therefore as a Muslims, automatically it becomes the duty to respect our motherland and the decisions of the fore-fathers of staying in BHARAT. No one questions the loyalty of a true Muslims. But some BHARATIYE Muslim falls under the influence of an enemy country or a traitor, and deviate from the true path of Islam, and do such acts that arises a question of the loyalty. Due to those few whole community is getting bad name.

After the First World War there was a rapid change in the functioning of the countries and whole world. Traditional monarchy changed to modern democracy. Whoever got the majority vote, regardless of anything became the ruler. World powers have their own policy to rule the world. Developed countries adopted the divide and rule policy, so that their weapons could be sold to different countries. Some countries also started the policy of playing the game of power in the name of religion. Many countries have adopted the policy of bringing instability in other countries so that the powerful country can rule the world. New technology has replaced traditional things. People adopted new technology and development was done in all the field.

After independence, the enemy country tried everything possible to weaken BHARAT. They chose religion as the easiest way to destabilize BHARAT and used religion as a tool. Due to poverty and some funding some enemy country took some Muslims into their fold, whom they misguided and made them do all the wrong things under the umbrella of religion.

There is no dispute in following Islam religion properly, believing in it, performing all rituals and being loyal to our country. Being loyal and loving one's country is an important part of the Islamic faith. The Quran says, "O believers! Obey Allah and obey the Prophet and obey those in authority among you" (4:59).

The meaning of the word "Islam" is the right way of living life, all works of humanity, i.e. "peace". But nowadays the whole community is being dragged in defamation due to- the behaviour of few Muslims. In an ideal society peace and harmony starts from home, then spreads to the community and then to the whole world. Allah has provided an ideal way of life for every aspect of human society. Islam urges love and peace between brothers, brothers and sisters, relatives, husband and wife, neighbours, fellow citizens etc. Islam urges to take care of neighbours irrespective of religion, cast, creed or sects. Islam instructs all to help others and at large Commands loyalty to the country of residence plus many commands of humanities. All these different responsibilities have one big goal - peace in the society. But are today's

Muslims specially in BHARAT doing all this? Are we obeying the commands of Prophet Mohammad pbuh?

As a citizens of any country, Muslims should always act and show absolute love and loyalty to their country which is mother land. It is the desire of every citizen that he and his country make progress and he should always strive towards this objective. History is full of examples that our fore-fathers have made sacrifices for our great country. 1, 2.

Prophet Muhammad pbuh declares: "He who obeys the ruler obeys me, and he who disobeys the ruler disobeys me" (Muslim); "Listen to your ruler and obey him, even if you despise him" (Bukhari). 3

In Arabic: "HUBBUL WATAN MINAL IMMAN" Translation: Loving one's motherland is a part of faith. There are many sayings about Prophet Muhammad (pbuh) yearning for Mecca, his birthplace.

Some Muslims have been so wrongly and falsely taught and brought up in such an environment that their characters has become distorted, and they are not loyal to anyone neither of their parents, brothers, sisters, neighbours, society or for the country. Some Muslims are becoming a burden on others. You will find live examples everywhere and in this book and in coming volumes of this book. Today some Muslims take pride in saying Insallah and Masa Allah, uses the name of Allah and Prophet Muhammad (pbuh) just to show supremacy and then deceive people. Some Muslims have completely gone against Islam. Just Because of few wrong Muslims, all Muslims are getting bad names.

Some teachings and some perverted system have created an illusion in the minds of Muslims that only Muslims will go to Jannah and all others will go to Jahannam. Some people have given wrong teachings and sowed the seeds of hatred. I ask how a person who lie and cheat others go to heaven. Muslims also say about other sects of Muslims that they will also go to hell. So what is right? Whether all Muslims will go to Jannat or only one Muslim sect will go to Jannat. Why few people are creating confusion? And with these types of confusion many controversy arises? Doing all evil and saying that only particular group will go to heaven is not justified. I think that any person irrespective of religion, cast, creed or gender, whoever is true to the commands of God and does humanitarian works and lead life like a good human being, only they will go to heaven.

Unknowingly due to limitation in education and limitation in upbringings Muslim children understand and learns to hate other. Under the influence of external people or due to the pressure of funding in few madrasa or in few mosque or any other place, people slowly bend to follow the wish and desire of the funder. People mind gets polluted by hate speeches in the name of religion, caste and sects, when the children grows up, they say the same hate speech which they have heard during upbringing. That's why hatred has entered every house today and peace is missing in every house. The Muslims are been misled. Nowadays, in every house, a brother does not have good relations with his own brothers and sisters, neighbours but they will try to keep good relation with outsider to show they are good. If you cannot be good to your own then how can you be good to other?

Now a days Muslims are insulting great Prophet Mohammad (pbuh) and their own fore-fathers. It is clearly found in each and every house that these days Muslims are not of their own brothers and sisters then what people are talking about brotherhood, supremacy and heaven. At least the Sanatanis, though they follow a different path of salvation are proving to be much better than the Muslims of today. Few misguided diverted Muslims who are insulting our motherland in the vain hope of Ghazwa e Hind, and because of such few misguided diverted Muslims entire Muslim community is suffering. Nowadays Muslims are being looked upon with suspicion. The big question is why? It is because of few Muslim people. Here one thing is very clear that BHARAT cannot be divided again. BHARATIYE Muslims are the citizens of BHARAT and cannot even move to another country now. Even no government can wipe out Muslims from BHARAT. Then for what and why some Muslims are trying to weaken our own country under the influence of enemy country or enemy of BHARAT. Our forefathers sacrificed for BHARAT freedom and lived in BHARAT. So it is our duty to honour the martyrdom of our forefathers. Some politicians may do politics to achieve something but it is the duty of Muslim leaders, Maulanas and influencers to spread the true philosophy of Islam.

It is the duty of all the influencers to at least start progressive work for the society and the country. The influencers shall stop to appeasement policy. It is the duty of influencers to inspire young generations and all Muslims to adopt contemporary education. It is our duty to be a true Muslim and a true BHARATIYE and walk step by step with the Government of BHARAT for the progress and development of our society and our country. There is no need to think that sanatanis are enemies of Muslims. If sanatanis disrespect Muslims then they are working against Sanatan Dharma and as per the sanatani philosophy the whole world is our home and all the humans are brothers and sisters. "Vasudhaiva Kutumbakam" the whole world is one family.

Some miscreant people are constantly trying to create a rift between Hindus and Muslims in BHARAT to get small benefits. It is against the act of humanity. We all know that 99% of the Muslims living in BHARAT are of BHARATIYE origin and can be said to be Sanatani Muslims. The religion name Islam came into this world from 7th century AD onwards. But whatever religion was there in the world since human civilization existed their only objective was love and peace. God did not created any religion, God only created humans to do humanity work and live happily. God messengers just brought and spread the words of GOD for peaceful existence. All the people living in BHARAT before Islam were the followers of Sanatan Dharma. May be due to some reasons like equality, goodness, simplicity, presentation issues, compulsions or many any other reasons the fore-fathers of today's Muslims became Muslims in different periods of time. So it is clear that the blood of every BHARATIYE is the same. 99% Hindus, Muslims and Christians living in BHARAT have the common ancestors and we all have the common DNA. The way the beauty of the garden increases with different flowers, in the same way the beauty of our country has increased with the different religions, sects and cultures in BHARAT having one objective that is of humanity and peaceful living. From history we find BHARAT is the only country in this world who has never initiated any war. We also find from history that India when forced into war has treated the captured soldiers with humanity.

It is the duty of Muslims to keep themselves away from evils and corruptions and to take responsibility to improve family and society. Muslims don't have to continue to act as a tool kit, they don't have to work only as a vote bank. Muslims have to act as a responsible citizen like our great scientist and former President Avul Pakir Jalaluddin Abdul Kalam and many other Muslims who brought glory to our country.

One important thing has to be kept in mind that when any enemy country's missile will come towards BHARAT, that missile will not be able to see who are Hindus? Who are Muslims? All have to beware of rotten thoughts of some crooked people. Now the time has come to break the shackles and bring the misguided Muslims on the right path of Islam. All Muslims have to contribute in the progress of the society. Loyalty is in the blood of all Muslims but due to some distorted mind-set people Muslims have gone in deep sleep, they have to be woken up and have to be taught to follow the Real ISLAM properly. The foundation of Islam is of humanity, honesty, loyalty and all such things those are for peace.

I take a true incident of humanity from the time of Prophet Mohammad pbuh. Some traders were going through a road, one of them said "it seems that no Muslims comes and goes through this road". The other trader asked "why and how?" The first trader said, look how many stones are scattered on this road and dirt is also spread. Good Living and kindness is the identity of true Muslims. He said that Muslim means one who has firm faith, the identity of a true Muslim is that they do all the work of humanity. There activities does not hurt others. It is the duty of Muslims to remove the things that hurt others. The stone or anything's on the road which hurts people are cleaned by the Muslims who passes through the road. "The loyalty of a Muslim is recognized not only by words, but by putting it into practice.

A Muslim saint Rabia was asked, "Do you love Almighty Allah?" He said yes. Then asked, "Do you hate Shaitan?" He replied – "Because of my love for Allah is so much that I do not have enough time to hate Shaitan". This is true loyalty, Divine love.

It can be said that a true and good person irrespective of religion or sects sees only good things and a bad person sees only bad things in each and every thing.

Reference

1. Namod Khokher, graduate student at the University of Illinois at The Daily Illini The Independent Student Newspaper. Loyalty to the religion of Islam, country of residence. July 8, 2013

2. https://dailyillini.com/uncategorized/2013/07/08/islam-about-loyalty-to-religion-country-of-residence/

3. https://trueislam.com/campaigns/Muslims-for-loyalty/

Chapter 22

Faith and Sect

The Quran advises us to think and understand properly before doing anything, to seek advice from those whom we consider wise. But the wise should be really a true wise person. Once the course of action is determined, we must place our trust in God, for "He loves those who put their trust in Him" (Quran 3:159). "And Allah will bestow upon him boons from such sources which he could never have imagined. And whoever puts his trust in Allah, He will be sufficient for him." (Quran 65:3) 1, 2.

Quranic verses remind us to trust God. "Nothing happens to us except what God has ordained for us. He is our Lord and Master. The believers will put their trust in God." (Quran 9:51)

Quran [3:159-160]... and put your trust in Allah. God loves those who trust in him.* If God is with you then no one can defeat you. And if he leaves you, who else can support you?

The currency of the USA is the only currency that contains the phrase: "In God we trust." It is a fact that the US dollar has been the strongest currency in the world.it is the standard by which all other currencies are measured. 3

Muslims in BHARAT have reached a pathetic condition because of their own actions and deeds. These days the name of Allah and

Prophet Muhammad (sallallahu alaihi wa sallam) is used only as a word to show off and to show one's supremacy over others. Today it is common in every Muslim household to hate their own brothers and sisters and even neighbours. This shows that Muslims are having no faith in Allah. Many Muslims are jealous of each other. No one wants to give away the rights of his own siblings. Brothers and their wives stop talking to their own sisters or sister-in-law thinking that if she comes home, the father's property will have to be shared with her. From where this hatred has entered among Muslims? Think and ponder! You will get the answers.

Naqab or Hijab is a very respectful thing but now-a-days some Muslims are misusing Naqab/Hijab due to which Allah has withdrawn his blessing from it also. Naqab/hijab is a very good thing if it is given respect and worn for right purpose. Some people are misusing and cheating their parents and society. I am not saying from my point of view but I have seen it many times. In big cities some girls wear naqab/hijab and goes out from house but after moving out a few distance they remove it and again while returning they wear it. I narrate a true incident once one Maulana Hakim sahab asked few females sometimes you wear nakab and sometimes you do not wear Nakab. Upon this some girls said "if they get time to do makeup then they do not wear naqab and if they are not able to do makeup then they wear naqab". It is a fact that because of few people everyone's name gets spoiled. Allah takes away his blessing. The love and peace of every home has been destroyed due to the bad deeds of some Muslims.

The Quran says about those who divide religion into sects: [6:159] Allah is not with those who divide themselves into sects. The Quran has not said anything about sects. But some Hadiths (Ibn Majah, Abu Dawood, Al-Tirmidhi and Al-Nisa'i) say that according to the prophecy of Prophet Muhammad (pbuh) the Muslims will be divided into 73 sects. Out of 73 sects, only one sect will go to heaven and all other sects will go to hell. This may be to show supremacy over other Muslims or other groups. The 73 Divisions of the Muslim Faith states that the Jews are divided into 71 sects (firqa), Christians are divided into 72 sects, and the Muslim community will be divided into 73 sects.

73 Sects of this Ummah 'My Ummah will be divided into seventy-three sects, seventy-two will go to the Fire and one will go to Jannah.' How authentic is this Hadith?

1. Sayyiduna Abu Huraira narrated that Rasoolullah (peace and blessings of Allah be upon him) said:

   'The Jews were divided into seventy-two sects, and so were the Christians. My Ummah will be divided into 73.' (Sunan Tirmidhi, Hadith: 2640 and Saheeh Ibn Hibban; Al-Ihsan, Hadith: 6247 and 6731)

2. Sayyiduna 'Abdullah ibn 'Amr ibn'il reports that Rasoolullah (peace and blessings of Allah be upon him) said: '...Indeed the Bani Israel (Jews) were divided into seventy-two sects. My Ummah will be divided into seventy three. Except one sect, all others will be in the fire.

   It was asked: 'Which one will it be?' The Prophet (peace and blessings of Allah be upon him) replied: 'He who follows my path and the path of my companions.' (Sunan Tirmidhi, Hadith: 2641) Imam Tirmidhi has declared this Hadith as hasan.

3. Sayyiduna Mu'awiyah narrated that Rasulullah (Sallallahu Alaihi Wasallam) said:

'See! Those who were before you were divided into seventy-two sects. This Ummah will break into seventy-three. Seventy-two will be in the Fire, and one will be in Paradise. It is he who follows the group (of my Sahaba and my path).' (Sunan Abi Dawood, Hadith: 4587) 4.

All Muslim sects happily claims that their sub-sect is the 'saved' (Nazis) and the 'others' are meant for Hell. There are two parts to this Hadith: one is the number of sects that are above, and the other is the salvation part. In contrast, we have another version of the Hadith which tells us a different story. Muqaddasi (a 10th-century geographer), according to Mottahedeh (Diversity and Pluralism in Islam), tells us that "there are 72 sects in heaven and one in hell, according to what he believes is a more sound line of transmission (isnad)" This shows that there is also variation in the Hadith reported on the 73 sects.

This discussion lead us to the realization that communal numbers and who 'owns' the truth are complex issues. We need to view Muslim diversity with respect, humility, responsibility and celebration rather than through the prism of sectarianism. The same applies to all human beings irrespective of caste, creed, gender, religion etc.

There should be no bloodshed just because a sect believes and practices its faith in a particular way or other way. Everyone is in search of truth. The Quran refers to this positive approach in several verses and one example is: **"If your Lord had willed, all the peoples of the earth would have believed in one. Will you (Muhammad) compel the people until they not be believers? It is not possible for any man to believe except by the will of Allah. He has cast impurity on the ignorant" (10:99-100). 5**

Some people have used the words heaven and hell in the sense of show off supremacy and greed. The followers take the word Muslim sects as a special guarantee that their sect will only go to heaven. Each sect proudly calls itself right and all others wrong. What is the policy where did it come from? The Prophet does not seem to have predicted this. And if Prophet Muhammad (peace and blessings of Allah be upon him) had predicted this, then one can understand that he knew that his followers would later go astray and get marred. The meaning is clear that Muslims should stop feeling proud and superior, and shall give due respect to all.

Because of all these types of Hadiths and non-cooperation's among each other's within Muslims, jealousy has entered in the Muslim society. Many fabricated Hadiths have become sources of such evils. Actually the Hadith was written 200 years after the death of Prophet Muhammad (peace and blessings of Allah be upon him). Different non authentic Hadith says different things.

I thank my mother, father and ALLAH who has provided me right education, made me experienced widely and showed me very closely the different types of evils, corruptions, difficult situations and irregularities in home, society, country and world. I have gone through every aspects of life, richness, toughness, poverty, big job, small job, fast, slow, comfort, pain, prosperity, happiness and depression. I have seen many people how and how much they get upset. I have seen very rich people becoming poor due to their bad deeds within just few years of their bad deeds. I have seen good and bad, Kindness and ugliness very closely. Many Muslims do not speak anything because of self-respect, shyness and family respect. Allah has created such a situation and made me write this book to bring the facts in front of everyone so that people return back to the original path of humanity as shown by our great Prophets. I am writing this book after seeing lots of pains and struggles so that the society relook within themselves and revive.

I remember when I was small boy and we used to go to Masjid and Ijtama and Milad ul Nabi. We used to hear from Maulanas the great activities of various Prophets. Maulana's used to give speeches of humanity, all the good deeds and practices of leading a good life. As a child, listening to the great stories of great Prophets and messengers of God, they used to become our heroes and role models. Parents living in joint family also had better control over the children. Parents also used to teach good moral conduct. We learned and practiced compassion, love and peace.

These days in Masjid or Ijtma or anywhere we only hear the hate speeches of "I / we are good and he/they are bad". One sect abuses other sects. During religious programme or ceremonies some Maulanas screams in such a way, as if they will start a fight from the mike itself. Worst of all is that even some sectarian Muslims have dared to put display boards at the entrance of some mosque that people of other sects are not allowed inside the mosque. How can a Muslim prevent other Muslims from entering a mosque to perform prayers? A mosque is a sacred place of worship and is not the property of any individual or any particular sect.

Actually during the translation of Quran people did not get success in changing the Quran. And judiciously the Quran was translated into different languages according to the originality. The word remains the same. We have seen earlier that Prophets Moses, David, Solomon and Jesus etc. brought revelations from God for humans to eradicate evils and spread humanity. In the same way God send Prophet Muhammad pbuh to eradicate evils from the Middle East and establish humanity. The revelations of the Prophets Moses, David and Jesus were seen to have been changed by their followers. That's why Allah sent the Quran with the words that no one can change the Quran. Like in Christianity the New Testament which was written about 200 hundred years after the death of Jesus. Similarly, the followers of Prophet Muhammad pbuh were unable to make changes in the Quran, so wrote the Hadiths according to their understanding, collections from people and through words of people in which many contradictory ideas also came. We have already seen that there are lots of controversies about the authenticity of different books of Hadith.

Now is the time to start introspecting and understand how evils and corruption have entered in our religion and sects, how we can rebuild the faith. For this, every faith has to be objectively tested by the truth. Supreme Power GOD is one so in Arabic Allah is one and is for all, so the essence of the messages sent by him through different messengers is the same. Truth is one, but wise explain it in many ways.

In the book Bhagavad-Gita Page 192 – 193 by Sarvepalli Radhakrishnan writes "O Lord, in every temple I see those who seeks you, in the different languages I have heard speaking, people praising you. Polytheism and Islam seeks you; every religion says that you are the one and unique; Because of your love, people pray in mosques and bells ring in Christian churches. Sometimes I go to the monastery and sometimes to the mosque, but you are the one I search for in the temple also.

Reference

1. Paola Garcia, The Salvation Principle of Tawakkul in Islam or Absolute Faith and Trust in God, November 15, 2020

2. https://insidearabia.com/the-liberating-principle-of-tawakkul-in-islam/

3. https://www.masjidtucson.org/God/trust_God_verses.html

4. https://Hadithanswers.com/73-sects-of-this-ummah/

5. https://www.siasat.pk/forums/threads/the-mystery-of-73-sects-by-jan-e-alam-khaki.

6. https://www.dawn.com/news/1035023

Chapter 23

Fatwa

Fatwa is an Arabic word which means "opinion" or "suggestion" given on a question or on any issue. The opinion or suggestions has influence from Sharia law. Fatwa is given only when a person or group seeks the advice from a qualified jurist (maulana or mufti) on any subject. The moulana or mufti gives suggestion or decision, but the question is on what basis do they give? The most authentic basis in this regard is the guidance from Quran Sharif and the second authentic is Hadith. Also sometimes it is taken from Prophet Muhammad pbuh life where he has given some advice to someone or in different issues or circumstances or he has presented any example through his conduct.

In due course of time, when Islam spread out of Arabia and after that many local traditions started showing their influence upon the Islamic law. Then many different sects were formed in Islam, Latter Muftis of all sects started giving different fatwas according to their own wish and will. This is the reason that today on one topic different types of fatwas are issued by different people. A common Muslim gets confused as to which fatwa is valid and which is illegitimate. Fatwa is just a suggestion or advice given by someone. Just like when we respect our elders then we follow their suggestions or advice. In case of difference of opinions in the fatwas given by different Muftis, an educated person takes the final decision easily according to the wisdom by using his discretionary power, but that section of the society, which has not been properly educated gets confused and often gets influenced by wrong fatwas. The situation has worsened to the extent that sometimes some clerics also mislead people by issuing false fatwas in personal and financial (property) matters for little benefits.

Muslims living in BHARAT are BHARATIYE citizens and are subject to BHARATIYE law. On the other hand, Muslims consider it their duty to follow the law of Sharia. Nowadays, most of the BHARATIYE Muslims are following the dual law. When the Muslims get benefits from Sharia law then they follow Sharia Law but when BHARATIYE Muslims get loss or suffer from Sharia Law then they go with Indian Penal Code. This dual policy is against the principle of ISLAM. If Muslims follow Sharia law then sharia law shall be followed by all Muslims in each and every matters.

Public or political fatwas are issued to form an opinion and a stand on doctrinal disputes, to legitimize government policies, or to clarify public grievances. Many a times it has been found that some Moulanas in BHARAT issue fatwas that to which party Muslims should vote and to whom to not. In a democratic country giving such fatwas is very wrong and it is clear violation of personal rights of the people.

Modern fatwa is marked by an increasing reliance on the process of ijtihad, i.e. making legal decisions based on an independent analysis in line with the opinion of earlier legal authorities (taqlid). While in the past muftis were associated with a particular school of law, in the 20th century many muftis began to assert their independence from traditional school of jurisprudence.

The most infamous result of the disregard for classical jurisprudence is the edicts of clerics regarding extremist. Some edicts support suicide bombings, indiscriminate killing of innocent people and declare some Muslims as unbelievers. Reforms have also given rise to fatwas that support notions such as gender equality and interest banking, but the process of reform has been very slow.

It is often seen in BHARAT that some Maulanas give wrong fatwas only for a little benefits. Once upon a time a brother got a false fatwa made from an Imam in the year 2010. Everyone in the locality and society knows and the Imam also must knew that the person is a big cheater and does all kinds of evils and corruption. At that time brother usurped the property and sold the land. For the sake of family respect, that person did not go to the court at that time. Like me many Muslims just for the sake of defamation and family respect does not go to court. Along with that, that Imam has also signed a duplicate will. Isn't this a serious matter of breach of law in ISLAM? Being an Imam, how did he get involved in those illegal activities? If that will was true then why didn't that Maulana discuss it with any brother or sister? And why hasn't that brother brought that will in front of everyone till now.

Now a days Muslims are going against the teachings of Prophet Muhammad (pbuh) only for little benefits. I have explained few in this book volume as a live example. I am pretty sure all these things are happening in almost all Muslim families in BHARAT. But people are not speaking because of shy, shame, defamation and respect. I am trying to bring the facts in front of everyone so that the evils can be eradicated from the society. Someone or the other has to come forward to show the mirror and bring back the misguided Muslims back on the right path of Islam.

Wrong or flexible fatwas give birth to too many evils and corruptions. How can any man justify any illegal act? The funniest thing is that no educated person takes the name of fatwa but less educated and illiterate people mostly use the name of fatwa. Muslims are ready to use any things to justify their wrong deeds and relate it with fatwa.

Many Muslim people go after fatwas or are ready to do anything to get any kind of disputes and decisions in their favour. The identity of Haq (rights) and Halal (legal) has been forgotten by Muslims. A question also arises that evils are present in other communities but I Why am I not quoting them? The answer is that first we have to improve ourselves then we should think about the evils of other. If I raise one finger on the other then three fingers automatically points towards us. I have heard from many Maulana that most of the literate Muslim people will go to hell because they have not propagated the correct teachings of Islam. Not raise voice against evils, wrong and bad deeds. Raising voice against illegitimate things is also a part of Iman. Today Muslim does not say anything even after seeing wrong things, it means that the community has become a living corpse.

Muftis should only give the fatwas free from their personal gains, selfishness, personal likes and dislikes, all kinds of discrimination and political influence. Sometimes people don't want to listen the facts and reality because they don't want to break their false notions.

Chapter 24
Jihad

Jihad is an Arabic word which literally means "struggle" or "strive" for humanity and existence. The word jihad occurs in several different contexts in the Quran. It includes various types of non-violent struggle for humanity, struggle to become a better human being. In the Islamic context almost all efforts which confirms personal and social life for the cause of humanity and peaceful existence as per the guidance of God can be called jihad. Such as the struggle against evil deed, the effort towards the moral betterment of human beings. 1, 2.

The Quran describes various types of jihad (struggle) and none of them allow terrorism or terrorist activities. **Jihad against Saitan is called the big jihad and jihad against the open enemy is known as the small jihad**. Prophet Muhammad pbuh explained Jihad on his return from war. "We are returning from the small jihad to the big jihad," he said. Means waging an open war is a small Jihad and avoiding evil in ordinary life is a big Jihad. This Jihad against oneself manifests itself in many ways. For example, **getting good and high education is a big Jihad**. Giving up vices, giving up smoking, giving up corruption, losing weight, overcoming cancer, learning skills, good parenting, living for others, giving up one's luxuries and desires are all forms of great Jihad.

The Quran clearly defines who is an "open enemy". The "open enemy" is not your government, people of another religion or your fellow citizens. The open enemy is anyone who are doing only unhuman activities and not letting you to live peacefully if you are right. The Quran allows Muslims to fight in this small jihad when dire circumstances arises which are only for self-defence and peaceful living.

The Quran clearly instructs Muslims not to attack any "churches, synagogues, temples and mosques". But can only fight in self-defence in dire circumstances. Quran also tells that a Muslim should immediately forgive the enemy if the attack stops. "And if they fight then fight with them until the oppression ends and they accept God freely". Also Prophet Muhammad (pbuh) strictly laid down the laws of war to prevent acts of terrorism and terror. No Harm to innocent human beings and livestock, damage to public property and greenery and forbid such acts which are against humanity. If a Muslim who takes the name of Jihad and harms innocents and does any such activity which is against humans and humanity is terrorism and is not in Islam. Terrorism has no place in Islam. Muslims just by name is not a true Muslim if he/she is not doing JIHAD within one self to be a true human.

The term jihad has been purposefully translated by few Muslims as "holy war". When Prophet Muhammad pbuh was helpless then only he took up arms for self-defence. But later many people misinterpreted it and misrepresented it as a means of propagating religion. The reality is that Prophet Muhammad pbuh was never in favour of forceful conversion. As it is written in **Quran - Chapter No. 2: 256 "There should be no compulsion in the matter of religion".**

Islamic scholars believe that out of **114 Surahs of Quran, 91 Surah's were revealed in Mecca and 23 Surah's in Medina**. It is found that 91 Surah's revealed in Mecca have only 5 verses related to Jihad while

24 Surah's revealed in Medina contain Jihad. There are 250 verses related to this. What is the reason for this? It can be concluded that in Mecca Muhammad was a social reformer, an accomplished fakir (a deep thinker) and a religious preacher. At that stage the purpose of Jihad for him was only to end unhuman practices and idol worship which was prevailing there. But in Medina Muhammad had to play three role simultaneously, the first one of a religious preacher, the second one of a social organizer and the third one of a ruler. These three roles could not be discharged simultaneously in the way of religious reformer of Mecca. There was a need to fight continuously against the invasions which they did.

The word Jihad in the Quran is a word with many meanings. During the Meccan period (610–622 CE), when the Prophet Muhammad pbuh received the revelation of the Quran in Mecca, emphasis was placed on the internal dimension of jihad, which refers to the practice of "endurance" by Muslims. To face the ups and downs of life and fight only against those who wanted to harm him. The Quran speaks of a jihad against pagan Mecca during the Meccan period (25:52), indicating a verbal struggle against those who rejected the message of Islam. In the Medinan period (622 AD – 632 AD), during which Muhammad received Quranic revelations in Medina, a new dimension of jihad emerged: fighting in self-defence against the aggression of Meccan oppressors known as kitl. In later literature—including the Hadith records of the Prophet's sayings and actions mystical commentaries on the Quran; These two main dimensions of more general mystical and didactic writings—jihad, sabr and qital—were named jihad al-nafs (inner spiritual struggle against the lower self) and jihad al-sa'if (physical combat with the sword) respectively.

Followings are the different types of Jihad:-

Jihad-e-nafs: killing and controlling one's senses, self-restraint.

Jihad-Bil-Qalam: Using the pen in support of the truth i.e. writing articles.

Jihad-Bil-Listan: Jihad with tongue in support of truth and raise voice against injustice.

Da'wat-e-Jihad: Call to fight in support of truth, Call to fight for the protection of truth.

Jihad al Akbar is a non-violent struggle

1. Efforts to fight against all the evils present within oneself and efforts to fight against such evils as manifested in the society.

2. Fighting against racial discrimination and striving for women's rights.

3. be a better student, be a better partner, be a better business partner and above all control your anger.

It should be noted that the Quran (2:190) explicitly forbids starting a war and allows fighting only against actual aggressors (60:7-8; 4:90). Although acknowledging political realism, many early Muslim jurists allowed wars to expand Muslim rule over non-Muslim territories. Military Jihad was announced only by legitimate leaders of Muslim politics. In addition, jurists cited statements from the Prophet Muhammad forbidding attacks on civilians and destruction of property. 3, 4

(Note: - Here we come to know that in order to expand Muslim rule some rulers and Muslim had called for war and linked it with Jihad. But **in real Islam Jihad is only a fight against devils within one's self**. In real Jihad we have to try and work for humanity.)

The concept of war which has been misinterpreted by the western world and few tyrant Muslims is totally wrong. And even some leaders and separatist groups have been misinterpreting the word Jihad. The effect of misinterpretation is that many innocent Muslims are falling prey to it and Islam is being brought into disrepute. Jihad in Islamic teaching provides positive effects if the original meaning as told by Prophet Muhammad (pbuh) is applied by Muslims. Due to wrong interpretations, the true spirit of Islam is dying and gradually all the impurities are entering. **A famous writer George Bernard Shaw said "Islam is the best religion but the followers of Islam are the worst".**

Jihad means fighting against one's own weaknesses, being morally virtuous and making sincere efforts to do good deeds and help improve society. When life is in danger during social reform and all options fails then war becomes the last option. It is clear here that Jihad is for good and only for improving oneself and improving society. Jihad is not a war of two religions. So first Muslims should do Jihad within themselves, in their home, family and society. War is the last option in Islam to stay alive only. That too Islamic law sets clear guidelines for the conduct of war and forbid acts of terrorism. The Quran provides detailed guidelines and rules regarding warfare, including who should fight (48:17, 9:91), when fighting should end (2:192), how to treat prisoners (47:4). It also stresses on proportionality in warfare. So those who ever talk about Jihad in Islam should first do Jihad within their own society and reform it not through fighting but through good deeds.

Now-a-days purposefully Jihad has been pushed towards terrorist acts. Many Muslims are being misled under the umbrella of religion. One big question is that why only poor students go to Madrasa? Does any government official/rich man or woman send their child to a madrasa for education? 99% only poor or orphans go to Madrasa. And usually when a boy reaches the age of 12 or 13 they start going to work for survival. Very few students complete the madrasa education and get a degree and become Qari or Mufti. Every Muslim parent whenever they get a chance they try their level best to send their kids to private school or good government school so that they can get contemporary education and become a capable human beings. Modern education is the latest and contemporary version of education that is taught in educational institutions. Contemporary education not only focuses on the core academic subjects of commerce, science and arts, but also aims at fostering critical thinking, life skills, value education, analytical skills and decision making skills in the students. All these were the teachings of Prophet Mohammad pbuh.

One special thing is that till date no student of any madrasa has become a big officer. In a rare case we have examples of one or two students becoming IAS officers who had madrasa base, but they latter left madrasa to pursue higher education of contemporary education system. It is difficult to survive without contemporary education. Now the time has come for all the Muslims to start thinking in the right way and practice the right teachings of Prophet Muhammad (pbuh) and do the right Jihad to improve themselves and do Jihad to eliminate the evil practices prevalent in Islam. A Muslim should have a Quran in one hand and a computer in the other hand, only then the society will come out of the shackles of oppressors.

BHARAT famous religious text book "Bhagavad Gita", which was said by "lord Krishna" on the battlefield. Shri Krishna is observed continuously motivating Arjuna to fight. The first satva-guna is a balanced state of knowledge and contentment. The second is Rajo-gun, which is the state of action and dualistic passion. The third is Tamo-gun, which is the state of ignorance and inertia. There are two options for a man to overcome worldly obstacles. First the alternative is to flee rather than confront those obstacles, this is the Tamo-guni state. The other option is to throw oneself in battle before him, this is the Rajo-guni state, which is needed for the threefold role of Prophet Muhammad in Medina. It was necessary. But when satva-guna predominates, then the purpose of that war is the establishment of truth, justice and peace. In the Hadith, what is called great Jihad means, that the conflict with passion is used to establish the ideal of peace with satva-guna?

In general even before and even today, we have the experience **that unrighteousness is always aggressive.** Gangs of criminals get organized very easily. But religion by nature cannot be aggressive. People in favour of humanity i.e. religion are **"good people", who are conscious of righteous conduct in life, but seeing the anger of the wicked on others, they keep quiet and do not dare to come forward and retaliate.** Lord Krishna does not like this gesture of righteous people. This is mere display of goodwill. In his view, there is no practical difference between evil people like Duryodhana of Kaurava side and good people like his supporters like Bhishma. Therefore, Shri Krishna Arjuna encourages him to fight against both Duryodhana and Bhishma.

When Prophet Muhammad Sahab pbuh was ordered to do Jihad during his stay in Madina, it only meant that he could start a war if necessary to stay alive and to propagate his faith. The aim of those war was always to restore peace. It is another matter that the consequences of war are always painful, and it results in the killing of innocents, the orphaning of women and children and the destitute of the elderly. In ancient times war was an age-religion. Today's era is not of war but of peaceful co-existence. "Vasudev kutumbkam". Today, the true meaning of Jihad can be accepted only as a "struggle against evils within oneself". Jihad in the form of any guerrilla warfare or direct attack is invalid in today's context. And these types of activities are totally against Islam. In Islam killing any innocent human is just like killing the whole mankind.

Reference

1. Roy Jackson (2014). What is Islamic philosophy? Routledge. P. 173. ISBN 978-1317814047. Jihad literally means 'struggle' which has many meanings, though often associated with warfare.

2. Asma Afsaruddin Jihad Islam Discussion

Chapter 25

Ghazwa e Hind

Ghazwa-e-Hind is a fictional word, it can also be called an idiom. Extremists use this idiom against BHARAT and purposefully associate it with Jihad. "Ghazwa" in Arabic refers to a war that is guided by faith rather than materialistic or territorial gain. This belief is largely a concept. The phrase was used by Muslim conquerors. There is nowhere mentions about Ghazwa-e-Hind anywhere in Quran. Also there is no concrete proof that Prophet Mohammad pbuh spoke about "Ghazwa-e-Hind". Probably someone has concocted it, so that benefits can be taken from it.

Of the many mistranslated words in Islamic terminology, the word "jihad" has been repeatedly misinterpreted and misused. Many ideologies and concepts in Islam have been distorted to a great extent based on baseless understanding of Jihad and Ghazwa e Hind is one of them. The term has been used for geopolitical gain and power. It gives a religious perspective to support radicalization by various rulers, religious establishments and extremist organizations. It is repeatedly cited by BHARAT enemies to make BHARATIYE Muslims questionable and suspected for their loyalty to the country, and to bring instability in BHARAT.

The word GHAZWA is derived from the word GHAZA which means to achieve something or to undertake a mission. Wars in Islam were fought even during the time of the Prophet but all of those were defensive in nature and commonly referred to as Ghazwa and Sarai (Sharia). Ghazwa refers to the battles in which the Holy Prophet (pbuh) himself took part, while Sharia (Sarai) refers to campaigns that were sent by the Holy Prophet, but he himself did not participate in them.

The Holy Quran strictly prohibits violence in the name of religion. It is absolutely neither allowed to attack anyone in order to propagate Islam nor openly or secretly harm those who do not follow Islam. The Holy Quran states that the killing of an innocent human being is equal to the killing of the entire humanity. Destruction of others worship structure or killing of non-Muslims or doing anything that harms the interest of any fellow human being is unacceptable in Islam, rather such acts of aggression and oppression are against the spirit of Islam. Actually Islam is a symbol of sacrifice, tolerance, peace and brotherhood with all human. Under no circumstances war is allowed, one can fight only for the sake of survival by following the rule of humanitarian. The rule of humanitarian is not to harm any innocent, not to attack anyone's religious place, not to destroy any tree or plantations, not to destroy any thing which is for the public use or which is bringing harmony in the environment.

Some scholars believe that if Ghazwa e Hind was a false or true prophecy, then that prophecy has already been fulfilled, when Mahmud ibn Sebuktegin (Ghaznavi) invaded BHARAT. After Mahmud Ghaznavi, invaders like Muhammad Ghori, Timur Lang, Zahiruddin Muhammad Babar, Nadir Shah, Ahmadshah Abdali etc. had fought in BHARAT. While some traitor and misguided people still believe that BHARAT victory is not yet completed. Historian Ibn Kathir in his book Al-Bidaya van-Nihaya under this prophecy included Ghaznavi's attack on the Somnath temple. 2

Hafiz ibn Kathir in his book "Al Bidaya Van Nihya" discusses the Hadith of Ghazwa-i-Hind and included the campaigns of Muhammad bin Qasim, Mahmud bin Subughtagin (Mahmud Ghaznavi) and many other kings. He interpreted these Hadiths to include China and Central Asia, in addition, Mahmud Ghori, Mughals, Turks and armies coming from Central Asia also tried to conquer Hind. 3

As per the history and by considering all the facts with open eyes and without being biased it is concluded that some one of the chiefs writing at that time must have included the words Ghazwa-e-Hind, either from his own idea or under the influence of the king for getting benefits in the expansion of their kingdom. So that the kings, people and warriors at that time gets motivation to go towards BHARATIYE subcontinents as BHARAT was very rich that time. The main objective would have been to inspire the warriors to attack BHARAT and rule BHARAT from within and outside. It was around the 10th and 11th century and before that there were several attempts by the Turks to capture BHARAT but they failed. They were able to expand their kingdom up to the west of the Indus River in the 8th century by war against King Dahir of Sindh. But the Arabs and Turks were unable to enter the mainland of BHARAT. So someone must have written Ghazwa-e-Hind to inspire people and warriors.

Now the biggest question is that we know that till date this fabricated Hadith is being miss understood by some Muslims that one day BHARAT will be under Ghazwa e Hind. It is clarified that Hadith is not the words of Quran. That's why Ghazwa-e-Hind is not a topic of discussion. Now it has no relevance in present day BHARAT. Many people are still using this Ghazwa-e-Hind to propagate and deceive the people and trying to weaken BHARAT. The people of enemy country who do not have power to stand in front of BHARAT are using these non-relevant words among the few uneducated and poor Muslims of BHARAT and misleading them to die in the name of religion. Whereas love for one's motherland is an important part of Islam. If Muslim is not loving his or her mother land then they are not a Muslim.

Only for the name shake they are Muslims. Prophet Mohammad pbuh has propagated that a Muslims has to love ones mother land and has to obey the rules and regulations of their country.

Initially Islam in BHARAT did not spread by the sword. Initially Islam spread by the principle of love, goodness, equality and truth in the 7th century AD during the life time of Prophet Mohammed pbuh. The first Muslims in BHARAT came to Gujarat coast and Malabar Coast as a trade delegation. Muslim pilgrims used to go for Haj, the first ship to go for haj was seen on the BHARAT coast in 630 AD during the life time of Prophet Mohammad pbuh. Cheramun Jumma Masjid in Malabar and Juni Masjid in Gujarat was built with love and compassion peacefully by the help of Bhartiye people. And for centuries Muslims in BHARAT used to live in peace and dignity under Hindu Kings.

In the name of Ghazwa-e-Hind the enemies of our country are misleading some of our youth and inciting them to die in the name of religion. Misguided leaders say that if you die for Ghazwa-e-Hind, you will get the reward of 72 Hoors in heaven. I ask that suppose if a woman dies in Ghazwa-e-Hind, what will she get in heaven? The man will get the hoors and the woman will get nothing.

Life is too short and fast, due to globalization this world has become too small. Be kind, patience and love human regardless of any caste, creed or religion. All people should love and respect each other. If you love others, Allah will shower his blessings and make others to love you.

It is the fault of Muslims that they think that it is the job of Maulanas only to decide and take any decisions related to religion. Everyone should understand the Holy Quran and try to live according to the message of Prophet Muhammad (pbuh). Why to blame only the Maulanas? All Muslims are guilty because Allah has given everyone the right to education, so why don't everyone study Quran and understand its true meaning. The first word of Allah that came in Quran is "iqra" which means read. Allah says to read.

It is the duty of all the Muslims of BHARAT to follow the path shown by Prophet Muhammad (pbuh) and not fall into the hands of BHARAT external or internal enemies. The concept of brotherhood just for name should be stopped. If at present own brothers or sisters are not giving rights to each other, then it is absolutely wrong to talk of universal brotherhood. Nowadays this word Ghazwa-e-Hind is being used a lot by terrorist groups. Actually the word Ghazwa-e-Hind is a myth. The enemies of BHARAT are misleading the Muslim youth to fulfil their nefarious desire to weaken BHARAT.

Muslims should feel proud to be a BHARATIYE and a true follower of Islam, which is "Hubbul Watan Minal Imaan." We all have to do our best as Abdul Hamid did and thousands and lakhs of Muslims have done earlier. Today youngsters needs to be careful from wrong people who mislead them. Islam is not so weak that Muslims resort to wrong doing. All Muslims should make their character like that of Prophet Mohammad pbuh to love all humans and even enemies. That's why this word Ghazwa-e-Hind has to be rejected. This word was never right and will never be right.

Jamiat scholar Maulana Mufti Salman Mansoorpuri has asserted that the enemy country is wrongly and mischievously linking the word to its differences with BHARAT. Maulana Mahmood Madani also disclosed this at an Observer Research Foundation (ORF) conference and renewed interest in the religious interpretation of the phrase.

Some terror groups are using Ghazwa-e-Hind as a Hadith to recruit, fund and justify their audacious terror attacks as a religious holy war against BHARAT. Some organizations falsely propagate that Jihad against BHARAT is considered sacred in Islam and that those participating in it [the "fight against the infidels] will be given easy entry into heaven". These claims have been rejected by Maulana Mufti Salman Mansoorpuri, and argued that no predictions and statements shall be used for political or material gain.

According to Mansoorpuri, there are many Hadiths mentioning the Ghazwa-i-Hind and its virtues, but the chain of narrators is very weak, confusing and relies on little known ones in the authentic collection of Hadith. The Narrator's Role is very much questionable.

It is important to understand how the Hadiths were collected and preserved. A Hadith consists of two parts - the matan (text) and the isnad (narrator's chain). A text may sound logical and reasonable, but it requires an authentic isnad with reliable narrators to be acceptable. During the Prophet's lifetime and after his death, his companions used to quote his sayings. The successors (tabi'un) followed suit; some of them quoted the Prophet through companions, while others omitted intermediate authority – such Hadith were known as mursal (loose).

We all have seen in the earlier chapter Hadith that Ismail al-Bukhari collected about 600000 Hadiths from more than 1000 scholars, of which he accepted only 7275 as authentic and arranged them in 93 chapters. Means only 1.2% Hadith is correct i.e. authentic.

Mansoorpuri argues that in addition to the faulty chain of narrators of the Ghazwa-i-Hind Hadith, it is also spoken in its entirety without indication of a specific time for its occurrence. He says, there are three possibilities as to which war is being referred to:

1. The fighting that took place in the BHARAT subcontinent in the early and middle ages of Islam, due to which the Muslims ruled the country for a long time. Like the battles fought by Muhammad bin Qasim and Mahmud Ghaznavi.

2. Another possibility is that the word 'Hind' mentioned in the Hadith may not refer specifically to BHARAT. Instead, it may

refer to HIND Territory and surrounding areas, specifically Basra and its neighbouring places AL HINDIYA, which is in present-day Iraq. This view is supported by some statements of other Companions who used to say: "We interpret Hind as Basra." Al Hindiya is a place that is still in Iraq today.

According to this explanation, Mansoorpuri adds, these Hadiths may refer to battles fought against Iran during the early period of Islam.

3. The third possibility is that the war mentioned in these Hadiths has not happened yet. Instead, it would occur during the period of the re-emergence of Christ and the Mahdi as mentioned in Islamic tradition.

"The above description makes it clear that it is completely wrong to exhort present-day Muslims in the BHARAT subcontinent for Jihad on the basis of Hadiths relating to Ghazwa al-Hind." 4

According to the principles of Muslim religion, the world is divided into two parts, one is the country where Muslims living are in majority and is called Darul Islam ruled by Muslim, and the other is Darul Harb where Muslims live but non-Muslims rule.

Today's BHARAT neighbouring countries like Pakistan, Iran, Bangladesh and Iraq are called Islamic countries but at the same time we should remember that many of these countries also have republics before their names, which means democracy. BHARAT is also having democracy. This means that people living in BHARAT whether Muslim or of any other religious sect can become the rulers of BHARAT. A. P. J. Abdul Kalam, who was a Muslim by religion, has been the President of BHARAT.

Ashraf Madani of Jamaitul Ul Ulema-e-Hind writes, is it possible that Pakistan will rule BHARAT? There is nothing like that. This is just a wall being raised by foreign Muslims against BHARAT Muslims to weaken Bharat.

Yunus Al Gohar author and co-founder of the British Messiah Foundation writes that people are being misled by associating Ghazwa-e-Hind with Hadith. Arif Mohammad Khan, the Governor, and writes in the name of Ghazwa-e-Hind in the country a false campaign is being run. The purpose of this is to fill the minds of the people that BHARAT will break into pieces. This is not possible.

The rumour of "Gajwa e Hind" is a part of terrorists' conspiracy to harass BHARATIYE Muslims. They want to divide BHARAT into pieces again in the name of religion and caste. Unfortunately, some anti-nationals who says that Bharat Tere Tukde Honge are living in BHARAT as agents. BHARATIYE Muslims should think for themselves that what was their personality in United BHARAT, when Maulana Abul Kalam Azad, Khan Abdul Ghaffar Khan and Ashfaq Ullah were here. Freedom lovers were born, today Muslims of United BHARAT are divided into three parts, Pakistani Muslims, Hindustani Muslims and Bangladeshi Muslims. Due to division and diversion from the right path as shown by Prophet Mohammad pbuh all these Muslims are in a pathetic situation.

If it is believed that regions which are different from each other geographically and in every way, can be tied into one on the basis of religion, then there is no bigger lie than that. It is true that Islam wanted to establish a society that transcends caste, linguistic, economic and political boundaries. But history has proved that after the first few century, Islam was able to unite all Muslims on the basis of religion alone. Could not organize the countries into a single unit. This is the fact and reality even today in Middle East look how many countries are there but even fighting within themselves.

So what was the condition in the past is the condition even today. Within just 25 years of the partition of BHARAT, the Muslims of West Pakistan committed countless heinous crimes against the Muslims of East Pakistan their own counterpart. And that part of Pakistan broke away and became Bangladesh an independent country. What is the present condition of Pakistan itself today? How one community is torturing the other community and how it has reduced its own people to the condition of beggars, it is not hidden. Why the great idea of Muslim brotherhood is not able to unite Shias and Sunnis?

I conclude this by a speech of Maulana Abul Kalam Azad at the Ramgarh session of the Indian National Congress on March 27, 1940. Maulana Azad had said "I am a Muslim and feel proud that I am a Muslim. Thirteen hundred years of glorious tradition of Islam has come to my share. I am not ready to let even a small part of it go away. The teachings of Islam, the date of Islam, the methods and arts of Islam, the culture of Islam is mine. Wealth is an asset and it is my duty to protect it. Being a Muslim, I have a special importance in the religious and cultural sphere and I cannot tolerate anyone interfering in it. I also feel that which has been created by the realities of my life. The spirit of Islam does not stop me from this and guides me on the way. I feel with pride that I am a BHARATIYE. I am a part of an integral nation of BHARAT. I am such an element without which the statue of its greatness remains incomplete. I am a component of its structure. I can never remain indifferent to this claim of mine.

Reference

1.   https://lightofislam.in/the-truth-about-gazwa-e-hind/

2.   https://daiyah.fandom.com/wiki/Ghazwa-e-Hind

3.   http://khilafah.daiyah.cf/the-prophecy-of-gazwatul-hind-conquest-of-BHARAT -by-Muslims.html

4. Everyone misinterprets Ghazwa-e-Hind, but a Jamiat scholar explains what it really means (theprint.in) News published in The Print news dated October 7, 2019 at 09:40 am

4. Everyone misinterprets Ghazwa-e-Hind, but a Jamiat scholar explains what it really means (theprint.in) News published in The Print news dated October 7, 2019 at 09:40 am

Chapter 26

Treatment with Violators from the Eyes of Quran

Dealing with those who violate human values from the point view of Quran

Surah Anam - Ayat 108 [6:108] translation by Ole Muhammad Farooq Khan and Muhammad Ahmad **"Do not use abusive words towards those whom they call upon other than Allah.** Otherwise they may go beyond their limits and start using abusive words towards Allah out of ignorance. In the same way we have made its deeds pleasant for every community. At last they have to return to their Lord. At that time he will tell them". 1

It is clearly mentioned in the verse of Quran that do not use bad language for anyone or do not abuse those who calls or worship other than Allah. Least the non-believers stoop so low by using abusive words that the non-believers, out of ignorance start abusing Allah and His Prophets. Allah has sent his messages among different groups/tribes/ societies through his messengers or avatars or incarnations to do good deeds. And in the end even the unbelievers will have to return to the GOD.

The Holy Quran only gives the message of love and peace. Many fabricated Hadiths shall be avoided. All people shall read and understand Quran thoroughly, follow and implement it completely and be progressive. Prophet Muhammad (Sallallahu Alaihi Wasallam) loved even non-believers. During the life time of Prophet Muhammad pbuh no tax was taken from the non-believers. At one place, there is a description in a Hadith that in a letter of Prophet Mohammad pbuh mention of Jizya has come, but according to some Islamic scholars it has been said about that incident that the letter of the Prophet pbuh was tampered and later some kings used it according to their wish and needs and to full fill their desire. Later kings started collecting taxes from non-Muslims to meet the expenses of their army. In the name of religion, the then kings used their powers. Any work that is against humanity is against religion, all religions say and accept that the supreme God is one for all and all humans are creation of one God. Prophet Mohammad (pbuh) preached humanity and through self-practice of goodness established and propagated the religion of Islam by love and peace. Prophet Muhammad (pbuh) fought only for self-defence. He never fought a war to spread Islam, yes he definitely fought a war for humanity.

SURAH AL-TAWBAHHH CHAPTER 9 REPENTANCE, AL-TAWBAHH 129 verses

The Surah declares for all time that Allah gave opportunity to his Prophets, Migrants and Helper Companions and to the believers to repent; And it offers equal opportunities to the unbelievers and the hypocrites, provided they forever give up enmity and duplicity; And which actually demonstrates the believability of this proposition in command of God's forgiveness for the repentant idolaters who fought the believers at a place called Hunayn.

Its name is mentioned in verse 3 and verse 5 by the name of "repentance" (Tawbahh) the surah opens by reporting the severance of the treaty with the idolaters as they broke it, but the bulk of the surah deals with preparation and recruitment. The hypocrites and those who stayed behind and failed to support the Prophet Muhammad pbuh for Tabūk's campaign are condemned. It is the only Surah that **does not begin with "Bismillah".** Because it is written about killing humans, it is written about unrest. Allah does not want to associate his name with any kind of violence or unhuman work. That's why this Surah of Quran does not start with Bismillah Heer Rahmanir Rahim that is Islam does not support violence. Actually no religion or sects supports violence.

The Surah is also known as: Dispensation, Immunity. Verse numbers 4, 5, and 6 are as follows: -

Translation of 4 (except the polytheists with whom you have made a treaty, and who have not violated [its terms] with you, nor supported anyone against you. So fulfil the treaty with them [to the end] Verily Allah loves all).

Translation of 5 Then, when the holy month (hajj) have passed, kill the polytheists wherever you find them, capture them and besiege them and wait for them everywhere. But if they repent and allow you to maintain the prayer and pay the zakat, then release them. Verily Allah is Forgiving, Merciful.

Translation of 6: If a polytheist seeks refuge with you, give him refuge, then recite the word of Allah to him. Then take them to safe place. This is because they are a people who do not know and do not understand.

Here it is clearly mentioned about the disbelievers of that time only, who violated the peace treaty for Hajj and Umrah in Mecca after the sixth year of migration to Medina. A treaty was signed between Prophet Muhammad pbuh and the people of Mecca to allow the followers of Prophet Muhammad pbuh of Medina to perform Hajj and Umrah peacefully every year without any hindrance. It has nothing to do with all unbelievers in other places or at any time. Also, it is clearly written that if those who do not believe in Islam apologize, then forgive them and Send to the safe place. But some people have misinterpreted the great holy book Quran without understanding its real meaning and true spirit. The Quran does not ask to force non-believers to convert and accept the religion of Islam. All this was happening during the life of Prophet Muhammad (peace and blessings of Allah be upon him). It clearly means that Prophet Muhammad pbuh never forced anyone to accept Islam, yes he delivered the message of God, just like all the approximately 124000 messengers and Prophets did. It was the goodness of Prophet Muhammad pbuh because of which people accepted the religion of Islam.

Why is Bismillah not in Surah Tawbahh? Because in it, a very harsh ultimatum was given to the infidels (violators) of that time. It talks about violence, punishment and war, all these are unhuman. That's why Allah does not want to use his name in any such work which is against humanity or hurts anyone. Violence and all types of war is against humanity. That's why Bismillah Hir Rahmanir Rahim is not used in this Surah. We can only fight war for our existence, which is justified and is mentioned in all religious book.

Today, if any Muslims fights or pelts stones on any minor issue then he is not a True Muslim. Because Allah does not like violence. ISLAM itself means peace. But Muslims have distorted ISLAM. If there is any issue or problem then both sides can sit, discuss and solve the issue. One thing has to be adopted in life to live peacefully be that "some things have to be ignored and tolerated, some small sacrifices have to be made. One has to be patience and one has to rely completely on Allah.

In fact that treaty is known as the Treaty of Hudaibiyyah. (Treaty of Hudaibiyyah)

The story is as follows: - The Prophet (PBUH) had a dream that he was performing Hajj. When he mentioned this to his companions about 1400 of them happily agreed to join the Prophet for Umrah. It was the sixth year after the Prophet's migration to Medina. The Prophet and his companions travelled from Medina to Mecca and stayed at a place outside the city of Mecca near Hudaibiyyah. People from all over the world were allowed to visit Mecca and worship according to their choice and wish during the holy month without any permission. Yet for peace Prophet Muhammad pbuh sent his message to the Quraysh seeking permission to perform the Umrah of the Kaaba in the city of Mecca. Because the people of the Quraysh tribe who were the relatives of the Prophet Muhammad had a harsh relationship with the Prophet, and the Prophet did not wanted any quarrel with them.

But the Quraysh instead of allowing for Umrah sent an army to fight Prophet Muhammad. The companions told the army that they had not come to fight but to perform Umrah peacefully. After performing Umrah they will return back to Madinah. On the other hand, Usman went into the city to convince the Quraysh, but Usman was taken into custody and this message spread like a fire. The companions of the Prophet started preparations of war for the release of Usman. Meanwhile Usman was released and the Quraysh came to negotiate a treaty with the Prophet Muhammad pbuh.

The Quraysh asked the Prophet (PBUH) to agree to their demands. The gist of the treaty was this: Muslims would return this year without performing Umrah, in the coming year the Prophet (PBUH) could come with his companions. If a person from Quraysh goes to Muhammad (i.e. accepts Islam) without the permission of his guardian, Muhammad will return him to them, but if a person from Muhammad comes to Quraysh, he will not be returned to Medina. The Prophet (PBUH) accepted the demands of the Quraysh, this is commonly known as the Treaty of Hudaibiyyah. But later the Meccans violated the treaty, and then came the revelation of Surah al-Tawbah and the message of war, which was only for that time and for those who violated the treaty. Fight only those people who were violating the commitment and peace. Today it is necessary to learn from that war that every possible effort should be made to establish peace, as Prophet Sahab and Hazrat Usman had done.

So the above verse of Surah Al Tawbah is true, fight only as a last resort, but it gives a clear message to deal (peacefully) with the enemy if they surrender.

In Surah Tawbah Chapter 9 Verse 123, the Surah talks about the fight with the non-believers of that time, who violated the treaty, is as follows,

O you who believe, fight those who are close to you from among the infidels and make them hard on you. And know that Allah is with the righteous. Sahih International

[9:123] Believers! Fight the unbelievers who are around you; and they find hardness in you. Know that Allah is with the one who fears Allah. Tafim-Ul-Quran - Abul Ala Maududi

It is written here to fight against the unbelievers. But why and when Allah has told to fight, it is explained in this chapter as follows:-

9:13 in Surah Tawbahh

Will you not fight those who broke their oath and conspired to expel the Messenger, and they were the ones who started (the fight) against you for the first time? Are you afraid of them? But Allah has a greater right than that you should fear Him, if you are believers. — Mufti Taqi Usmani

Will you not fight those who broke their oath and determined to expel the Messenger, and they attacked you the first? Are you afraid of them? But Allah has more authority than you to fear Him, if you are [truly] believers. Sahih International

[9:13] Will you not fight those who broke their vows and did whatever they could to drive away the Messenger and started hostilities against you? Are you afraid of them? Surely Allah has a greater right than that, if you are a true believer then fear Him. - Tafim-ul-Quran - Abul Ala Maududi 2

In fact, Quran talks about love, reconciliation and peace and fighting is the last resort when there is no other option left.

Surah Al Mumtahanah Surah Al Mumtahanah

This Surah tells how to deal with the enemy and how to deal with non-Muslims. Surah No. 60 verse no. 7,8 and 9 translation are as follows:

60:7 In time, may Allah bring about goodwill between you and those of you whom you now regard as enemies. Because Allah is most capable, Allah is the most forgiving, most merciful. - Dr. Mustafa Khattab.

60:8 Allah does not forbid you to deal kindly and justly with those who have neither fought you nor driven you from their homes. Surely Allah loves the righteous. - Dr. Mustafa Khattab, The Clear Quran

60:9 Allah forbids you to befriend only those who have broken "your" faith and fought you, driven you from your homes, or supported "others" in doing so. And the one who makes them his friend, then he is the 'true' oppressor. - Dr. Mustafa Khattab, The Clear Quran

In all the above verses we see that Allah is asking to live in peace and respect all the disbelievers who have not harmed you. Don't fight with people who are not harming you. Treat all people equally because all human beings are the creation of Allah. Then I say who are we to say that unbelievers are bad. Here the Surah also comes in the context of Surah Kafirun. "Lakum deenakum wa liya deen" (for you is your religion and for me is my religion). Those who are not harming non-believing Muslims are worthy of friendship and those who are against Muslims should also be given respect, love and be assured of peace.3

Surah Fussilat

This Surah Fusilat asks non-believers to live in love and peace. Prophet Mohammad pbuh who was alone during his life time and every Qureshi wanted to kill him, Prophet Mohammad pbuh through his behaviour made all his enemy his friend.

"Good and evil cannot be equal." (Verse 34) The followers of the divine message cannot return evil like this. A good deed cannot equal its effect or value to a bad one. Endurance, tolerance and rising above the desire to return evil ultimately bring people to their senses. Their earlier harshness softens and they become friendly: "Repel evil with that which is better, and that which is your enemy will become as close to you as a true friend." (Verse 34)

This rule proves true in most cases: a stormy attitude will be replaced by calmness, anger by cordiality, and arrogance by humility. All this can result in a kind word, a soft tone and a smile in the face of the anger of the person whose anger gets the better of him.

Due to the good behaviour of a person, one day even the enemy becomes his devoted friend. Because it seems that I am throwing pebbles at him and he is giving me flowers in return. Therefore it is the duty of all Muslims to be true Muslims and not oppressors. 4

Surah Al Furqan Chapter 25 Verse 63

This Surah of Quran also tells how to deal with unbelievers or enemies.

25:63 The servants of the Most Gracious are those who walk humbly on the earth and when the ignorant speak to them, they answer in peace. — Mufti Taqi Usmani

The (faithful) slaves of the Beneficent are those who walk humbly on the earth, and when the fool addresses them they answer: Peace; Pickthall

And the servants of (Allah) are those who walk humbly on the earth, and when the ignorant address them, they say, "Peace!".—Yusuf Alik

And the servants of the Most Merciful are those who walk smoothly on the earth, and when the ignorant address them harshly, they utter words of peace. Sahih International

The true servants of the Merciful (Allah) are those who walk humbly and slowly on the earth and when the fool addresses them, they simply say: "Peace be upon you". Tafim-ul-Quran - Abul Ala Maududi

So if the Quran says to love even the enemy, then who are the present few Muslims who disobey the Quran. Yes if the enemy wants to harm, then fight and defeat the enemy, says Quran. But the best option is to avoid war and enmity. 5

Many times we see that some verses of Quran are misinterpreted by some people in other language under someone's influence or to fulfil some wrong or someone's wish. Muslim youths are misled by those translations. We see in history that due to the goodness and teachings in Islam during the lifetime of Prophet Mohammad (pbuh) Islam reached different parts of the world peacefully by winning the hearts of human beings. We can see from the Quran and all the incidents of the Messengers of Allah that love and peace were taught.

There is a true example about Prophet Muhammad (pbuh) that daily garbage was thrown upon him by an old Jewish woman. But one day when she did not throw dirt upon the Prophet, Prophet

Muhammad (pbuh) went inside that woman's house. Prophet saw that she was suffering from illness. The Prophet brought some medicines and water for her, then she wept and asked for forgiveness from the Prophet. Prophet Muhammad pbuh won her heart by love and compassion. All Muslims should follow the path shown by Prophet Mohammad pbuh and try to remove evil practices in Islam. The actions of Muslims should be such that they win the hearts of all human beings.

Reference

1. https://www.islamicfinder.org/quran/surah-al-anaam/118/?translation=hindi-muhammad-farooq-khan-and-muhammad-ahmed&language=id

2. https://islamstory.com/en/article/3409208/Miracle-at-Hudaybiyyyah:-Prophet's-Visionary-Decision

3. https://quran.com/60

4. https://quran.com/41/34?translations=18,19,20,21,85,95,22,84,101

5. https://quran.com/25/63

Chapter 27

KAFIR

"Kafir" is an Arabic word meaning a person who denies the authority of God. The word is often translated as "pagan", "reject", "unbeliever", and "disbeliever". The word is used in different ways in different places in the Quran, with the most basic meaning being "ungrateful" to God.

Some misguided Muslims see infidels as enemies of Muslims and believe that God will punish them for this by putting them in Hell. What is at stake here is not just social harmony, but theology as well. Islam never teaches hatred. All of these themes can be found in the Quran, but we must not forget that there was a context for these verses. The infidels are mentioned in the Quran primarily as polytheists. Condemning these infidels, the Quran urges Muslims to understand and see the nuances between them and other non-Muslims. One verse says: "God asks you to deal kindly and justly with a person who has not fought you or driven you out of your homes for your faith and religion." 1, 2.

The Quran has made a clear distinction between polytheists and infidels, logically speaking we can only say that there are some who are infidels even among believers. So the word Kafir sometimes becomes a very confusing word. Fighting is permitted in Islam only to save/protect one's life and not for any other reason. The faith of the oppressor and the oppressed is unimportant. Those who fight to protect the weak and the oppressed, they fight for humanity and they are the believers.

God is one and is for all the people of the world. The Quran says: "Whoever call Allah/God (by whatever name) does good, he will receive from his God his reward; there will be no fear for them, no sorrow" (2:112).

The supreme power is only one i.e. GOD. God only recognizes the good deeds of people. There are people in all religions and sects who stand for justice and against oppression, those who are in love with God. We find that a Muslim can also be a Kafir who commits Kufr i.e. who does not follow the path of Prophet Mohammad pbuh. No one becomes a true Muslim just by reciting Kalma and using Muslim name. It is the duty of Muslims in Islam to promote co-operation with all people of other religion and sects.

Muslims should not be victims of some wrong religious people or leaders who uses Muslims for their benefit. The purpose of leadership shall be to bring the misguided into the right path, all together to find a solution to the current malaise of growing fundamentalism among the community.

The opposite word for Kafir is Imaan or faith. Prophet Muhammad pbuh also said to spread the authority of law and the rights of humanity. Let all people unite within Muslim community and try to stop all the evils and corruptions in the society. Now-a-days Haji, Mufti and Maulana uses the word Kafir to condemn other sects within Islam also. This has become dangerous for the society and country as this has become a source of hatred within the community and this hatred is slowly spoiling the whole society. Who is responsible for these things? This is a serious matter of discussion and needs special attention?

I will share one interesting incident, after the first lock down in 2020 I went to Hazaribagh and was sitting at a grocery shop where people were coming to purchase from the shop. There some people were talking in the shop that the imam of the mosque has said to stay away from non-believers because if you associate with infidels you will lose your faith and Corona will attack you. I asked till when and where will you stop talking and meeting the infidels. Is it possible? Wherever you go in BHARAT, you will have to meet people of other religions and sects and work together. I said that now a days many Imams call Muslims of other sects as Kafirs. So non-Muslims are infidels and there are infidels even among Muslims. That means there are infidels everywhere, so is it possible to live life without infidels. The man remained silent and argued, but finally he surrendered. I said Imam has misinterpreted the message which was given by W.H.O. to every country. During Corona call was to be clean and maintain social distance and avoid going out without any emergency work. This is what all the messengers of God taught about cleanliness and not to roam around anywhere without any work.

Till when people will be fooled by these type of religious leaders and some political parties who do not even have proper knowledge of Islam and who want to keep community in darkness. These people are not true Muslims. They have forgotten the words of Prophet Muhammad (peace and blessings of Allah be upon him) that if you have to go too far-away places for education, then go to that far-away place to get good education. Prophet Muhammad pbuh wanted everyone to develop and without education no development is possible. Education means to acquire knowledge not just to get degree but for gaining proper knowledge and become wise. Knowledge gives success. And according to the times contemporary education is the education. That's why Science has discovered many things present in the Quran written 1400 years ago. That is, the Quran also approves many of the latest technologies. New discoveries are being made in science. Clinging to some traditional education is taking away the Muslim community from modern innovations. If one understand Quran properly, then that person will go towards contemporary education. Today is the era of computers, but science has not stopped here, it will go further on and on. It will continue to grow and will continue to move forward. Muslims will have to open their eyes and come forward and has to walk step by step with the world.

Reference

1. Who is Akyol Mustafa, the 'Kafir'? What is at stake here is not just social harmony, but sensible theology. November 4, 2019

2. https://www.cato.org/publications/commentary/who-kafir

Chapter 28
Surah Kafirun

"Surah Kafirun" is the 109th Surah of the Holy Quran. Its meaning in English is "The Disbeliever" and it has 6 verses...

The Quran says: "Do not despise the deities that people worship besides Allah, otherwise out of ignorance they will begin to despise Allah out of envy."

The verses of Surah Kafirun are as follows: - Surah Al Kafirun (The Disbeliever)

Bismillah Heer Rahmanir Rahim (I begin in the name of Allah, the Most Gracious and the Most Merciful)

Another way we can translate this is "I begin in the name of Allah, the Most Merciful." Here it can be seen that the same line is translated with different ways. But both have the same meaning.

Kul ya Ayyuhal Kafiroon (Say, "O disbelievers)

La Abudu Maa Ta Budoon (What you worship, I do not worship.)

Wa la antum abiduna maa abud (Nor do you worship that which we worship)

Wa la aana abidum ma abattum (Neither will I be a worshiper of that which you worship.)

Wa la antum abedum maa abud. (Nor will you worship that which I worship.)

Lakum Dinakum Va Liya Din (To you is your religion, and to me is my religion.)

In above verses it is clearly written about different religions and sects, these are the words of Quran and not of any Hadith.

The translation of kafirun is unbeliever. The word Kafir is derived from this word. They may have a different name of GOD and may follow a different path. That person may be wrong or right it is for that person to decide. It simply means that the Kafir takes a different route to reach the truth i.e. God. Just like all the rivers flow separately but finally goes into the ocean. If you want to go to Delhi, you can use a plane, train or motor vehicle. It is up to you to choose how to reach the destination.

Surah Kafirun clearly states that "Kul ya Ayyuhal Kafiron means, O infidels. It means that one who does not believe in Quran or Prophet Muhammad (peace and blessings of Allah be upon him) is a Kafir. There is nothing wrong if they are following other paths of higher attachment. The right path has been shown by different messengers/ Avatars of the GOD in different parts of the world at different times in different ages. It simply means that the person who does good deeds and work for the betterment of humanity then he is a good person either he is a Muslim or a Kafir. Just as some Muslims are bad, similarly some infidels can also be bad if they are not following the teachings of their messengers or Avatars properly. The messeages of all the 124000 prophets are same that is of humanity. So Prophet Muhammad (pbuh) said that what we are worshiping is not worshiped by the infidels and what the infidels are worshiping is not worshiped by Muslims. So my religion is mine and his religion is his.

Let us see an example, in a house many times husband and wife do not have a common opinion on certain points, sometimes wife does not trust husband, sometimes children do not trust parents, sometimes brothers do not trust each other. The own sisters do not trust each other. At some point friends don't believe the other friend. There is difference of opinion among people. Even sometimes each one deceives each other's. Nevertheless, everyone leaves the differences and lives together. People sometimes quarrel in the house on disbelieving upon some topics or things. That doesn't means that they become enemy for ever.

If there are some points of mistrust in a house then how can we expect that in a large society everyone will trust each other or only one person? As there are different languages to communicate, there are different paths to follow. People call the different path of humanity as a sects. If Prophet Mohammad pbuh has given respect to other religions, then who are we to insult other religion or sects. We cannot say that I am right and they are wrong. It is wrong to say that you have to trust me or I will kill you. It is the right given by Allah to believe or not to believe in certain things or other things. But the ultimate objective shall be of humanity only.

Since the beginning of civilization, God has sent about 124000 messengers or Avatars in different parts of this world among different communities and in different eras. And it is clearly mentioned by Prophet Muhammad (pbuh) that all the messengers of God eradicated the evils and corruption prevalent in the societies at that time. And the followers followed the teachings of those messengers and their generations followed it. Later some followers or other brought distortion in the religion to fulfil their selfish personal desires and wishes. So Allah send Prophets one after another.

The Surah says "La Abudu Maa Ta Budoon" (I do not worship that which you worship)" So there are different path of salvation. It is the birth right of a person to follow any path of salvation.

Then it says "wa la antum abiduna maa abud" (Nor do you worship that which we worship).

Wa la aana abidum ma aabattum (Neither will I be a worshiper of that which you worship.)

It is clearly written in the above verse of Quran that neither I am worshiping that which you are worshiping nor I am forcing you to worship that which I am worshiping.

"Lakum Di nakum Va Liya Din" (To you is your religion and to me is my religion)

It is clearly written in this verse of Quran that for the infidels their religion is their religion and for the believers their religion is their religion. Then who are we to disregard others religions. The aim of all religions is to do only good deeds and to live and work for the cause humanity. But some people have perverted the teachings of religions for their own benefit and evils have come inside the religion.

It is clearly preached by Prophet Muhammad (pbuh) to respect all the approximately 124000 messengers of Allah. Therefore it is the duty of all the Muslims to respect all religion and sects of the world and all the messengers of Allah. Because all religions lead to the path of salvation only if followed properly. The word Kafir has been misinterpreted by some people and has slowly dragged towards hatred. Prophet Mohammad (pbuh) never forced anyone to convert into Islam, he only preached the good things of humanity and worked for humanity so during his life time people voluntarily converted to Islam due to its truth, purity, goodness, love, peace and all kinds of work of humanity.

In the present time in almost all Muslim houses be it son, daughter, brother or sister all are disbelieving each other on one or the other points. So one can also call them Kafir in a way or other because they are not believing each other. This is the time to open eyes and accept the facts. In many houses we can see that own children is neither giving food to their own parents nor taking proper care of own father, mother, Brothers and sisters. It means that the son is not trusting his own father, due to which the son becomes a disbeliever in the eyes of his father. Grabbing the property of own brothers means they are also in a way Kafir because they do not believe in the ethics and teachings of Islam.

So now it's time to understand exactly who are we? It is the duty of all citizens to follow the rules of the country in which they live in. In today's era, every BHARATIYE (Muslim, Sanatani, Sikh and Christian) will have to utilise their senses, shall tolerate something, shall have some patience, shall ignore few things, shall think something and shall take humanity and country forward. We have to become a human first then only we all can be a religious person.

Chapter 29

Sharia Law or Indian Law

Sharia is a religious law that is part of the Islamic tradition. The traditional school of Islamic jurisprudence recognizes four sources of Sharia: the Quran, the Sunnah (authentic Hadith), qiyas (equal reasoning) and ijma (juristic consensus). Thus Sharia is not only a system of law but also a comprehensive code of conduct that covers both private and public activities. 1, 2.

Sharia is a code of conduct for all Muslims to live life in a good and healthy environment. It guides the observance of prayer, fasting, charity, eating, drinking, sleeping, and helping others, sharing of wealth, business and every aspect life according to humanity. The purpose of Sharia law is to guide Muslims how they should live every aspect of life in accordance to the will of Allah. The right guidance of humanity. But later like any legal system Sharia law was made into a complex law and it started being practiced in different places in completely different ways by taking into the account of the local culture and traditions.

There are different types of Sharia law. They are for Sunni:- Hanbali, Maliki, Shafi and Hanafi, for Shia is Jafari.

All five schools differ in ideas and practices, but they all have the one main objective and that is of humanity. They all depend on how they interpret the texts from which Sharia law is derived. Interpretation also depends on local culture and customs. Sharia law looks quite different in different places in the world. Sharia law divides crimes into two categories. They are "crimes" that are serious offenses and have prescribed penalties. The second is "tazir" offences in which punishment is left to the discretion of the judge.

Islam was a spiritual, social and legal reform fourteen centuries ago. At the height of its civilization between the seventh and eleventh century, Islam was neither oppressive nor regressive. It was a progressive, humanitarian and legal force for reform and justice. Everyone understood Haq (rights) and Halal (legal) and followed the teachings of the Prophet properly. But after the mid of 13th century when Baghdad (house of wisdom) was destroyed by the Mongols, from that time the decline of the Muslims began. Later on some mangols generations also accepted Islam religion. Those kings started using the religion as a tool-kit to expand their territories and powers. They and their descendants continued their attacks and became great invaders. Most important to remember is that Mongols (Genghis Kan, Halaku) who burnt Baghdad were not Muslims, Nadir Shah and Taimur Lang were Muslims who did massacred in Delhi during Mughal emperor's rule.

Other sources of Sharia law are ijma' (consensus), qiyas (analogy), ijtihad (progressive reasoning by analogy).

Direct revelation from Allah ceased after the death of Prophet Muhammad (pbuh). The revelation that came upon the Prophet Muhammad pbuh was interpreted in different ways and in different languages. The ulema had the monopoly on the interpretation of the laws also. Muhammad (pbuh) had served as the supreme judge of the community during his lifetime. But after his death lots of issues came and slowly as the time passed many types of issues began coming up. The Prophet solved all legal problems by interpreting and expounding the Quran. After his death, the legal tradition continued through his successors called as the Caliphs.

With the expansion of the Islamic country, Sharia law passed into the hands of regional ulema (educated Person). Because of the different regional culture and traditions, complexity arose within Sharia law. Therefore, the Caliphs appointed judges in different provinces and thus the judiciary came into existence. Later when problems and crimes increased, the idea of a book came which can give guidance on the law. This need also came because a lot of disputes started between the practice of the Sunnah and the local customs and traditions. So according to local tradition and local customs, sharia law began to be formed in every kingdom and state. There are some similarities in sharia law everywhere but there are also some dissimilarities which can be seen in every country or state, according to the cultures prevailing there. As we can see in BHARAT today that the customs and traditions of BHARATIYE Muslims are different from those of Arab Muslims.

We have already seen that about 200 years after the death of Prophet Muhammad (pbuh) a new development came and that was the writing of Hadith. After writing the Hadith, the Ulemas also tried to end the legal disputes. But due to the different local traditions and cultures Hadith was also not able to be 100% solutions provider. So one after another many Hadith came into existence.

Al-Shafi's emphasis on the importance of the Sunnah as a source of law stimulated great activity in the collection and classification of Hadith reports, especially among his own supporters, who formed the Shafi'i school. The Ḥanbalī School was formed. The compilation of Hadith by Muslim scholars, notably Al-Bukhari (d. 870) and Muslim (d. 875) created an authentic record of the Prophet's sayings. Al-Shafi'i's thesis formed the basis of the classical theory of the roots of jurisprudence (ul al-fiqh), which became accepted in the early 10th century. The judicial "attempt" to understand the terms of the Shari'a is known as ijtihad and Legal theory charts the course that ijtihad should follow. The answer to any legal problem must first be sought in consultation with the Quran and the Hadith. If no specific solution is found in divine revelation, the jurist must employ analogy (qiyas) or some auxiliary principles of logic, such as istishan (judicial prudence) and istillah (welfare consideration). As an attempt to define Allah's law, the ijtihad of individual scholars can only result in a tentative conclusion called a zann ("conjecture"), which is based on certain knowledge. 5

The point here is that Sharia law is a very good law if followed properly. In Sharia law there is a punishment of chopping off hands for a theft, punishment for rape is death in the middle of the city, and punishment for misbehaving with a girl is gouging out. Sharia law has strict punishment for all evils. Islam has strict laws so that no one dares to do wrong.

As I am a BAHARTIYE so I will talk about BHARTIYE MUSLIMS, nowadays Muslims in BHARAT uses Sharia law only for benefits. If Sharia law harms the interests of Muslims then the Muslim goes with Indian Penal Code. In this way Muslims waste the time and energy of IPC. I say that Muslims should either follow Sharia law completely or follow the Indian Penal Code. Lawyers use both Sharia law and IPC laws during arguments in court. What is this? Where are the Muslims going? Where are we taking our generations? Due to this dual nature, the character of BHARATIYE Muslims is getting distorted. Muslims have become only consumer whereas our beloved Prophet Mohammad pbuh has given us the teaching of becoming a contributor. Faith in religion is just for the name shake. The real teaching of Islam has been twisted and distorted.

Now the time has come for Muslims to ponder and become a true Muslim for the betterment of future generations and for the betterment of the world. All shall strongly favour oneness in law for country. One country, one president, one prime minister, one currency and one law.

There should be no word Hindu or Muslim in the law. Only the word BHARATIYE shall be used in the law. Law should be one for all the citizens of Bharat. If Muslims want to follow Sharia law then they shall be made to follow all the rules of Sharia be it civil or criminal. Those Muslims should not be allowed to approach the INDIAN Penal Court for any issue. And according to Sharia law, the government should appoint an executioner in every district of BHARAT and the culprits should be given punishment according to Sharia law only. If complete Sharia law is implemented for Muslims, then Muslims will run after the government to abolish Sharia law in Bharat because it gives harsh and severe punishment for all evils and corruptions without any delay and lengthy process. And if Sharia law is strictly implemented for Muslims, then I am sure that within a month half of the Muslim population will be physically disabled and many people will be put to death due to strict punishment provisions as per Sharia laws.

There is also a point that about 15% to 16% of the population in BHARAT is of Muslims and 99% of Muslims are the native of Bharat and are sanatani's Muslim, no one can erase it. If BHARAT has to become a world power, then all have to respect the growth of all citizens. If 15% to 16% of the population is left behind due to any reason, then our country cannot make progress. If there are some issues and problems within the Muslim community, then it is our duty to rectify them. Not all Muslims are bad. Hardly 2% or 5% Muslims are bad. But many are poor. It is the poverty of the person due to which he/she starts committing crime. At the same time, the enemy country tries to take advantage of the poverty of the people and persuades them to turn against our country.

In 1969, the birth centenary year of Mahatma Gandhi, the son of ZAMBODEEP Sarhadi Gandhi came to BHARAT. After fasting for three days, he concluded the plight of BHARATIYE Muslims to be the reason for the selection of wrong leaders by the Muslims. BHARAT was divided on the basis of religion. Pakistan was formed after partition, but within just 25 years, the Muslim country was divided into two parts. Having one religion did not work. Everyone should take a lesson from this and make sacrifice for the unity and peace in our country.

Reference

1. https://en.wikipedia.org/wiki/Sharia

2. https://www.britannica.com/topic/Shariah/Development-of-different-schools-of-law

3. https://www.mei.edu/publications/islamic-law-shariah

4. M Cherif Basiouni: Islamic Law - Sharia: January 24, 2012

5. https://www.britannica.com/topic/Shariah/Reform-of-Shariah-law

Chapter 30
Status of BHARATIYE Muslims

There are many reasons for the pathetic condition of Muslims in BHARAT. The first reason is the difference of language and its specific nature. The language of Quran is Arabic, while the general public of BHARAT including Muslims do not know Arabic, so they have to rely on translators. And one have to trust the clerics.

Even today the majority of the population of BHARAT is of Hindus. The prosperity of BHARAT was destroyed in the beginning by the few Muslim invaders, their remnants and atrocities has created a kind of suppressed hatred within the Hindus, which is incited every now and then. On the other hand, it has been instilled in the hearts of the Muslims by the people that once they were the rulers of this country.

Due to certain things Muslims irrespective of anything consider themselves to be the best of all humans. They lives in a limited area and confine themself, consider themselves to be superior beings, they do not learn from others, keep themselves aloof, all these are the hallmarks of foolishness. Muslims believe that there is no religion like theirs. Such is their arrogance that if you name any other science in front of them, they will call you not only ignorant but also infidel. Due to being kept separate from the main stream, today Muslims are lagging behind in education, health and economic matters.

Knowledge is truly international and the benefits of ideas and major inventions reach all nations in the world. Many BHARATIYE Muslims are world famous for science, art and technical research etc. but unfortunately Muslims instead of considering them as their ideal. Fanatics consider other people as their ideals. Why shouldn't "A.P.J. Abdul Kalam", "Bismillah Khan" or "Azim Premji" be the ideals of BHARATIYE Muslims? In the field of religion too, there is a difference between the beliefs of the educated class Muslims and the non-educated common Muslims. Where the BHARATIYE Muslims of the educated class understand the universality and depth of religion are humbly engaged in worshiping God and spreading humanity. Whereas the common people goes after Fatwa and acts of terrorism. Which have often been associated with Jihad and are making the mistake of considering the same as their religious identity by falling into the trap spread by the extremists.

The Quran (17:37) says "Do not walk haughtily on the earth. You can neither tear the earth nor can you reach the height of a mountain by stretching yourself".

Then a big question arises who is responsible for the pathetic condition and poverty of Muslims in BHARAT? If we talk about universal brotherhood, then why don't the rich Muslim brothers from all over the world come to BHARAT to help the poor Muslims, they cannot come because they are foreigners. Today, if a foreign nation helps another nation, it does so for the expansion of the economic empire only. In today's world religion-ideas, enslaving nations is not an issue. Today's issue is trade which is international and is the basic foundation of relationships.

Means only BHARATIYE in BHARAT can help each other. At present in BHARAT when people are not tolerating their own brothers and sisters and their neighbours, then it is futile for Muslims to talk about brotherhood either universal or national. The cause of poverty among Muslims is lack of proper education and some wrong guidance and wrong understanding of things.

The Prophet taught to use the pen first then the sword only for self-defence. Today the era of the sword is no more, but the era of the pen continues. Lack of modern education is the biggest reason for the poverty of Muslims. Today's general Muslim lacks education. The maximum rank they are able to achieve in BHARAT is only that of semi-skilled labour. This tragedy of BHARATIYE Muslims started with the partition of our great country because of some leaders. The biggest cost has to be paid by the Muslims living in BHARAT on their own free will. It looks like BHARATIYE Muslims are the lost children of partition. If BHARATIYE Muslims want to rise economically and socially, then all have to live amicably together in this country and contributes towards development of BHARAT.

There has been a wrong preaching by some wrong people within Islam, that Islam is incompatible with nationalism. These are baseless. Islam is a faith based on one God and one holy book. At the same time, loyalty to the mother land is a part of Iman. Hubbul Watan Minal Iman.

At present look at any two Muslim countries which have one border, do they live peacefully as brothers? Religion and nationalism are fundamental aspects of modern life. But for Muslims, these have often been described as conflicting concepts that make people's lives miserable. Pakistan has been embroiled in a conflict with Afghanistan for a long time. In contrast, Bangladesh is a successful country because all its neighbouring countries are non-Muslim countries. 1

The percentage of poor's among Muslims in BHARAT is as follows: - Less than 2% of Muslims in Hyderabad come under the elite class economically. And according to surveys 63% of Muslims fall below the poverty line and survive on government donations or meagre daily income and charity. A survey by the National Council for Applied Economic Research (NCAER) states that 3 out of 10 Muslims are below the poverty line. 2, 3

Muslims among minorities are more economically disadvantaged than other religious groups and are dissatisfied. According to the National Council of Applied Economic Research in BHARAT, Muslims have more people living below the poverty line, which is 31% as compared to national 26%. 4

Here a big question arises that why there is more poverty in the Muslim community? No one can deny that the ancestors of BHARATIYE Muslims were once the followers of Sanatan Dharma only. When the conversion took place (whatever may have been the reason) then after the conversion in BHARAT the converted Muslims in BHARAT were left to their condition i.e. left like a hanging piece of cloth, whichever way the wind blows Muslims fly like a cloth. There has been a lack of education among Muslims since the beginning. One commendable work is that most of the Muslims live on self-sufficient works. In the beginning, some madrasas were established for education, which was right for that time, because at that time the education of madrasas was the contemporary education. Slowly century passed the world kept changing and the education systems and pattern also changed, but the madrasas never tried to adopt contemporary education. Madrasas and Maulanas emphasized on traditional education and are doing the same even today. Today times have changed, the contemporary education of 1000 - 1200 years ago has become obsolete today. In today's modern era, Muslims are left behind because they have not adopted the right education. New technology is initially ignored due to wrong fatwas by some Maulanas. But later all of them were adopted under compulsion. For example, when photography came into existence, in the initial period some Maulanas gave a fatwa that photographing any living things is against Islam. But now can anyone justify that fatwa. What can you think about? Some would have thought that if contemporary education is adopted and the public becomes literate, then there will be a decrease in their respect. This is the reason why contemporary education has not been adopted in Madrasas till date. This is the main reason for the backwardness of Muslims. Jealousy has entered in the Muslim community because of the wrong education system and sects division and hatred speeches.

The Industrial Revolution began in England around 1750. It was one of the most remarkable turning points in human history. At this stage, human and animal labour technology changed to machinery, such as the steam engine, spinning jenny, coke smelting, peddling and rolling processes for iron making. The Industrial Revolution was renewed for global economic growth, increasing production and consumption. Transport communication through canals, roads and rail improved. Along with this, banking and other financial systems were improved for smooth running of industries and business firms. The infant mortality rate decreased and the fertility rate increased. As a result population grew. On the other hand, there has been an increase in women and child labour in dangerous and unhygienic conditions. To save the family from starvation, the factory workers had to work sixteen hours a day. The Industrial Revolution created a widening gap between the rich and the poor. 6

On the other hand, Muslims all over the world were busy with their monarchy and did not pay attention to the changes happening in the world. The Muslim kings used to think that Maulana and Mufti would do all the work for the Muslims. Slowly Muslims had gone astray from Allah's command, they had taken up sword instead of pen. Even during Mughal period, Muslim kings from Iran and other places had also invaded BHARAT. It means brotherhood among Muslims prevailed only for the name shake. The word brotherhood is only to mislead the Muslim youth. If the word brotherhood exists in Islam, then how

Nadir Shah looted the Mughal emperor and brutally massacre millions of Muslims at Chandni Chowk in Delhi. The Persian emperor Nader Shah invaded the Mughal Empire in March 1739. Nadir Shah took away so much valuable treasures from Delhi that he stopped taxation in Persia for a period of three years after his return from Delhi to Persia. It can be easily understood from the above incidents that the word Universal Brotherhood is false only to mislead people. At present one's own brother is deceiving own brothers and sisters then what to talk about the brotherhood.

Jealousy has entered the Muslim society due to wrong education and perverted social environment. Jealousy is the source of evils and corruptions. In today's BHARAT, we see that if a Muslim progresses in the society with hard work, then due to jealousy, another Muslims and even his relatives tries his best to humiliate that Muslim and do something so that the progress of own people gets hampered. This is because knowingly or unknowingly from childhood one keeps hearing about hatred. During Friday prayers different Maulanas in different mosques keep on speaking badly about other Muslims and Maulanas of other sects, they call their counterparts as infidels and says every bad thing. In some places only love for religion is taught during education. Which is against the spirit of ISLAM and humanity and hence it becomes against Islam. Jealousy, envy have spoiled the Muslims so much that gradually it is becoming a big obstacle in the development of the society and the country. Sometimes even good Muslims/developed Muslims become victims of evils under the influence of non-performing and jealous Muslims. They also start doing bad things and slowly they get spoiled.

Let me give a live example of jealousy factor. There are five brothers in a family. Elder brother left home after marriage. At that time the family were not wealthy. The second and third brothers worked hard together with their father and GOD gave them good progress. The third brother became a very successful businessman. Elder brother and fourth brother had the base of Madrasa education. They did not succeed in their life due to wrong mind-set and weak educational background. Seeing the progress of other brothers they both became very jealous and started doing all the evils because they were unsuccessful. Specially they were jealous of the third and youngest brother because they worked hard and got success in his career. The third one was giving employment to more than 100 members through his business. Due to jealousy, the first and fourth brother and their wife did everything like backbiting, black magic to destroy their own brothers. Under the influence of elder and the fourth brother, the third brother started doing all the evils. The third brother also turned towards evil and corruption because of wrong ideas with bad brothers. His own brothers pushed him on the wrong path due to jealousy. And a rich and famous person became a poor person due to bad eyes, jealousy and black magic of own people. Although he had a lot of wealth but he died in a very pathetic condition. Due to his bad conduct GOD had taken away his blessing from him.

How did he become a liability for the country, this must be a big question coming in everyone's mind? The third person was a very successful person but due to the jealousy factor by his own people and society, he became poor. He had property but no cash. His deed punished him to such an extent that he was paralyzed and became dependent upon other. People used to feel pity on him. Because everyone had seen his high personality, name and fame. He started taking money from the minority educational fund of the government for his children education. So it is a liability for the country. A person who used to give money to others for education and other welfare was turned to take money from the Government Education Welfare Fund. All this is the result of jealousy and evils inside our community. We can see that when own brother cannot be own, then how we can talk and look at the matter of Muslim brotherhood. The word Muslim brotherhood was used by the invaders for their benefit to fulfil their desire, and is still in use by the enemies. It is time to understand and realize that Muslims will never develop if they continue to be victims of jealous and unhuman people.

Today the old education and social environment of Muslims has become like a frog inside a well. When the frog comes out of the well, he sees how big the world is and how many different things are there in the world. Similarly traditional education looks very sweet in childhood, but when children grow up and come in contact with the world for sustainable living, they come to know how different and how big the world is and they are lagging far behind. Nowadays Madrasa educated people find themselves far behind. A feeling of backwardness and left behind comes so even without wanting some people enter into the factors of jealousy.

Some political parties in BHARAT have kept Muslim society only as vote bank. Since independence they have used Muslims, only for their benefits and think that if Muslim society gets educated or developed then their grip will become loose upon Muslims. BHARATIYE Muslims today needs educational and economic development. They do not need to sing a separate song, but they need to sing country-song together with their fellow citizens. Only then we all BHARATIYE Muslims will be able to make progress educationally, scientifically, economically, socially, politically and spiritually.

Reference

1. https://indianexpress.com/article/opinion/columns/Muslims-population-in-BHARAT-nrc-caa-protests-secularism-6205149/ This article was first published in the print edition on January 8, 2020. Titled "Let's Reclaim the Muslims". The writer is a human rights activist based in Vadodara, MS University

2. https://timesofindia.indiatimes.com/city/hyderabad/63-hyd-Muslims-are-poor-survey/articleshow

3. https://timesofindia.indiatimes.com/India /31-Muslims-live-below-poverty-line-ncaer-survey/

4. https://news.gallup.com/poll/157079/Muslims-India -confident-democracy-despite-economic

5. https://www.britannica.com/topic/Hadith/The-compilations

6. https://mpra.ub.uni-muenchen.de/96644/1/MPRA_paper_96644.pdf Journal of Social Sciences and Humanities, Vol. 5, No. 4, 2019, pp. 377-387 The First Industrial Revolution: Creating a New Global Human Age Hardhan Kumar Mohjan Department of Mathematics, Premier University, Chittagong, Bangladesh

7. https://educatebox.com/names-of-Prophets-in-islam-list-of-Prophets

8. https://islam.stackexchange.com/questions

Chapter 31

Prophet Muhammad (pbuh) about BHARAT

It has been mentioned in many places that Prophet Muhammad (peace be upon him) used to say that he gets cool air (breeze) from Hind. He used to get a special fragrance from Hind.

Hadith narrated by Umar Qays bin Mihsan, "I heard the Prophet (peace and blessings of Allah be upon him) saying: "Treat the scent of BHARATIYE incense/substance, as it has healing for many diseases, apply it to the throat and different parts. Should be used by a person in trouble, and put on one side of the mouth of a person suffering from pleurisy." Sahih al-Bukhari, Book 71,

Hazrat Imam Bukhari (d. 875 A.D.) in his book "Al Adab Al Mufarad" wrote about the period of Companions that once Hazrat Ayesha (Prophet's wife) fell ill, her nephew brought a Jat (BHARATIYE) to treat him. It means that the process of love and trade between BHARAT and Arabia was since ancient times.

Shah Waliullah Muhaddith Dehlavi quoted a Hadith referred by Al-Tibrani-al-Aust, the Holy Prophet (PBUH) said, "I am Arab but Arab is not in me and I am not in Hind but Hind is in me".

Allama Iqbal used a part of this Hadith in his couplet of Bang-e-dara. 1

The Prophet said that love for one's country is a part of faith. This Hadith has been copied by Imam Sakhavi in Al-Maqsid-ul-Hasnah.

1. Al-Masnu Fi Ma'rif Al-Hadith Ali Moudu, Imam Suyuti, 91/1

2. Al Silsila ul Deefa Shaikh Naseer ud Din Albani, 36

3. Tazkeerat ul Mauduat, Allama Muhammad Tahir Hanafi, 11/1

4. Al Mauduat ul Saghani 2/1 6. Ad Darar Al Muntasara 9/1. 2

Huzoor's love for HIND i.e. Bharat:

Huzoor turned his face towards hind and said, I get cold breeze coming from the hind.

Hadith has got the status of shahi and its rabbis are Hazrat Ali and Ibn Abbas.

[Mustadrak Al Hakim Hadith 4053 Hakim said that this Hadith [Sahih] is correct on the conditions of Muslim. 3

It can be concluded from the above Hadith that Prophet Mohammad (pbuh) being the messenger of Allah knew very well many good things about BHARAT / HIND. Prophet Mohammad pbuh was so great that his attachment was direct with Allah as well as with BHARAT. This could be because may be most out of the 124000 messengers of Allah would have come in the BHARATIYE subcontinents in different ages. The first Homo sapiens, Prophet Adam also descended on the BHARATIYE subcontinent and many messengers have come here since the beginning of civilization. Long before Prophet Noah as mentioned in Quran and this mention justifies the era system of Sanatan Dharma. The exact time of the beginning of human civilization is not yet been confirmed. It may be more than three lakh years or four lakh years or may be more for different species. Even the exact time of Prophet Adam's arrival on this earth has not been known yet. The essence of the teachings of the many messengers who came to Hind must have been realized by Prophet Muhammad (pbuh).

In history we have seen that BHARATIYE soldiers went to Arab lands to save the grandson of Prophet Mohammad (Sallallahu Alaihi Wasallam). At the same time, it also shows that although Prophet Mohammad was not born in BHARAT, he respected BHARAT and loved BHARAT. All Muslims are lucky that they are born in BHARAT and therefore it is imperative to have respect and love for BHARAT. Muslims will be a true Muslims only when they have faith upon Prophet Mohammad pbuh. And faith tells to love one's place of birth. **If Prophet Mohammad (pbuh) loved BHARAT then it becomes Sunnah for all the Muslims of the world to love BHARAT.**

Reference

1. https://www.siasat.pk/forums/threads/pak-aur-hind-in-Hadiths-and-religious-literature-of-islam.679858/

2. Source: Famous Deef A Hadith, Hafiz Imran Ayyub, Volume II, page 48

3. From: Al Mustadrak Ala Al Sahihayn Al Hakim Al-Nisaburi Jild 2, Book: Tawarikh ul Mutaqadamin Min Al Ambia'i by Wal Mursalin

Chapter 32
Hubbul Watan Minal Iman

Translation: Loving one's motherland is a part of faith.

There are many sayings about Rasulullah (Sallallahu Alaihi Wasallam) love and yearning for the birthplace Makkatul Makarrama. This is absolutely correct because we find that Prophet Muhammad left the city of Mecca and went to Medina. But Prophet Mohammad pbuh always looked for an opportunity to go to Mecca and later started living in his place of birth.

Actually Islam is a way of living a good, peaceful and healthy life in a scientific way. But nowadays the true spirit of Islam is missing among the Muslims. The fact is that Islam was accepted as a good religion in different parts of the world during the life time of Prophet Muhammad (pbuh) and even after the life of Prophet Muhammad (pbuh) for a few centuries. Islam initially spread by winning heart of people because of its truth and goodness. The Prophet had given the light of hope in the time of darkness. He had given respect and rights specially to girls, women, slaves and all underprivileged persons.

Initially in the first few centuries Islam spread by its own spirit of truth, peace and love in many places, countries and continents. Different kings living away from Mecca in different countries wanted to expand their territory. Many small kings wanted to become more and more powerful. They were looking for some opportunities and tools to fulfil their selfish desire of becoming a powerful king. About 200 years after the death of Prophet Muhammad pbuh some kings started using religion as a tool kit to expand their kingdom and become powerful. Those kings started misleading the public in the name of religion and appointed some people to write different books as per their wish and need of that time. In the name of Sunna the kings got different books written through some people and gradually those books became the book of law. The books were translated in different countries and in different languages according to the wishes of the kings who wanted to use the fabricated Hadiths to their advantage and wanted to expand the territory and become more powerful. Seeing one king, other kings also appointed someone to write another book and thus different books were written one after the other. The question why there are different books?

"Hubbul Watan Meenal Iman" has also been deliberately misinterpreted by some people so that Muslims can be misled and the tyrant king can easily expand his territory.

Various translations of this HUBBUL WATAN MINAL IMMAN have been misinterpreted as follows:-

According to Muhaddithun Ali al-Qari, this statement is considered to be a mythical one. (Moudu'atus Saghani, 81 and al-Masnu', 106)

Mullah Ali al-Qari writes that if this Hadith is proved to be authentic, then the correct meaning of 'homeland' would be Jannat or Mecca. (Al-Asrul Marfu'ah, pp. 190-191)

Such translations cannot be considered correct. How can we understand that Watan means Jannat or Mecca? In simple language, "Watan" means the country that is the place of one's residence. We cannot tell that the Sun means the Moon because both shines. Now Muslims have to think for their future generations. Muslims have to be true followers of Prophet Muhammad (pbuh) and not fall prey to some people who are dragging Muslims into darkness by some fabricated Hadith.

Prophet Muhammad pbuh taught love and peace throughout his life. But today's Muslims specially in BHARAT are going against the teachings of Prophet Muhammad pbuh. Not only Prophet Mohammad pbuh but all approximately 124000 messengers of GOD have taught peace and love, and acts of humanities. Shree Ram sacrificed his luxurious life for 14 years only for peace and love, and to honour his father words. The irony is that people take the names of all the messengers or avatars of God but do not follow their teachings. Muslim calls many Prophets and feel proud, but Muslims do not adopt their characters. Prophet Muhammad (pbuh) never harmed those who used to harm him except in a war which was the last option for survival. He kept patience and by his good deeds won the hearts of those who used to harm him. Prophet Muhammad (pbuh) has given the message of love and peace with everyone including the enemy throughout his living. He used to find ways and means to forgive people and even forgive the enemy. Because forgiveness is the best deed in front of God and it is in almost all religions. But these days we are just finding ways for selfish desire.

When Prophet Muhammad (pbuh) returned to Mecca from Medina with his followers, at that time he was looking for the means and ways to forgive the people of his homeland i.e. motherland Mecca. The Prophet was harassed by them in many ways. They even tried to kill Prophet Mohammad (pbuh). But Prophet Mohammad forgave all his enemies. He announced, before entering the city of Mecca, that he would pardon Abu Sufyan, as well as the people living in Abu Sufyan's house, on the condition that they stay inside the house. Abu Sufyan was the head of the city of Mecca, who led the war against Prophet Muhammad (pbuh). He further announced that the rest of the people who will stay inside the houses will also be forgiven. He also announced that those who are taking shelter inside any place of worship will also be forgiven. This happened because of the Prophet's love for his countrymen.

All have to love our roots, our motherland and our country. There is a saying in English (go back to basic) that means go to your roots. It is the duty of all Muslims to know about the life of Prophet Mohammad (pbuh) correctly and Follow the path shown by him and become a patriot.

Dharma (religion) is the practice and process of living a good, healthy life. It calls for living in the country and following the rules and regulations of that country. If Muslims follow true Islam then it automatically leads to following all the rules of that particular country where Muslims live.

I am going to give a true example. Just about a century ago there was a fatwa that photography is not allowed in Islam. Muslims kept Maulana's fatwa on their heads and eyes. Is that fatwa valid in present 21st century? Can we imagine that we can do anything without photos?

Islam does not forbid anyone to accept the laws of the country of residence. There are different continents and all continents have different countries and each country has different languages and laws and each country has its own rules and regulations. Islam asks to follow the rules and regulations of country where we live in. Islam does not ask to disrespect our motherland.

If a person lives in America, he has to follow the laws of America, if a person lives in Africa he has to follow the laws of Africa, if a person lives in Russia he has to follow the laws of Russia. Australians has to follow the rules & regulations and laws of Australia. So a person living in BHARAT should follow the rules and regulations and laws of BHARAT. "Hubbul Watan Minal Imaan" is to be adopted.

When we talk about Sharia law in BHARAT. If all the laws of Sharia law are implemented then they are so strict and good that more than half of the Muslims in BHARAT will be handicapped and many will be killed according to Sharia law. Because Sharia law directly gives severe punishment for evils and crimes. Everyone should feel proud to be a BHARATIYE. We have to be like our beloved President of BHARAT Dr. Avul Pakir Jainulabdeen Abdul Kalam. Muslims have to be like Major Abid Hasan Safrani of the BHARATIYE National Army, the father of the slogan "Jai Hind". Safrani was a close associate of Subhash Chandra Bose. There are many patriotic Muslims like Khan Abdul Ghaffar Khan, Abdul Hamid, Allama Iqbal, Bismil Azimabadi "Sarfaroshi ki tamanna ab hamare dil mein hai", Abdul Hameed, etc. and there are countless patriotic Muslims, we have to be like them. We have to live and die for our country and follow the right path as shown by the Prophet with honesty. So it is the duty of all BHARATIYE Muslims to consider Hubbul Watan Minal Iman and make themselves true citizens.

During any international event, we all are known by the name of our country and not by the name of our religion. Even when Muslims go for Hajj, they all are known by the name of country i.e. BHARATIYE Muslims are also called as HINDUSTANI MUSLIMS.

The most important thing is that Muslims born in BHARAT, they die in BHARAT only. Their dead body also is buried inside the mother land BHARAT. The body is taken by mother land inside herself. What a respect by the mother land even after death. During life time mother land give us all the required things for happy living and allow us to enjoy life as per our wishes and gives us all the freedom just like our mother who give us birth. So we have great responsibilities towards both the mother one who give us birth and one who has given all means and materials to consume and leave happily. So love and salute to both the mother becomes an integral part of iman.

Chapter 33
Diverted Muslim

Some Muslims in BHARAT are not only being misled by wrong teachings, but are also being misused by the enemies of BHARAT by giving some inducements. After independence, Muslims in BHARAT have been used as a tool kit by some people and some political parties. A lot of misconception has also been created, Few Muslims are intimidated. Muslims today are in a dilemma for many reasons. Poor and less educated people easily fall in the trap of wrong leaders and start doing some illegal and inhuman acts. They unknowingly think that they are doing good for the community, while those acts are against Islam. Islam never teaches terrorism, jealousy, violence and hatred.

No one can deny the fact that whatever happens in the world it happens only by the will of Allah. So today if there is pain and suffering in the Muslim society, the society is in trouble, then it is happening only by the wish of Allah. Because Islam says whatever happens, it happens only by the will of Allah. Knowingly or unknowingly, Muslims are doing wrong things, they have gone astray. I am going to give many live examples which shows that how many Muslims are walking in wrong path, adopting evils but pretending to be a true Muslim.

A true and an interesting incident which I experienced in the year 2018, we 4 friends were having dinner in a hotel in Ranchi city.

The funniest thing was that two friends were drinking Alcohol, I and a friend were having soup. A man who was claiming to be a very good Muslim was drinking alcohol and was literally crying after drinking and said that Modi has made the lives of Muslims miserable. I laughed and said how? Next I said are you a true Muslim? He got angry. I said being a true Muslim can you drink alcohol? If you don't have control over yourself then how are you accusing PM Narendra Modi? Is MODI forbidding you from doing your religious work? Today some Muslims are doing all the evils, illegal and harmful activities for which Allah is punishing the Muslims, but the misguided Muslims are blaming PM Modi. This act is against Islam. Because of which some Muslims are suffering.

I told him that you need to do Jihad within yourself. He glared at me! And in a drunken state he asked me where he would have to go to do Jihad. He was under the impression that for Jihad he need to go and fight with other people. I laughed and said that you are educated person but you have not become wise. The real meaning of education is to gain knowledge from which discipline can be learned and a person can choose right and wrong. I told him that do Jihad within yourself and eradicate evils and corruptions from your heart and mind. Think carefully, religion only teaches humanity, he was surprised and angry. He called me a Kafir. I laughed and said you are drinking wine and I am drinking soup. You can better understand who is what? Anyhow I told him the real meaning of Jihad. Jihad is not just about fighting another person. The real meaning of Jihad is to struggle with the evils within oneself and to end them. Jihad is to restrain oneself from evils and corruptions. War is the last option which is allowed only and only when the enemy is not letting you live in peace or the enemy is trying to kill you. Further I said that if a person believes in Allah then he will respect the words of the Quran and understand and apply the Quran instead of just reading it. Also will follow path shown by Prophet

Muhammad (pbuh) which gives the message of humanity and peace. He was shocked and felt ashamed and told me that he will look into it and do true Jihad in himself (i.e. Will remove the evil from within).

Being born in a Muslim family and having a Muslim name does not make one to be a true Muslim. The fore most condition to be a true Muslim is that one must first be a true human being. This is possible only when a Muslim will understand the true meaning of Islam i.e. he will stay away from dishonesty, theft, violence, hatred, cheating, looting, jealousy etc.

Prophet Mohammad pbuh has said to love one's motherland i.e. the country in which you are born and are living. Neither these days some Muslims love their motherland nor do they have good relations with their own brothers and sisters. Then how do they show love and affection for the people of other countries whom they have not even seen. Now the time has come that Muslims has to bring reformation and follow the path shown by Prophet Muhammad pbuh. All Muslim brothers and sisters are requested to think again and rethink and then decide. By thinking with open mind one cannot become a kafir. Prophet Mohammad pbuh has himself told to acquire knowledge. If one will take right education and think beyond limitation then only one can acquire the knowledge. Today if anyone cannot love his own brother and sister or relative, then how can he love other and our country?

In history we find that the golden age of Islam was from 7th century to 11th century. During that time the Muslims were actually true Muslims and Islam had reached almost all parts of the world. So we see that the Muslims were progressive till the first 4th century Hijri and later on as they expanded their territory and did not adopt the changing contemporary education, the progress among the Muslims stopped because they did not follow the path of education as shown by Prophet Muhammad (pbuh). Slowly they went away from ISLAM and hence Allah started punishing the misguided Muslims. Today we see that Muslims are suffering in every corner of the world.

We also see in history that various Muslim leaders who ruled BHARAT from Slave dynasty to Mughal dynasty never remained stable and kept fighting among themselves to establish their kingdom. Their ancestors were also non-Muslims earlier but later converted to Islam. Most importantly, none of the kings came from the Gulf countries. All came from Central Asia. The world was busy inventing new things while the Muslims were busy getting praise themselves by small groups. Gradually the Muslims kept getting divided into sects. As they moved away from the teachings of the Prophet, the Muslims became weaker.

I am not saying that the evils are only in Muslims and not in other religions. There are evils and corruption in other religions too but it is our duty to first reform ourselves then we talk about others.

After independence the condition of Muslims in BHARAT worsened due to illiteracy, poor education system and lack of proper leadership and unity. The world started changing rapidly but the Muslims kept lagging behind. Poor education system and poverty have been the reason behind the backwardness. Political parties also exploited Muslims as a vote bank. Some people thought that if Muslims adopt contemporary education, their leadership position would be weakened. The result of being used as a vote bank is in front of everyone in BHARAT. Much later when Muslims opened their eyes they found themselves far behind others and became victims of jealousy, hatred and poorness. So many differences have arisen in the society that today the development of Muslims is hampered by own people and as a result the development of BHARAT is being hindered. Because BHARAT cannot become a world leader without the development of all of its citizens. To become a world leader every person of BHARAT has to make contribution which is possible only through progress of every citizens of country. The government also has to see that every citizen of the country contributes in the development of BHARAT and this is possible only when all the citizens are equally treated and happiness index of country is high.

Muslims fight in the name of religion, do not keep relation with their own brothers and sisters and talk about Muslims all over the world this is wrong. War happens between countries, war has nothing to do with religion. Perverted people associate war with religion, which is wrong. Suppose if there is a war between BHARAT and Pakistan, and suppose Pakistan fires a missile towards BHARAT, the missile will not be able to differentiate between Hindu and Muslim. Some people are fooling everyone in the name of religion.

Muslims have no option today except to adopt contemporary education along with the traditional education. Contemporary education keeps changing according to time as per development so it has to be renewed as per the development. Once Muslims understand the value of Islam then the evils and corruptions from the society will automatically vanish. The community will grow and develop and BHARAT will become a superpower. People of other religions or sects never opposes true Islam. Everyone opposes the misguided people. So it is the duty of all Muslims to take care of themselves and save others from going astray.

Chapter 34

People in Different Form

The Author has lived, studied and worked in different cities in different states with different people, from different societies, communities, religions, sects, castes, creeds, families, cultures and environment. The author has worked well with many different people and gained diversified experiences and knowledge. While living and working in different parts of BHARAT, the author found and understood that Allah has not created any thing called caste or religion. God created only two types of human beings, one is male and the other is female.

Humans have bifurcated themselves in different sects and castes. One who is good always sees and look for good and goodness in everything and one who is bad always sees and look for bad in everything. People have to learn from the life of great Prophets like Prophet Mohammad pbuh, Jesus, David, Abraham, Gautama Buddha, Rama, Krishna, Shiva and many Prophets and avatars to forgive other, to keep patience, to sacrifice selfishness and evils and lived for the cause of humanity and peace.

I have lived with and in homes of many other sects and casts people, studied together, eaten together, worked together, travelled around etc. I have found only difference in food resources and local cultures, that too according to the nature (place) and according to the season.

Like in South BHARAT Anna Sāmbhar, Idli Dhosa etc. In North BHARAT Roti sabji, Bhaat in East BHARAT, Roti, Dhokla, Thepla in West BHARAT etc. Means we find that in every state or region not according to religion, but the foods and drinks are taken according to the resources available there. Nowadays, due to globalization, all things are available everywhere, but there are still some ingredients that are not able to consume despite globalization. Like difference in coconut and mustard oil. North BHARATIYE do not like to cook food with coconut oil and in South BHARAT mustard oil is not liked. All these are external qualities, but the inner qualities are the same that the oil is used for cooking food by every humans, all humans eat food, everyone gets to sleep, washes hands and face after getting up in the morning, one has to eat, does some work to make a living. All Remembers God for peace and prosperity.

Living in different places and with people of different religions, I have found that there is some evil in everyone because man is a social animal. The only difference is that there is intelligence and strength, humans has the power to think and understand that separates humans from animals. Saitan misleads human and incites them to do wrong, but God who is inside every human being in the form of a soul prevents them from doing wrong. The person who suppresses his soul that person does wrong things means he gets away from God and gets closer to the devil. I have found that whatever religion and sects I have lived with like Sanatana Dharma, Buddhism, Christianity, Sarna religion, Jainism, Zoroastrianism, Punjabi religion, Jewish religion, etc. after making a mistake, everyone's eyes shows some shame feelings. But nowadays, many of the Muslims don't even have shame in their eyes. It means that some people have no fear of Allah. After making a mistake, they uses every trick to prove themselves right. If there is a benefit, Sharia law is adopted and if there is loss from Sharia law then BHARATIYE law is adopted.

A live example: In 2012, a Muslim family was struggling and his sister's marriage was at stake. He had reached me through a common friend. He needed money to save his house and sister marriage. He had nothing except unclear house papers and some unclear land papers. The house in which he lives had neither land mutation nor municipality receipt. I gave him money so that all his problems could be solved. At that time I had money, so I gave him five lakh rupees through bank cheque. His father was not alive, so seeing their helplessness and poverty, as a human being and a true Muslim I continued helping them in every possible way. I had helped him many times with money, moral supports and also given employment to his brother as a car driver. Earlier he used to do all evils and illegal things. But when he came in contact with me, I tried to make him a true Muslim and told him to leave all evils and illegal things. I had also given training to him and his brothers in construction works, but they did not wanted to earn through hard work. Later in the year 2017 he quarrelled with me because I forced him to stop doing illegal work which I did not liked. He forgot all my help that I had done to him and to his family in their difficult times.

In fact, at that time 2018-2020 he had brought lots of money from somewhere, while he had no source of legal income. With that money he had opened a shoe shop as well but later closed that too because that shop business needed attention and hard work. Where did he get the money from is a big question? Whereas he did not return my money to me at once. On the other hand in covid during lock down, from where did he brought so much money that he has made a new multi storied building? The person who had no money to eat, no source of income, suddenly his lifestyle changed completely raises a point of concern. In one year 2020 without any business he made a building worth more than crores, he roamed in a car along with his so-called Haji brothers. This is also a serious case of hiding tax money also. His brothers are hajjis? Why won't Allah punish such people and such community? Such people are cheating their own people and country by not paying any tax on their earnings. Can we call such people Muslims? Are these people not oppressors? Such people make holes in the same plate upon which they eat.

There is a lots of concern upon the Muslim community. All do illegal things and blame others for their difficulties. Allah is giving all kinds of trouble and stress because the Muslims has gone astray and are disobeying Allah and Prophet Muhammad pbuh. Muslims are not true to their religion and even forget the compassion and kindness of people. That's why Muslims are losing respect in front of others. Allah has taken away his blessings from Muslims due to bad deeds. History is full of examples.

One big reality is that some Muslims earn money by doing unrighteous works, then they go for Hajj and after returning from Hajj they feel proud to be called Haji Sahab. It is regrettable to say that some of the Hajis of today keep on doing illegal activities because of which Allah has ignored Muslims. Islam says to treat the neighbours nicely, do not let the neighbour sleep hungry. We can find lots of Muslim families who has been living together for long times but just to grab properties one does all types of unhuman activities to get them out of their own house and grab property. We have lots of live examples that many Muslims has got his own brothers, sisters and neighbours electricity and water supply cut off, forced own people to live in the dark under a broken house. What would you call such a Muslim? In front of Muslims everything is happening but even seeing all the struggles and pains no one is ready to solve the problems. Where is the word brotherhood? If Muslims harms Muslims then no Muslims open their mouth but when any non-Muslims harms any Muslims then all Muslims starts doing all things. Is this right?

Let me give you another example. I helped a shopkeeper in my locality on humanitarian ground. Once during Eid festival he asked me for a loan of Rs. 20,000/- and he promised to return my money on the second day of Eid festival. I gave the money to him without any greed because I have a basic mantra that "If someone helps another human, then GOD will help him in some way or the other". But after Eid he did not return my money. With these types of experiences who will help the needy people? Why will Allah's punishment not come upon such a community?

As per the teachings of Prophet Muhammad PBUH I have always helped other people specially marginalized and needy people. And I am sure many Muslims help other needy people. This is the basic principle of Islam. Islam religion is a very good religion but at present few Muslims have diluted the spirit of Islam. Upon thinking deeply we come to understand that this is the fault of our environment, poor education system, hate speeches, society and upbringing of Muslims. That means if our education system improves then automatically environment will improve and the upbringing of children will automatically become better and Muslims will be a true Muslim.

Let me give you another live example of betrayal. In fact in the area where I live in, many people live on the basis of daily earnings. A man needed money for his wife's treatment in the hospital. He asked me for help by lending Rs.50, 000/- in the month of September 2020. At that time I had only Rs.27000/- so I helped with that amount. He promised me to return my money within a month. But till date he has not returned the full money. Not only this, he said that he has CCTV footage, that my son has taken Rs.15000/- from his shop. He didn't show any footage because he was lying. Actually I don't have any son. What would you call such Muslims?

I don't know what Allah has made me of? Why after being badly cheated by so many people even by own Brothers and relatives, I keep doing the same mistakes of helping other again and again. Seeing a human suffering it is the duty of a good person to help the suffering person. This is what I am doing according to the teachings of Prophet Muhammad pbuh, who have told to help others and be a contributor. I have helped not only Muslims but also my Hindu and Christian friends. I have also given them time, service and money and some of them have also cheated me. But the percentage of cheating is very high among Muslims as compared to people of other religions and sects. Also I found that the sense of shame is present in the eyes of non-Muslims but is not present in the eyes of many Muslims. We have found that some people steal as well as sew. My observation on this is that the nature and character of a person never changes. Education and upbringing by parents and society also play an important role in shaping the character of an individual.

There are many more live and true examples of tyrants and this has become the story of each and every house in present Bharat. Is it a crime to help Muslims? I am taking the name of Muslims because Muslims think that they will only go to Jannat (Heaven) and others will go to Hell. Everyone does bad things and says that they will go to heaven. Allah leaves everything upon deeds and it is the deeds which gives reward and punishment according to the deeds of people, not as per the religion, because Allah has made humans not any religion. So in front of Allah all the humans are equal and they gets rewards or punishment as per their activities.

Also a question arises? Will only Muslims go to heaven? Then what would one say about those messengers of God i.e. Prophets who came in this world other than Prophet Muhammad pbuh. Where will the approximately 124000 Prophets will go? Here it is clear that only the people who is good and does work of humanity will go to heaven irrespective of religion, cast, creed or gender.

Now a day's one more important thing about bad activities inside Muslims community is that for little benefits and due to jealousy a brother and sister cheats his own brothers and sisters. It can be seen from registered documents that land which was in the name of brother and sister, that has been sold illegally by own brother. In the beginning that person complained to father but left them all to save the honour of the house. But later on when he saw that the matter has gone too far away and one after another own brother and relatives are doing only evils and corruptions under the umbrella of religion. I went in depression then Allah prompted me to write this book. And series of volumes of this book will come. I am bringing this facts in front of everyone so that our future generations are saved from evils and all misguided Muslims can return to the path of humanity, love and peace as shown by Prophet Muhammad (pbuh). If I keep writing about oppressor Muslims and present live examples, this process will go on and on.

Such incidents are present in almost all Muslim families but they hide many things because of family honour, respect and self-honour in the society. Initially I also did not go to the court because of my father regards and respect. Our family was one of the most reputed Muslim family in Hazaribagh in terms of power, money, business and education. After the death of my mother my elder brother and the fourth brother due to poor education, madrasa background, greed and jealousy did all the illegal things and destroyed the house, property, reputation and everything because they were not successful. A successful brother who used to employee more than 100 people was brought to death in a pathetic condition just because of jealousy by own siblings.

The most surprising thing is that during the writing and completion of this book many people and friends supported me morally but few so called own came in front tried to demoralise me, suppress me, threatened me indirectly and did all the activities so that this book may not come in market. But as I said truth can be suppressed for time being but cannot be erased. After facing lots of difficulties and by the blessing of Allah I am able to bring this book in front of all.

All types of evils, corruptions and incidents are present in almost every Muslim families but they hide many things because of family honour. All this is happening because of poor education system, hatred religious speeches and jealousy factors. The environment of our society in which we are living is so much corrupted that the essence of ISLAM is just for the name shake. The Muslim has been the victim of few fabricated translations of Hadith. Due to artificial translation and impurity imposed on common Muslims, today few Muslims has been diverted and the result is that whole society is under lens and is suffering.

Today for the peaceful living amicably the true spirit of the religion is to be adopted. That is to adopt eternal religion in the right way. The true spirit of all religion is the religion of son, religion of daughter, religion of Brother, religion of Daughter-in-law, wife religion, husband religion, father religion, mother religion, friend religion, neighbour religion, teacher religion, disciple religion, food religion, Work religion (Karya Dharma), Civilian religion, Rashtra Dharma (country religion), Yug Dharma (time religion), Shiksha Dharma(education religion) etc. etc. (i.e. duty and all right works) is needed which every human being specially Muslims have to adopt, only then peace and progress will come in society. There is a need to spread the message of humanity to every corner of the world and that can happen only when the right education with moral values and ethics is given to every human. People have to leave the feeling of envy and jealousy. GOD only likes the work of humanity, so everyone has to understand this before doing any activity. It has to be taken into consideration that whether our work or conduct is causing problems to others. If any of our work is causing problems to any

other then that is against religion. Whoever is in trouble today, he himself is responsible for that. God does not punish anyone, it is the actions and deeds of a human being that punishes a human being. So before blaming others, assess oneself. Today there is a need of the most important religion that is Yug Dharma. Today we all living in BHARAT, identified as a BHARATIYE. Religion is only one that is the humanity works. Humans have given different names to the different path of salvation as different religion.

It is the duty of every citizen to cooperate and contribute in all forms in the interest of the country, specially the Muslims should come forward and increase their contribution in the interest of the country. At the end of this volume, I would like to say one precious quote to every person of the world, *"If anyone wants to fight, then why to fight in the name of right, fight in the name of duty"*.

Kind attention:

One organization by the name **"DHARTI AABA FOUNDATION"** is doing humanity work. The foundation have plans to provide good education to the marginalized boys and girls. The foundation wants to upgrade the people so that the people become self-dependent with quality Skills and Works and generate employment for others. The foundation wish to promote livelihood skills and agriculture. Self-sustainability through agriculture programme is the need of the time. To promote various programs the foundation need supports from all of you. Therefore it is a kind request you all to kindly support by giving small donations of rupees 500 in the foundation. Your contribution will help the foundation to spread the teaching of humanity among people.

Our bank details are as below:-

Account Holder name	**: - DHARTI AABA FOUNDATION**
Account Number	**: - 496310110013359**
IFSC	**: - BKID0004963**
Bank	**: - Bank of India**
Branch	**: - Lalpur Circular Road, Ranchi.**

Our motto is to make humans become a contributor rather than becoming a consumer.

The below is the QR Code for mobile payment